Why We Need a New Welfare State

Gøsta Esping-Andersen

with

Duncan Gallie,

Anton Hemerijck,

and

John Myles

OXFORD

UNIVERSITY PRESS

OXFORD

UNIVERSITY PRESS

Great Clarendon Street, Oxford OX2 6DP

Oxford University Press is a department of the University of Oxford.
It furthers the University's objective of excellence in research, scholarship,
and education by publishing worldwide in

Oxford New York

Auckland Cape Town Dar es Salaam Hong Kong Karachi Kuala Lumpur
Madrid Melbourne Mexico City Nairobi New Delhi Shanghai Taipei Toronto

With offices in

Argentina Austria Brazil Chile Czech Republic France Greece
Guatemala Hungary Italy Japan South Korea Poland Portugal
Singapore Switzerland Thailand Turkey Ukraine Vietnam

Oxford is a registered trade mark of Oxford University Press
in the UK and in certain other countries

Published in the United States
by Oxford University Press Inc., New York

British Library Cataloguing in Publication Data

Data available

Library of Congress Cataloging in Publication Data

Esping-Andersen, Gøsta, 1947–
    Why we need a new welfare state / Gøsta Esping-Andersen with Duncan
    Gallie ... [et al.].
       p. cm.
    Includes bibliographical references and index.
    1. Welfare state.   I. Title.
JC479. E86 2002   361.6'5'094–dc21   2002066250

ISBN 0-19-925642-X (hbk.)
ISBN 0-19-925643-8 (pbk.)

Typeset by Newgen Imaging Systems (P) Ltd., Chennai, India
Printed in Great Britain
on acid-free paper by
Biddles Ltd., King's Lynn, Norfolk

Why We Need a New Welfare State

For today's children who will provide for our welfare when we are old. It is for you—and hence for ourselves—that we desire the best possible welfare state.

Contents

Foreword: Sustainable Social Justice and 'Open Co-ordination' in Europe

In March 2000, the European Council held a special meeting in Lisbon, at which a new and ambitious strategic goal was assigned to the European Union for the next decade. In the broadest terms, this goal is 'to become the most competitive and dynamic knowledge-based economy in the world capable of sustainable economic growth with more and better jobs and greater social cohesion'. The modernization of the European social model was part and parcel of this new strategic goal: 'Investing in people and developing an active and dynamic welfare state will be crucial both to Europe's place in the knowledge economy and for ensuring that the emergence of this new economy does not compound the existing social problems of unemployment, social exclusion and poverty.'

The Lisbon Summit not only promoted social policy as a distinct focus of attention for European co-operation; at the same time it laid the methodological foundations for a new Europe-wide approach to social policy, called 'open co-ordination'. Succinctly stated, open co-ordination is a mutual feedback process of planning, examination, comparison, and adjustment of the social policies of Member States, all of this on the basis of common objectives.

Expectations ran high after the Lisbon Summit. The next step was to turn these solemn declarations and new principles of co-operation into practice. One immediate challenge was to make 'open co-ordination' operational and effective in the field of social inclusion and pensions, two areas singled out as priorities for co-operation. This was a key ambition during the Belgian Presidency of the European Union in the second half of 2001. We were able to finalize a first round of effective open co-ordination on social inclusion, which was launched in December 2000, with a set of common conclusions drawn from the first Member States' National Action Plans on Social Inclusion. And we reached a political agreement on common quantitative indicators to monitor the Member States' performance with regard to social inclusion. We also reached agreement on common objectives for our pension systems, and a procedure for applying open co-ordination to pensions from 2002 onwards.

In order to put the pension challenge into a broader perspective, I asked Gøsta Esping-Andersen, together with Duncan Gallie, John Myles, and

Anton Hemerijck, to present a scientific report on the evolving architecture of the European welfare states to a conference organized by the Belgian Presidency in Leuven in October 2001. Their brief was to reflect upon the *Gestalt* of social policy at the beginning of the new century, both from the point of view of desirability and feasibility. Admittedly, such a brief encompasses difficult and far-reaching questions. The report had to be explicit on the underlying issues of social justice (what are common European objectives of social policy?) and on issues of political methodology (how can European nations co-operate to enhance their performance, in view of these common objectives?). This book is based on their excellent conference report.

The analysis of this book strongly supports the idea that open co-ordination of social policies in the European Union, if applied judiciously, can contribute significantly to the achievement of sustainable social justice for Europe's citizens. In this Foreword I would like to comment briefly on the idea of sustainable social justice and on the role of open co-ordination.

Sustainable Social Justice through an Active Welfare State

The Lisbon conclusions refer to 'an active and dynamic welfare state'. The Belgian government coined the expression 'active welfare state' in 1999 to capture the combination of three ideas. First, it refers to a goal, namely a state of *active* people. We want to enable all citizens to participate in the mainstream of social and economic life. Second, it is no coincidence that our objective is still called a *welfare* state: the traditional ambition of providing adequate social protection for those who cannot participate actively, or who have reached the age of retirement, is entirely preserved. Third, the notion suggests that we need an *'intelligently active state'*, i.e. it refers to the way in which government should conduct and manage its social policy.

The idea of the active welfare state builds upon some widely shared convictions with regard to social policy that came to be accepted during the 1990s in most European countries. These boil down to four main points.

First, welfare policy cannot be reduced to questions of employment and unemployment, but employment is nonetheless the key issue in welfare reform. Moreover, the nature of the employment objective has changed. Full employment as it was conceived in the past in most European countries, was employment for men. The social challenge today is employment for men and women. This is linked to the transformation of family structures and our changed conception of women's role in society. It points to the need to rethink both the architecture of the welfare state and the distribution of work over households and individuals as it emerges in the labour market.

Second, during the 1990s there was growing consensus that active labour market policies should be higher on the agenda and made more effective, both in quantity and in quality, by tailoring them more effectively to individual needs. Active labour market policies presuppose a correct balance between opportunities, obligations, and incentives for the people involved. Hence, taxes and benefits must not lead to a situation in which the poor (or their families) face very high marginal tax rates when their hours of work or their wages increase, or when they take up a job. More generally, mechanisms in the current social security systems that discourage people from being active should be discarded as much as possible.

Third, the welfare state should not only cover traditionally defined social risks (unemployment, illness, disability, and old age), but also new social risks, such as single parenthood or a lack of skills causing long-term unemployment or inferior employment. And it should respond to new social needs, such as the reconciliation of work, family life, and education, and the need to be able to negotiate changes within both family and workplace over one's entire life cycle. This is crucial. Yes, the traditional ambitions of welfare policy still remain and are subject to greater pressures than ever, as a result, for example, of demographic change. But now they coexist with new challenges. It should therefore be obvious that rolling back the welfare state is the worst conceivable option: we don't need less, but more welfare.

This brings me to the fourth point that is now accepted by most policy makers. The traditional welfare state is, in a sense, predominantly a passive institution. It is only once an undesirable outcome has occurred, that the safety net is spread. It is surely much more sensible for an active state to respond to old and new risks and needs by prevention.

An intelligently active state recognizes the individual vulnerability that is the result of social dependency. But it recognizes at the same time that this dependency can often be avoided. Increasing dependency is no law of nature but the result of socio-economic changes, which in turn react to human intervention. What is needed, in addition to social spending, is social investment, such as in education and training. I concur with the authors that social investment is not a substitute for social spending. The idea that the 'social investment state' can replace much of the traditional welfare state is unrealistic, especially given that we live in an ageing society, with ever more people dependent on benefits and social spending because of age. For that reason, the term 'active welfare state' is to be preferred to the notion of a 'social investment state'.

What I have said, so far, about the active welfare state is probably not controversial. Certainly, most people would agree that 'getting people back to work' is an important ambition. Let me nevertheless ask a question that, at first sight, seems redundant: why does this matter? Why should we aim at more 'active participation' in our society?

A first possible answer is that of a macroeconomic book-keeper with a social conscience, pointing to the ageing of the population. If demographic ageing increases the ratio of non-working to working members of the population, then the ratio of the average social security benefit of the inactive population to the average wage of the working population can be maintained only by increasing the financial burden on those who work. Those who want to keep social benefits at the same level as wages without increasing the financial burden on the latter, have to counteract the ratio bias between the non-employed and the employed. This argument of sustainability, which people on both the right and the left of the political spectrum accept, is valid and important. But it is rather limited in scope. What if there was no such demographic shift? Would a low activity rate then no longer be a problem?

There is a subtler argument as to why participation matters. Encouraging active participation, it is said, is the best weapon against poverty and the best guarantee for a fair income distribution. However, this argument too is not really sufficient. Obviously, for many individuals access to the labour market is crucial to escape from poverty. Yet, a cross-country comparison shows that promoting labour market participation is no substitute for income redistribution and the fight against poverty: more work does not necessarily mean less poverty. In the United Kingdom and the United States, for example, more people are at work, and for longer hours. But there is more poverty—in the active age bracket—than, for example, in Belgium. By contrast, countries such as Denmark succeed in reconciling extensive social protection with high participation. It is necessary and possible, therefore, to aim at both high levels of employment *and* social protection.

My defence of participation consequently stems neither from the concern of the macroeconomic book-keeper nor from the belief that we have discovered a substitute for social protection. What justifies fundamentally the importance I attach to participation is a conception of equality.

Since participation in social life is crucial for gaining respect from others and self-respect, the opportunity to participate actively in society is one of the basic opportunities that should be the right of everyone. Borrowing some terminology from John Rawls, the argument may be developed as follows. Rawls considers self-respect as perhaps the most important of his 'social primary goods' (social primary goods are what social justice should distribute fairly). Rawls takes it that in a well-ordered society self-respect is secured by the public affirmation of the status of equal citizenship for all. But, he adds that self-respect requires that there should be 'for each person at least one community of shared interests to which he belongs and where he finds his endeavours confirmed by his associates'. In Rawls's conception of social justice 'the social bases of self-respect' are to be distributed *equally*. If I am right to include the opportunity to participate in the social bases of self-respect, then justice requires that the opportunities to participate be shared equally too. Or, at least, an unequal distribution can only be just when it works to the greatest benefit of the least advantaged.[1]

This normative rationale necessarily refers to participation in society in the broadest sense, rather than participation in the labour market. Indeed, if the defence of more active participation draws its strongest argument from the postulate that participation is a Rawlsian 'social primary good' for every individual, it cannot be narrowed down merely to participation in the labour market. In that case, participation should also include other activities that can be used to build up respect and self-respect. These may include caring for a friend or a family member, voluntary social or cultural work or education. From this point of view, the growing number of women in the labour market may equally lead to policy measures aimed at activating men in the household, and social participation may also stand for active ageing, where the elderly are no longer regarded as dependent but rather as productive people who can make valuable contributions to society.

This normative justification directly feeds back into labour market policy. If participation is seen as a social primary good, the quality of jobs becomes as important as the quantity, as rightly emphasized in Duncan Gallie's chapter. Also, this broad interpretation of participation implies new rules for the organization of tomorrow's full employment of both men and women. I am, for philosophical reasons, no supporter of a universal, unconditional basic income. But I do support a labour market in which it is easy to enter and exit on a temporary basis, perhaps to care for children or parents or to take refresher courses, or perhaps just simply for a battery recharge. The existing enterprise culture, which drains people's creativity and energy between

---

[1] My summary of Rawls's complex argument on self-respect, developed, for instance, in §67 and §82 of his *Theory of Justice* (Rawls, 1971), is so brief that it cannot do justice to his theory. Moreover, Rawls does not explicitly refer to 'participation' in the sense in which I use it, and the relation I assume between equal opportunities to participate and 'self-respect' requires a more elaborate argument than I can present here. One should also note that Rawls raises the issue whether or not 'maximin' might apply to the social bases of self-respect (thus deviating from the equality benchmark) but does not develop it.

25 and 40 and considers those above 55 often as increasingly unproductive, is not compatible with the 'full employment' model of the future.

My egalitarian argument for the importance of participation has yet other consequences, notably for the way in which we have to integrate the idea of 'individual responsibility', an expression often used in the context of activation. Let me elaborate upon this, with specific reference to my own social-democratic stance. Responsibility can be a slippery notion, and social democrats are sometimes hesitant about referring to responsibility in the context of social policy: they fear it is a euphemism for the sort of mindset which holds that benefit recipients are guilty of sloth until they provide proof to the contrary. But as a simple matter of fact, the increasing emphasis on individual responsibility is not only the result of the popularity of such a dislikeable ideology; it is also nourished by sociological developments, namely the nature of new risks (such as skills shortages and single-parent households) and the link that is made, rightly or wrongly, between these risks and personal behaviour. These developments cannot be ignored. The traditional social security approach of insurance against unpredictable risks was mechanistic and based on supposedly objective statistics and probability theory. Judgements about individual behaviour were pushed into the background. That is now changing, also for the sociological reasons I mentioned.

But apart from this sociological observation, we owe it to ourselves to clarify what we mean by 'personal responsibility', at least if we assume that real equality of opportunity is the essence of social democracy. Indeed, one cannot explain what equality means if one doesn't make clear what individual responsibility, on the one hand, and societal responsibility, on the other, really stand for.

Allow me to give a trivial example. Suppose that we lived in a world without social security. Two sons inherit from their father. Although they have had the same education, they are very different. The elder brother is very sober and fully satisfied with what life has to offer. He is much 'happier' than his younger brother who needs champagne and caviar each day to be happy. If their father splits his inheritance exactly in two, the elder will be happier with his share than the younger. Yet nobody doubts that the equality principle has been adhered to. Now suppose that the two brothers have the same consumption patterns but that the elder is perfectly healthy and the younger has been paralysed since birth and requires all kinds of medical equipment. If their father divides his inheritance in two equal parts, we may find that the equality principle has been violated. Why? Because we generally regard a difference in taste as a matter of individual responsibility—for example, because we classify it as produced by 'free will'—whereas no one would ascribe an innate physical impairment to an individual's responsibility.

My egalitarianism is based on the conviction that it is unfair that individuals should be put at a disadvantage by characteristics or circumstances for which they cannot be held responsible. Two conclusions follow. First, pursuing equality is by definition responsibility-sensitive. Otherwise we end up with absurd implications (holding, for example, that equality requires the father to bequeath more money to the son with luxurious habits). Second, since the equality principle is the very cornerstone of social democracy, the principle of individual responsibility requires a context of full solidarity with those who have become victims through circumstances beyond their control.

Viewed in this way, the pursuit of equality is not a question of equal outcomes, such as equal pay, independent of personal choice and effort. Yet it requires more than what is usually understood by 'equal opportunities'. Individual choices are not determined solely by formal social institutions, but also by natural gifts and talents which individuals received at birth and through their early childhood. Those who want to give everyone the same opportunities but ignore such differences hold a narrow, meritocratic view of individual responsibility. In the view I am committed to, people cannot be held responsible for differences in talents, only for what they do with those talents. Here again, our philosophical stance has clear policy implications: even in a situation of formally equal opportunities (an objective that has so far not been attained) and full employment, there is still a case for income redistribution.

So a social-democratic commitment to participation and responsibility affects the shape of the welfare state. For a social democrat the active welfare state must meet four tests. First, the government's task is not simply to invest in people in order to prepare them for confrontation with the market. A meritocracy, which offers equal opportunities but ignores any differences in talents, is no ideal goal. Even if opportunities are formally perfectly equal, differences in reward by the market do not necessarily reflect individual responsibilities. There is a fundamental argument for giving income redistribution (notably progressive taxation) a role of its own for the purpose of social justice. Second, society as a whole—including the government—is responsible for ensuring that the labour market can actually offer a sufficient number of opportunities. Third, the plea in favour of participation as a social primary good gives rise to a broad definition of 'active participation' in a labour market that is positively flexible from the point of view of individual and family needs. And fourth, it continues to be the duty of social democrats to make provision, in addition to the easy rhetoric about the moral responsibilities of the poor and the powerless, for a more difficult rhetoric about the social obligations of the rich and the powerful.

My account of the normative rationale for active welfare states is certainly not complete. If we were to pursue the reference to the Rawlsian basket of 'social primary goods', which social justice aims to distribute fairly, we would have to include not just participation (as a social basis of respect and self-respect), but also income and wealth. How should we treat such a multidimensional basket of primary goods in a conception of social justice? I will not enter into this complex discussion. Moreover, if we were to stick to a literal interpretation of Rawls's *Theory of Justice*, we would be confronted with ambiguity concerning citizens' individual responsibility.[2] Let me however conclude by adding a qualification to my own emphasis on responsibility, or rather by raising a problem. Not all the dilemmas we face when implementing social policy can be reduced to 'equality with responsibility'. Some consequences of individual choices—choices for which people are responsible—are so dramatic, and the ensuing vulnerability so overwhelming, that we want to correct these effects anyway. Intensive care units admitting two critically wounded drivers will not ask themselves, for example, which of the two violated the traffic regulations and which one did not. The same applies to a great number of decisions where the question 'How did you get in such dire straits?' is simply not asked. This is compassion—a notion which some think has no place in the rigorous field of justice but rather supplements it. But surely protecting the vulnerable can claim an independent place as a requirement of justice when we speak about the welfare state? Protecting the vulnerable, sometimes irrespective of the cause of their vulnerability, is a positive responsibility which society should assume.

---

[2] There is ambiguity in Rawls's theory when it comes to the question whether or not people are to be held responsible for their effort at work, as G. A. Cohen and others have pointed out. (Rawls writes: 'That we deserve the superior character that enables us to make the effort to cultivate our abilities is also problematic; for such character depends in good part upon fortunate family and social circumstances in early life for which he can claim no credit. The notion of desert does not apply here' (1971: 89). However, when it comes to differences in 'taste' Rawls's approach to character is rather different, and contradicts what he writes about character here.) I think differences in 'effort' can legitimate differences in result, without violation of the principle of equality: what we equalize are opportunity sets. Elsewhere, I use the expression 'responsibility-sensitive egalitarian justice', borrowed from Stuart White, John Roemer, and others, to denote the ensuing conception of justice. However, this conception is not a textbook Rawlsian approach to social justice. Yet, it is possible (albeit with some difficulties) to apply Rawls's 'difference principle' (i.e. the maximin criterion) to a conception of justice based upon opportunity sets. What we take from Rawls, then, is not his whole theory, but rather the 'difference principle'.

Where are we to draw the line? Which principle should we appeal to in concrete situations? This is not an easy question since the two starting points I mentioned earlier—responsibility-sensitive egalitarianism on the one hand, protecting the vulnerable on the other—do not arise from one key principle; they may even be at odds. We must dare to admit that this is probably inherent in any such philosophical reflection. Some will stress the first basic principle rather than the second. Perhaps social democrats differ from others in that they want to take both principles explicitly on board.

The Life Cycle, Financial Sustainability, and Justice

Gøsta Esping-Andersen and his co-authors explicitly refer to a broadly Rawlsian conception of justice. Their highly interesting 'life-cycle approach' also fits well into a broadly Rawlsian framework, since Rawls explicitly reasons in terms of citizens' 'life prospects', or 'expectations of well-being'.[3] I fully support this innovative search for an explicit normative position, which is often lacking in social policy analysis. The life course dynamics perspective is also highly relevant from a practical policy point of view. Indeed, we should firmly keep in mind that good pension policies—like good health policies—begin at birth. Investment in real equality of opportunity for children and the concomitant welfare policies that are needed, should be at centre stage, as Gøsta Esping-Andersen argues.

John Myles moreover raises issues of intergenerational justice, and so ventures into a domain where the political and philosophical issues at stake are extremely complex. Formulating an unambiguous, philosophically justifiable standard for intergenerational justice that is politically acceptable for the various (European) actors involved is everything but easy. The living conditions of different generations can be as different as chalk and cheese, which makes reasoning in terms of *equality* (which is our benchmark for intragenerational justice) rather precarious. Also, a satisfactory forum for discussion does not exist. However 'a-historical' our conception of social justice may be, it still is our view and we use it to think about the problem 'here and now'. By definition, other—possibly more sophisticated—future views on justice may evolve but this does not help us decide today.

---

[3] I write that the authors' approach is *broadly* Rawlsian, since, in comparison with the pension question that Myles focuses on, Rawls examines a larger and somewhat different question when he discusses intergenerational justice and introduces his 'just savings principle'.

Myles provides an extremely useful input into this complex normative discussion, by drawing attention to Richard Musgrave's proposal for inter-generational risk sharing. Let me introduce the argument as follows: a basic precondition for any pension system is that it must be 'time-consistent'. A pension system must be robust and flexible enough to avoid that some generation would one day feel entitled to abandon the prevailing implicit intergenerational contract. In other words, we must construct pension systems so that they will be considered 'fair' by successive generations; time-consistency in this sense requires an accepted notion of fairness, which leads us to the realm of social justice.

Now, financial sustainability and social justice are often seen as uneasy friends at best, sworn enemies at worst. This is a mistake. Financial sustainability is not an 'external' constraint befalling our pension systems independently from their internal logic. On the contrary, intergenerational (and intragenerational) fairness is a precondition for their sustainability. Consider the budgetary debate on pensions expenditure: the sustainability of the public pension system will be jeopardized, so it is assumed, if essential future government spending is crowded out by the costs of ageing; or if the system is sustainable only on the basis of unacceptably high taxes. 'Crowding out other essential spending' and 'unacceptably high taxes' are statements that signal problems of fairness towards future generations.

Musgrave suggested a conception of intergenerational fairness by proposing a solution for optimal risk sharing based on the *relative income position* of the working age population and pensioners: an implicit contract between generations based on a stable and 'fixed' definition of relative living standards. Musgrave's point was that this divides the demographic and economic risks between the actives and retirees.

Admittedly, a 'fair' spread of risks between generations on the one hand and intergenerational social justice on the other hand, are two different things. Or, as the Dutch Scientific Council for Government Policy put it in a report on 'Generationally-aware Policy': 'It is not so that sustainable solutions per se are either just or not, and that just solutions per se are either sustainable or not.'[4] But there is common ground in the two approaches: creating a situation that is unsustainable in the long run is unfair to the generations to come. We want sustainable social justice in Europe. In that perspective, the Musgrave condition is an interesting reference point, but not

---

[4] Wetenschappelijke Raad voor het Regeringsbeleid (2001), *Generatiebewust beleid*, Den Haag, Sdu Uitgevers, 89. I discuss the problematic relationship between stability and justice (in a different context) in Vandenbroucke (2001).

necessarily an absolute and immovable criterion. Yet, although I endorse the relevance of Musgrave's 'fixed relative income position', I would immediately like to amend his point slightly by introducing the dimension of care. When we focus on the relative income position of pensioners, we may neglect potential expenditure differences between the working age population and pensioners, such as expenditure differences related to health care and care for the elderly.

It is safe to assume that spending on care is relatively more important in pensioners' budgets. William Baumol's *unbalanced growth theory* would help us predict the likely long-run consequences. If, like Baumol, we were to divide the economy into two sectors: the care sector on the one hand, and the non-care sector (that is, all the other sectors) on the other hand, no doubt productivity would grow more slowly in the former. If we don't want wages in the two sectors to diverge, the cost 'per unit of care' will probably increase more than the cost 'per unit of product' in the rest of the economy. If the 'price per unit of care' increases faster than the 'price per unit of product' in the rest of the economy, the cost of living will increase relatively faster for pensioners, because the share of care is relatively larger in pensioner's budgets. Pensioners and the working age population have as it were, different consumer price indices: given our assumptions the real value of the euros of pensioners will decline faster than that of the working age population. If we were to base our reasoning purely on nominal income, we would therefore do pensioners an injustice in such a context. However, the argument that care will inevitably become more expensive for consumers crucially depends on the extent of public investment in the care sector: public intervention may protect the consumer's budget, by increasing subsidies for the care sector, by higher levels of reimbursement of care expenditure, etc.

This issue is obviously connected with the increasing professionalization of care and, inevitably, also with the increasing employment of women (and of both men and women over 55). Since we now prioritize the goal of raising female activity rates, we must simultaneously recognize that this has enormous consequences for the provision of care to the frail elderly. I believe our analyses of Europe's social future have failed, so far, to integrate the challenges posed by the family–work–pension nexus with the challenges posed by the care nexus.

Obviously, the significance of all this requires empirical assessment. But, whatever the outcome, it makes more sense to require a 'fixed relative position' between the generations (if that is the yardstick) in terms of *well-being* than to require it in terms of income. Depending on public investment in the care sector, it may well be that unchanged relative incomes yield a fall in relative well-being for the elderly.

Since the pension challenge is compounded by the increasing cost of health and elderly care in our societies, an adequate assessment of the future of social protection requires an integrated approach. After launching open co-ordination on pensions, preparing open co-ordination between the European Union Member States on the challenge of health and care for the elderly may well be the next step to take.

These summary and incomplete reflections on rather abstract problems of social justice may appear surprising, coming from someone whose *métier* is politics. Yet, I firmly believe that politics and policy making need normative debate. Being a somewhat reconstructed Rawlsian myself, I am obviously pleased with the authors' reference to a broadly Rawlsian framework. To say, as the authors do, that 'the European debate is quite close to the Rawlsian ethos', seems an overstatement; a Rawlsian conception of social justice would entail far more redistributive efforts than are currently undertaken in most European nations. Yet, I believe there is such a commonality of social values in the European Union, based on solidarity and the rejection of social exclusion, that it makes sense to reason in terms of a 'European social model' (and to probe it along Rawlsian lines), notwithstanding the variety of institutions and social traditions in the Member States. However, it is high time to specify this rather vague notion of a European social model by means of more precise definitions of our common social objectives. That is, I believe, the principal role of 'the open method of co-ordination', to which I turn now.

Open Co-ordination and the Definition of the European Social Model

Open co-ordination is a process where explicit, clear and mutually agreed objectives are defined, after which peer review enables European Union Member States to examine and learn from good practices. The method respects and is in fact built on local diversity; it is flexible, and aims to promote progress in the social sphere. To do so, it requires that we use comparable and commonly agreed indicators in order to monitor progress towards the common goals. The exchange of reliable information aims at institutionalizing 'policy mimicking', at least to a certain extent. Intelligent policy mimicking needs to be actively managed and 'contextualized', as Anton Hemerijck emphasizes. Well thought-out 'benchmarking' requires three elements:

- First, reliable information on social policy and its results.
- Second, evaluation of this information in the light of the commonly defined objectives.
- Third, evaluation of this information in the light of the local context of policies.

The latter is important, because otherwise benchmarking would easily appear 'compulsive' to actors who find themselves in a completely different local situation. If we are insensitive to context, the 'open method' will lose credibility and the whole exercise is unlikely to be successful.

This 'open' approach is pragmatic, and this is why it can be an *effective* instrument for social progress. Thus, we have found a way that implies a credible commitment to a social Europe. This signals an important message to the European citizen, namely that Member States will defend our welfare states against a possible retrenchment, as a result of intensifying competition in an integrated European market and a globalizing economy. Or, to use more popular terms, it is a signal that we will counteract 'social dumping'. With regard to 'social dumping' there is, however, a need for nuances. First, economic and monetary integration is only one of the many challenges. Today, adjustment is necessary because (*a*) the traditional fields of social protection, such as pensions and health care, will require more resources and (*b*) because new social risks and needs have emerged. Second, experience, so far, does not suggest that European integration necessarily leads to welfare retrenchment. To the contrary, in many countries the single market has reinvigorated the formation of broad social pacts and the need to rethink—rather than roll back—welfare state programmes.

Nevertheless, it would be naïve just to extrapolate from current experience. Increased factor mobility within the Union will undoubtedly affect welfare states in the long run. We should not forget that we are still at the dawn of a long process of European Union enlargement. In light of these developments, the need for an explicit definition of the European social model is now greater than ever. This brings me to what I consider to be the principal added value of the open method of co-ordination.

This added value is far greater than, simply, the fruits of policy learning or a defence against a competitive 'race to the bottom'. Common objectives are *essential* because they allow the much discussed but rarely specified 'European social model' to be translated into a tangible set of agreed objectives, to be entrenched in European co-operation. For the first time, thanks to the open method of co-ordination, the rather vague idea that the European Union embodies a distinct social model, based on common social values, is given content by means of precise definitions.

Open co-ordination is both a cognitive and a normative tool. It is a 'cognitive' tool, because it allows us to learn from each other. This learning process is not restricted to the practice of other Member States; national policy makers can also learn a lot from the underlying analyses and normative views within other Member States. Open co-ordination is a 'normative' tool because, necessarily, common objectives embody substantive views on social justice. Thus open co-ordination gradually creates a European social policy paradigm.

The 'soft' character of open co-ordination is often met with scepticism. Yet by means of 'soft' co-operation and consensus building we can go far beyond solemn but vague declarations at European Summits. This is, at this stage, the most promising way to give concrete shape to 'social Europe', as a large region in the world in which sustainable social justice will thrive. Open co-ordination can fulfil that ambition if it is used in a judicious way.

Open co-ordination is not some kind of fixed recipe that can be applied to whichever issue. The methodology we have now applied for the first time in the field of social inclusion differs from the open co-ordination that, via the so-called Luxembourg process, has been developed already since 1997. The methodology with regard to pensions will again be somewhat different. In December 2001 it was agreed that Member States would be invited to present a 'national strategy report on pensions'; the European Commission and the Council will then agree on a joint report at the European level 'to analyse the national strategy reports with regard to the broad common objectives and to identify good practice and innovative approaches of common interest to the Member States'. Common conclusions on pension policy should be integrated into the Broad Economic Policy Guidelines, drawn up by the European Union every year. Thus the methodology in the field of pensions, agreed upon at the end of 2001, envisages a fairly 'light' process in comparison with the other existing open co-ordination processes.

To ensure a successful application of the open method of co-ordination, five key principles have to be met.

1. This is only one method amongst others. It is no panacea we can apply to all European social issues. We cannot rely solely on open co-ordination to reach social Europe. Legislative work is important, as is evident in the need for the portability of social security rights when we move within the European Union.

2. We must not mix up the objectives and instruments of social policy. Mixing up these elements goes against the spirit of subsidiarity that is

fundamental to the open method of co-ordination. But that is not the only reason why I emphasize this. *How* we achieve something is undeniably important, but thinking ahead about *what* we want to achieve is obviously what matters most. This may seem a trivial point, but in practice it is sometimes forgotten. For instance, the debate on the future of our pensions has been dominated for a long time by elaborate comparative analyses of the relative efficiency of pension *instruments*, that is, of pay-as-you-go systems versus funded systems. This involves definitely important questions but the debate should not get bogged down in a debate on instruments. When we apply the open method of co-ordination, we must focus first on the objectives.

3. All possible instruments should be included in the analysis. 'Comprehensiveness' is particularly important in the field of pensions, as John Myles's analysis in this book illustrates very convincingly. Let me elaborate a little on this.

In discussions on the demographic transition and financial sustainability, it is often assumed that countries with a relatively strong first (public) pillar have a particular disadvantage. But this may well prove to be an illusion.

According to the basic rules of macro-economic accounting, pensions represent a claim on the output of services and goods. For any pension system, the real cost of the retirees boils down to their expenditures on services and goods that have to be provided for by the people who are active at that given time. So conceived, the demographic problem is one of an increasing share in spending. From this angle, it makes no difference whether these expenditures are accounted for within the public ledger, or not.

As Myles argues, adequate benchmarks and indicators must therefore be based on the total social cost of pensions, and not only on public expenditures. Such a comprehensive approach requires the establishment of reliable, and indeed comprehensive, social accounts. A shift of costs to the private sector lightens the budgetary burden, but offers few solutions to tricky questions like intergenerational equity and intragenerational justice—it may even lead to less equity and justice. A comprehensive approach to the pension challenge requires us to revisit not only our public pension pillars, but also the regulation of our private pillars.

Shifting to private systems under budgetary pressure is no solution in itself: it does not require less government, but a different kind of government, capable of regulating the private sector. Thus we are far beyond the primitive stage where the question was 'for or against' the second pillar, or alternatively 'for or against' pay-as-you-go. With reference to the reform of the second pillar that is currently underway in Belgium, I would say the crucial question is: to what extent can private systems provide a supplementary *social* protection, which is easily accessible for the many, not just the few? I am pleased that such a comprehensive approach, including all the relevant pension vehicles, is an agreed feature of the process of open co-ordination that will be launched in the field of pensions.

4. The fourth principle concerns the choice of 'benchmarks' used to put objectives into practice: when we define our standards, we have to be realistic and ambitious at the same time. We definitely need *best practices* in the learning process: feasible 'standards of excellence' instead of already acquired standards of mediocrity.

5. The fifth principle for a useful application of the open method of co-ordination is eminently practical. Progress cannot be measured in the field of social exclusion and poverty without comparable and quantifiable indicators. For this reason, developing a set of common EU indicators with regard to social inclusion was a top priority for the Belgian Presidency, and we were very pleased to reach a political agreement on this by the end of 2001.[5]

This fifth principle is the actual litmus test for the political readiness to engage in open co-ordination. However, I should emphasize that the purpose of a common set of indicators is not a naming and shaming exercise. If there is a 'rank order tournament' at some stage of the process, it should exclusively serve the purpose of improving the overall record of all European welfare states through, amongst other things, the identification of best practices. Indicators are not a vehicle for defining any pecking order among Europe's nations, but a tool to preserve and reinforce the quality of social protection for the benefit of all Europe's citizens.

A final question, raised at the Leuven conference where we discussed the content of this book, is about the relation between open co-ordination and democratic decision making in Europe. One of the potential gains of open policy co-ordination is that it requires all national governments to prepare and discuss their policy reforms 'in public', and this, moreover, simultaneously. Open co-ordination definitely implies 'openness' in that sense too. On the other hand, the intergovernmental nature of open co-ordination, without formal involvement of the European Parliament, points to a democratic deficit. In my opinion this constitutes an important question for the debate on the future of Europe's institutions that will be prepared by the Convention, decided upon at the December 2001 Laeken Summit.

[5] Atkinson *et al.* (2002).

Let me conclude by emphasizing again that open co-ordination is not a panacea, let alone a magic formula. Yet, an effective open method of co-ordination is more than an intelligently managed learning process and a defensive instrument. If we employ it judiciously, open co-ordination is a proactive and creative method that allows us to define 'social Europe' in more specific terms and to anchor it firmly as a common collective good at the heart of European co-operation. This method can provide the key for people to be able to identify Europe with sustainable social justice. At this stage of European co-operation, open co-ordination is clearly a promising way to realize this ambition. We should sail thoughtfully, but we should embark on the voyage with all due speed.

Frank Vandenbroucke
Minister for Social Affairs and Pensions
Belgian Federal Government

Preface and Acknowledgements

This book has its origins in contemporary European politics. It is based on a report 'A New European Welfare Architecture' prepared at the request of the Belgian government, in the context of the Belgian Presidency of the Council of the European Union (EU) in the second half of 2001. It was commissioned by Mr Frank Vandenbroucke, Minister of Social Affairs and Pensions. We are most grateful to him for his support, both material and intellectual.

The report was presented at a Belgian Presidency conference, 'Towards a New Architecture for Social Protection in Europe? A Broader Perspective of Pension Policies', at Leuven, 19–20 October 2001, and we have benefited from the constructive comments made by the speakers and conference participants.

Of course, it is one thing to write a report intended for a policy making forum, another to author an academic publication. This book incorporates most of the analyses and arguments of the original work, but it has been substantially revised. Indeed, large parts of the final book would be unrecognizable to anyone who had read its progenitor.

Within the social field, the Belgian Presidency gave special attention to the development of the 'Open Method of Co-ordination' in the area of pensions, as is explained in detail by Minister Vandenbroucke in his Foreword. Our report was conceived as a contribution to this project, even though it casts the net far wider. Its authors believe that long-term and sustainable solutions to ageing and retirement must take a broad life course perspective, analysing the retirement process as part and parcel of citizens' life span. Hence, the report attempted to draw systematic policy links between old age, adult working age life, families and children.

This life course framework has, if anything, been strengthened in this book. Indeed, as a result the book can no longer be regarded as 'retirement' or 'pension' focused. It is, simply, life course focused. Our conviction is that this is a first *sine qua non* condition if our more lofty goal is to define a just and efficient welfare architecture for the twenty-first century.

The book concentrates on four major life course related issues: childhood and families with children, gender equality and the compatibility issues facing working mothers, working life, and retirement. We attempt to demonstrate that the welfare problems distinct to each life phase are, at the same time, directly linked to the other phases. It is this principle of interconnectedness that spurs us to speak, perhaps with undue pretentiousness, of a new welfare 'architecture'.

The entire idea of the book came from the Belgian Presidency, and for this we must doubly thank Minister Frank Vandenbroucke. First, because he provided us with a unique opportunity to try to piece together the many puzzles involved in a major overhaul of contemporary welfare states. Second, because of the enormous and incredibly generous personal and intellectual investment which he dedicated to our project.

The report enjoyed the support of a Scientific Steering Committee and an Institutional Steering Committee (the members are listed below); many members made valuable comments on earlier drafts that led to considerable improvements. Our work for the Presidency was also helped hugely by Michelle Pritchard and Tom Van Puyenbroeck for their decisive and constructive editorial work.

In addition, the authors benefited from what turned out to be the indispensable scientific collaboration of Sebastian Sarasa, at the University of Pompeu Fabra, and Koen Vleminckx, at the University of Leuven. Together, they provided most of the data analyses presented in the book.

And, of course, the authors of the various chapters in this book have also, jointly or individually, drawn upon the wisdom and critical spirit of other colleagues. We would in particular like to acknowledge the help of Anthony Atkinson, Maurizio Ferrera, Kaj Frick, Janet Gornick, Anne Marie Guillemard, Peter Hicks, Michael Littlewood, Josep Mestres, Judit Montoriol, John Morley, Fritz von Nordheim Nielsen, Einar Overbye, Jill Quadagno, Phillippe van Parijs, Emmanuel Reynaud, Martin Rhodes, Sebastian Sarasa, Fritz Scharpf, Anne Mette Sorensen, and Axel West Pedersen.

None of these people should however be held responsible in any way for the contents of the book. Also, even though the book originates from a report commissioned by the Belgian Presidency of the European Union, all responsibility must be placed squarely on the shoulders of the authors.

Members of the Steering Committees

Scientific Steering Committee

Chairman: Mr Yves Chassard, Bernard Brunhes International, France
Professor Jonathan Bradshaw, University of York, United Kingdom
Professor Gøsta Esping-Andersen, University of Pompeu Fabra, Spain
Professor Maurizio Ferrera, University of Pavia, Italy
Professor Jean-Paul Fitoussi, President of the Observatoire Français des Conjonctures Economiques, France

Professor Duncan Gallie, Nuffield College, Oxford, United Kingdom
Professor L.J. Gunning-Schepers, University of Amsterdam, The Netherlands
Professor Anton Hemerijck, University of Leyden, The Netherlands
Professor John Hills, London School of Economics, United Kingdom
Professor Peter Mohler, University of Mannheim (ZUMA), Germany
Professor John Myles, Florida State University, United States
Professor Pierre Pestieau, University of Liège, Belgium
Professor Fritz Scharpf, Max Planck Institute, Germany
Professor Luc Soete, University of Maastricht, The Netherlands
Professor Panos Tsakoglou, University of Athens, Greece
Professor Philippe Van Parijs, Catholic University of Louvain-la-Neuve, Belgium
Professor Jan Vranken, University of Antwerp (UFSIA), Belgium

Institutional Steering Committee

Chairman: Professor Jos Berghman, Catholic University of Leuven, Belgium
Mr Raoul Briet, Chairman of the Social Protection Committee
Professor Paolo Garonna, University of Padua (Italy) and Deputy Executive Secretary, United Nations Economic Commission for Europe (UNECE)
Ms Anna Hedborg, National Social Insurance Board, Sweden
Ms Beatrice Hertogs, European Trade Union Confederation, Belgium
Mr Ludo Horemans, President of the European Anti-Poverty Network (EAPN), Belgium
Ms Marie-Thérèse Join-Lambert, President of the National Observatory on Poverty and Social Exclusion, France
Mr Allan Larsson, Former Director General, Directorate General Employment and Social Affairs, European Commission
Ms Odile Quintin, Director General, Directorate General Employment and Social Affairs, European Commission
Mr Emmanuel Reynaud, International Labour Organization (ILO)
Mr Peter Scherer, OECD
Mr David Stanton, Chairman of the Social Protection Committee's Sub-Group on Indicators
Mr Frank Vandenbroucke, Minister for Social Affairs and Pensions, Belgium

Notes on Contributors

Gøsta Esping-Andersen is professor of Sociology, Universitat Pompeu Fabra in Barcelona. He has previously taught at the Universita di Trento, the European University Institute in Firenze, and at Harvard University. He is the author of a number of books including *Social Foundations of Postindustrial Economies* (Oxford, 1999), *Why De-regulate Labour Markets?* (with Marino Regini, Oxford, 2000), *Welfare States in Transition* (Sage, 1996), and *Three Worlds of Welfare Capitalism* (Polity Press, 1990).

Duncan Gallie is an Official Fellow and Professor of Sociology at Nuffield College, Oxford. He is a Fellow of the British Academy. His research has focused both on changes in employment conditions and on the experience of unemployment in Europe. His recent publications include *Restructuring the Employment Relationship* (co-authored with Michael White, Yuan Cheng, and Mark Tomlinson) and *Welfare Regimes and the Experience of Unemployment in Europe* (co-edited with Serge Paugam).

John Myles is Canada Research Chair in Sociology at the University of Toronto and Visiting Research Scholar at Statistics Canada. He is the author of *Old Age in the Welfare State: The Political Economy of Public Pensions* and *Relations of Ruling*, a comparative study of class and gender relations in North American and Nordic countries. Recent publications include studies of the contemporary politics of welfare state retrenchment and of trends in earnings inequality, child and old-age poverty. His current research focuses on issues related to urban inequality with a particular emphasis on immigrants and race.

Anton Hemerijck is deputy director of the Netherlands Council for Government Policy (WRR) and senior lecturer in the Department of Public Administration, Leiden University. Between 1997 and 2000 he was research affiliate of the Max Planck Institute, working on the large comparative project, *Welfare and Work in the Open Economy*, directed by Fritz W. Scharpf and Vivien A. Schmidt. Publications include: with Jelle Visser, *'A Dutch Miracle': Job Growth, Welfare Reform and Corporatism in the Netherlands* (1997); with Maurizio Ferrera and Martin Rhodes, *The Future of Social Europe: Recasting Work and Welfare in the New Economy* (Report for the Portuguese Presidency of the EU in the first half of 2000), an updated and revised version will be published by Oxford University Press shortly.

List of Abbreviations

ECB	European Central Bank
ECHP	European Community Household Panel
EES	European Employment Strategy
EMI	European Monetary Institute
EMS	European Monetary System
EMU	Economic and Monetary Union
FRC	Fixed Rate Contribution
FRP	Fixed Relative Position
FRR	Fixed Revenue Rate (defined contribution schemes)
GAI	Guaranteed Annual Income
GDP	Gross Domestic Product
ILA	Individual Learning Account
LIS	Luxembourg Income Study
NAP	National Action Plan
NIT	Negative Income Tax
OECD	Organization for Economic Co-operation and Development
OMC	Open Method of Co-ordination
PAYGO	Pay-As-You-Go
SERPS	State Earnings Related Pension Scheme
SOU	Sveriges Offentliga Utrednigar (Swedish Government Commission Reports)
SSI	Supplemental Security Income

Towards the Good Society, Once Again?

Gøsta Esping-Andersen

Two distinctive features stand out in the long history of western welfare states. In the first place, we see long phases of consolidation and institutional path dependency being punctuated by two epochs of intense reform. The closing decades of the nineteenth century heralded a path-breaking burst of welfare reform; the 1930s–1940s produced a second, and equally decisive, wave of regime-shifts. In large measure, today's advanced welfare states are but elaborations on the post-war 'welfare capitalist' edifice—although the Scandinavian shift towards a servicing and 'activation' bias since the 1970s may arguably constitute a third instance of fundamental regime overhaul.

In the second place, most historical regime shifts have one thing in common, namely an intensification of ideological competition between rival visions of the 'Good Society'. Late nineteenth-century reformism pitted absolutist and often anti-capitalist defenders of the *ancien régime* against liberals and occasionally also Christian reformists. What was at stake in Bismarckian Germany, in Disraeli's Britain, or in Giolitti's Italy was not merely the urgency of social amelioration but, far more to the point, huge questions of nation-building. Moving forward to the second reform era visions of the Good Society emerged once again, but now by a rather different set of political actors. With the authoritarians pretty much gone, the contest now stood between liberals, social Catholicism, and social democracy. The diversity of contemporary welfare models bears testimony to the kinds of historical compromises that were forged in that epoch.[1]

In some countries, particularly in the US but increasingly also the UK, the compromise favoured individualism and markets with the welfare state cast as a minimal and residual player. In Scandinavia it favoured social

---

[1] Excellent historical treatments of welfare state evolution can be found in Rimlinger (1971), Flora and Heidenheimer (1981), Alber (1982), and in Ferrera (1993). For an analysis of welfare regime variations, see Esping-Andersen (1990; 1999).

democracy, universalism, egalitarianism and comprehensive social citizenship. And a third model fused social insurance with corporativist and often also social Catholic subsidiarity traditions in much of Continental and, especially, Southern Europe. In each and every case, these were not simply technical solutions to social security but also a promise to resolve the 'social question' and put an end to class inequalities. To this end, the policy repertoire, albeit not its ambitions, contents, or design, appeared quite similar everywhere: the expansion of mass education as the vehicle for equal opportunities and an end to inherited privilege; income maintenance as a means to equalize living conditions and eliminate social risks across the life cycle.

The New Welfare Challenge

We live in an era in which rival forces, once again, promote their blueprints for a Good Society. Indeed, much suggests that we are heading towards yet another historical regime shift. We are in the midst of a revolution in demographic and family behaviour, spearheaded by women's embrace of personal independence and lifelong careers. Marriage is less an act of economic necessity and more a question of individual choice. This also means a proliferation of new and far less stable household and family arrangements. The average child is increasingly unlikely to stay with *both* mother and father throughout childhood. All this mirrors heightened individual freedom of choice, but also insecurity and risk.

We are also in the midst of economic upheaval, the emergence of a very different kind of integrated global economic order from that which reigned in our grandfathers' time. Technological transformation and the dominance of service employment provoke major changes in the social risk structure, creating a wholly new set of societal winners and losers. The standard production worker and the low-skilled could by and large count on a decently paid and secure job in the welfare capitalist era. This is unlikely to be the case in the twenty-first century. The basic requisites needed for a good and secure life are growing and changing at the same time. Those with insufficient skills or cultural and social resources may easily slide into a life course marked by low pay, unemployment, and precarious jobs. Our contemporary preoccupation with social exclusion appears very much like an echo of the 'social question' that permeated debates in the 1930s.

The unfolding service economy is potentially dualistic. The overwhelming thrust is in favour of skilled and professional jobs but a sizeable market of low-end, routine services may easily emerge. And this is especially so if wage disparities continue to widen. The hard trade-off is that, in the absence of a low wage market, the alternative is likely to be mass unemployment.[2] Those with weak human capital are therefore likely to face either low wages or unemployment. Whether they shall be condemned to a lifetime of exclusion or of precariousness is, we underline, not preordained. The duality of the post-industrial employment structure need not coagulate into a post-industrial class abyss if—and this is *the* big 'if'—our society can extend guarantees against lifelong entrapment. And this implies a system that ensures strong mobility opportunities. But it probably necessitates more since widening inequalities at the individual level may easily harden at the household level. Marital homogamy is definitely not in decline and, hence, the post-industrial losers and winners are likely to bundle within households.

All this seems to add up to one great ironical twist of historical change. Probably far more due to structural transformation than to the efficacy of existing welfare programmes, the traditional class divide is, no doubt, eroding. This would, as many social scientists claim, indicate that class no longer matters.[3] The irony is that class may be less visible, but its importance is arguably far more decisive. In knowledge-intensive economies, life chances will depend on one's learning abilities and one's accumulation of human capital. As is well established, the impact of social inheritance is as strong today as in the past—in particular with regard to cognitive development and educational attainment.[4]

The post-war welfare state no doubt succeeded in equalizing living conditions, but it failed to deliver on its promise of disconnecting opportunities from social origins and inherited handicaps. Ideological predilections aside, it should be evident to all that we cannot afford *not* to be egalitarians in the advanced economies of the twenty-first century. There are inevitably basic questions of social justice involved. But there is a very good argument that equality of opportunities and life chances is becoming *sine qua non* for efficiency as well. Our human capital constitutes the single most important resource that we must mobilize in order to ensure a dynamic and competitive knowledge economy. We are facing huge demographic imbalances with very small working age cohorts ahead, and to sustain the elderly we must maximize the productivity of the young. Finally, to put it bluntly, no country would willingly opt for a dualistic or, worse, polarized future scenario with 'islands of excellence in a sea of ignorance'.

---

[2] For recent treatments of this basic dilemma, see Scharpf and Schmidt (2000) and Esping-Andersen (1999). [3] Notable examples are Bell (1976) and Clark and Lipset (1991).
[4] See e.g. Shavit and Blossfeld (1992). This will be examined in more detail in Chapter 2.

Emerging Blueprints for Reform

For two reasons, the continued viability of the existing welfare state edifice is being questioned across all of Europe. The first is simply that the status quo will be difficult to sustain given adverse demographic or financial conditions. The second is that the same status quo appears increasingly out-of-date and ill suited to meet the great challenges ahead. Our existing systems of social protection may hinder rather than promote employment growth and competitive knowledge-intensive economies. They may also be inadequate in the face of evolving and possibly far more intense social risks and needs. It is on this backdrop that new political entrepreneurs and welfare architects are coming to the fore with calls for major regime change.

Sidelined and muted for decades, in the 1980s the libertarians and neo-liberals spearheaded the call for a recast model. Much inspired by Hayek, their blueprint advocated a return to rugged individualism, de-regulation, and privatization of social protection. They even believed that their formulae would attack class inequalities because, as they saw it, it was primarily big government and excessive regulation that were responsible for social segmentation and the reproduction of poverty.[5] If markets were allowed to reign more freely, pathological barriers to individual initiative and mobility would fall. With the debatable exception of Britain, New Zealand, and the US, the neo-liberal vision of the Good Society failed to ignite the passions of most ordinary citizens or even their elected representatives. Their concrete accomplishments remained limited even where their ideology was vocally embraced (Pierson, 1994). The neo-liberal vision was evidently far too radical— even to most of the European right.

'The Third Way' of the 1990s heralded the arrival of a second grand formula for the post-industrial Good Society. No doubt, it succeeded better in catching the mood of the times, in large part by retaining some of the more credible and popular aspects of neo-liberalism, including its accent on individual responsibility and a more competitive reward structure, while fusing these with a concomitant *public* responsibility. Contrary to the extreme transparency of neo-liberalism, it is broadly viewed as an emperor without clothes. Indeed, the Third Way does remain frustratingly vague and generic, but if one attempts to piece together its broad objectives with the few concrete measures actually introduced, the outlines of a basic architecture do seem to emerge.

---

[5] Charles Murray (1984) is probably the most explicit voice along these lines.

First and foremost, it proposes one sharp break with the past: rather than tame, regulate, or marginalize markets so as to ensure human welfare, the idea is to adapt and empower citizens so that they may be far better equipped to satisfy their welfare needs within the market. At its core, it is a supply-driven policy attempting to furnish citizens with the requisites needed for individual success. Hence its flagship policies are training and lifelong learning. The assumption seems to be that the social risks and class inequalities that emanate from markets can be overridden if we target policy so that all compete on a more equal footing.

Towards a Viable New European Welfare Architecture?

It is probably fair to say that British Labour's Third Way has been received rather coolly in most of Europe. When it moves from vague catchwords to some degree of concreteness it seems to have little novel to offer or, alternatively, what it offers is perceived as problematic. There appears, for example, to be a widespread unease with its enthusiastic—and many say, naïve—embrace of markets. Additionally, Britain's steady move from universal social security towards income-tested assistance has not been halted during Labour's rule in the 1990s, and this will appear wholly incongruent with basic principles across most of Europe.

To Northern European social democrats, its accent on activation and strengthening individuals' capacities would appear old hat. With mixed results this is indeed what the Danes and, especially, the Swedes have been pursuing for decades. As many critics have suggested, the Third Way may be little more than a very belated British discovery of Nordic social democracy.

The Third Way may be criticized for its unduly selective appropriation of social democratic policy. First, it has a tendency to believe that activation may *substitute* for conventional income maintenance guarantees. This may be regarded as naïve optimism but, worse, it may also be counterproductive. A leading theme in this book, and especially in Chapter 2, is that the minimization of poverty and income insecurity is a *precondition* for an effective social investment strategy. Second, British Third Way policies of activation tend to be slanted towards remedial programmes like adult training and job insertion. Another leading argument in our book is that remedial policy is unlikely to be very effective unless participants already possess the necessary abilities and motivation in the first place. It is not difficult to demonstrate that a truly effective and sustainable social investment strategy must be biased towards preventative policy.

The book we have written would seem to promise a complete blueprint for 'a new welfare architecture', lock-stock-and-barrel. To stave off accusations of hubris, we readily admit that we are not selling the reader a completed house, let alone cathedral. Nor do we pretend to propose a set of policy *panacea* that will solve all problems, once and for all. Important pieces of the welfare edifice are simply absent in our treatment, health care in particular. Still we do believe that our work may help contribute to the ongoing project of constructing a new and workable welfare model. What we shall offer is perhaps more accurately a partial formula, a set of building blocks. The first of these is a more effective analytical methodology.

The Need for a Method

Normal policy making is inevitably short-sighted and fragmented into specialized areas and compartments. As such it is powerfully biased in favour of improving upon existing practice rather than questioning the *Gestalt* itself. Additionally, the identification of problems in need of attention is too often based on what we might call a static methodology, on snapshots of today's reality: how many people fall below the poverty line? How many elderly require a nursing home? How many children abandon school?

If society remains very stable, snapshot diagnoses can be quite valid. They become problematic for policy making if, as is now the case, we are undergoing very rapid change. Fragmentary, compartmentalized and static policy diagnosis is of questionable value if our real challenge is to construct a new welfare model for the twenty-first century. For this we need a method that satisfies three criteria: that it allows us an informed 'peek' into the future; that it links fragments to the whole (after all, we are concerned with the architecture and not simply a window here or a doorstep there); and that it captures the dynamics of citizens' life chances.

The latter criterion requires elaboration. The core welfare issue is not so much how many people at any given moment are low-paid or ill-housed, but how many are likely to remain persistently low-paid or ill-housed. Our society will probably *not* be able to avert that some people, for some period of their lives, will encounter social ills. This may not be as bad as it seems because social ills are not, by definition, socially problematic. Low-wage jobs, for example, may play a positive role as entry ports into the labour market for youth or newly arrived immigrants. *The foremost challenge we face is to avert that social ills become permanent, that citizens become entrapped in exclusion or inferior opportunities in such a way that their entire life chances are affected.*

For these reasons we require a diagnostic methodology which focuses on dynamics. Our work adopts what we believe to be a powerful such tool, namely a life course framework. The life course framework allows us, first, to connect fragments because welfare conditions at one stage of the life cycle are often directly linked to events earlier in life (and may influence well-being later on in life). Poverty in old age is usually the result of a problematic employment career or of the death of a spouse. In turn, precarious employment tends to be powerfully correlated with insufficient educational attainment and this, we know, reverts back to conditions in childhood. Second, as discussed above, it is only via a life course perspective that we can adequately separate momentary (and possibly inconsequential) from lasting hardship. And, third, this is a methodology which does help us take a peek into the dim future. If we know a lot about today's youth cohorts we are in a fairly good position to make informed forecasts about tomorrow's parents, workers, or welfare clienteles. For example, given what we already know about labour force demand, it is reasonable to assume that contemporary youth without secondary level education are likely to find themselves locked into the low-end labour market a decade hence. And considering ongoing pension reforms, most of which will come to full fruition thirty or forty years down the line, it is equally reasonable to believe that these very same youth will face welfare problems as they reach pension age in, say, 2050.

Principles of Social Justice

A second necessary building block involves the basic ground rules for making choices and selecting priorities. Anyone who has suffered an introductory economics course knows that the promotion of economic efficiency can only be justified if it enhances welfare. The strong side of the neo-liberal Good Society lies in its promotion of efficiency through more market clearing. Its credibility problem, to most Europeans, lies on the social justice side and this is no doubt what sealed its fate. European welfare states espouse a number of different models of solidarity, but in all there exists a fundamental dedication to basic social citizenship, to pooling social risks collectively.

The welfare state implies a social contract with the citizenry. It has now been one of the chief organizing principles of the lives of several generations and, hence, it represents a deeply institutionalized contract. Indeed, herein lies an obstacle to possibly *any* reform. As so much attitude research has shown, the welfare status quo remains very popular.[6] And as recent reform

---

[6] See Svallfors and Taylor-Gooby (2001) for a recent comparative overview.

efforts (especially in pensions) demonstrate, masses of citizens will take to the streets and force parties from office if they seem to change the rules of the game. We must be certain that any design for a new social contract conforms to prevailing normative definitions of justice. This means specifying the bases of rights and reciprocity, and delineating the claims that citizens can justly make on society. And, to use Herbert Simon's expression, it also means defining our collective patrimony and how it should be allocated. In brief, what principles of solidarity do we wish to realize?

Everyday politics usually represent a hodgepodge of principles of justice. Policy is being made in favour of groups because they may be victims, unfortunate, or vulnerable. In order to extend more welfare to children it might suffice to appeal to their innocence. Paretian principles are also frequently invoked, i.e. a change of the status quo is positive if it generates more efficiency with noone being worse off as a result. Neither constitute durable and solidarity-building decision principles. Paretian welfare is often not suitable to welfare *state* policy. It may be that no one would be visibly harmed if government helped millionaires triple their fortunes, but this would nonetheless violate most citizens' idea of fairness. And, as American policy making reveals, redistribution on the mere basis of arguing victimization or discrimination easily degenerates into a spiral of competing victimization claims.

Strong and durable solidarities spring from a principle of social justice according to which a benefit to some is demonstrably also beneficial for all, when societal welfare depends on individual well-being. The right has a strong case when it attacks welfare dependants because most citizens fail to see how more generous benefits to, say, welfare mothers will improve upon societal (i.e. *their*) well-being. The Third Way's accent on activation will, in comparison, appear less objectionable in so far as recipients are also asked to contribute something. The coincidence of individual and societal welfare may be regarded as a 'bottom-line' criterion of social justice. But it is obviously a very insufficient and potentially dangerous criterion if it ends up standing alone. It presumes a *quid pro quo* that is too often inapplicable or unreasonable to expect.

The need for a stronger criterion of justice stems from the heightened uncertainties that accompany far-reaching social transformation. Social risks are no doubt intensifying, and their incidence is changing markedly. Groups that once could count on security, like the standard manufacturing worker, now face major job risks. Similarly, young families with children are increasingly vulnerable. More broadly, when society is in flux citizens *perceive* their lives as being more insecure, and may therefore refrain from taking risks.

When we simply do not know whether we, personally, will fall victim to the kinds of risks we face, we would most probably opt for a Rawlsian criterion of justice.[7] Here, according to the maximin principle, a rational, risk-averse citizen would opt for egalitarianism and would accept a change of the status quo only if assured that the welfare of the weakest will be safeguarded.

The European social debate is quite close to the Rawlsian ethos when it prioritizes social inclusion and the reduction of inequalities as essential ingredients in any strategy to boost economic competitiveness. In other words, our adoption of a Rawlsian yardstick should resonate well with the prevailing view among European welfare states.

Welfare as Social Investment

National accounting systems distinguish between current consumption and investment, but social accounts do not—except in rare cases such as building hospitals. It is basically assumed that social outlays are an unproductive, yieldless consumption of a surplus produced by others. Human capital theory does, however, provide a good theoretical framework within which we might revise such practice. Nowadays most people would agree that educational expenditures yield a dividend because they (may) make citizens more productive, but we need to push the logic much further.

We shall argue that a recast family policy and, in particular, one which is powerfully child-oriented, must be regarded as social investment. Since it is well established that the ability and motivation to learn in the first place depends on the economic and social conditions of childhood, policies aimed to safeguard child welfare must be regarded as an investment on par with and, perhaps, more urgent than educational investments. Good cognitive abilities to start with will yield individual returns later on because they are an absolute precondition for educational attainment, lifelong learning, or for possible remedial intervention at some point in life. They also yield a social dividend because we need to offset the limited numbers within coming cohorts with greater productivity.

We shall apply the same logic in two other key areas of urgent welfare reform. Gender equality policies should not be regarded as simply a concession to women's claims. If society is not capable of harmonizing motherhood with employment, we shall forego the single most effective bulwark against child

---

[7] I here use Rawls's concept more loosely than originally intended. Kangas (2000) presents a similar analysis which leads him to conclude that rational risk-adverse voters facing a choice between existing welfare models would most likely opt for a Scandinavian type model.

poverty—which is that mothers work. We shall, additionally, face very severe labour force shortages or, alternatively, a shortage of births. And, as women now tend to be more educated than men, we shall be wasting human capital. Gender equality is becoming a lynchpin of any positive post-industrial equilibrium. The quality of working life becomes detrimental the more we pin our social inclusion strategies on job growth. Stressful and insecure low-grade employment has severely negative spill-over effects on families and children; low-grade jobs tend to become low-skill traps in which people easily experience an erosion of their learning abilities. If we pin our strategy to a lifelong learning model, we will need to invest in working conditions as well.

Much of what we call social protection of children, youth, and families—or what we call 'women-friendly' policy—is a mix of 'consumption' and 'investment'. It is admittedly difficult, perhaps impossible, to draw a precise line between the two. But the need to rethink our social accounting practice is gaining urgency for every year we move closer towards a full-blown knowledge-dominated production system.

Rethinking Security in Old Age

Those who adopt the standard 'snapshot' policy diagnosis will easily be led to conclude that the elderly and the young are on a collision course. The elderly are ever more numerous and yield formidable lobbying power while children do not even have the vote. Hence, many fear that the former will benefit disproportionately. This is not a very fruitful way of examining the coming challenge of population ageing. If instead we adopt a life course perspective, the issue will look quite different. Let us begin with today's retirees who on average, no doubt, enjoy solid welfare and income security. Is this due to exaggerated public largesse? In part, perhaps, but the real reason is that those who retire now were the main beneficiaries of the post war full employment boom, allowing them to accumulate strong resources. This is what mainly explains why the elderly fare well, regardless of whether they rely primarily on public or private pensions. Were we to turn the clock back to our grandfathers' generation, we would see a completely different retirement scenario, one replete with poverty. Granted, in the 1950s and 1960s public pensions remained modest indeed. But the main reason was that they had suffered, as a generation, extraordinarily poor lives: young during World War I, their careers dominated by the Great Depression and then World War II.

If we apply the same generational life course logic to those who are now young, what retirement fate might we predict? One closer to our grandparents, or one more akin to our luckier fathers and mothers? If we are unable to check the potential for social exclusion that lies ahead, it is a safe bet that a substantial proportion will face the lot of our grandparents. We are back to the Rawlsian problematic. Under conditions of heightened uncertainty, we should give policy priority to the most vulnerable. In other words, a redesigned social model cannot satisfy basic criteria of justice unless it offers an adequate retirement guarantee. As longevity increases, so do the risks of severe disabilities and this implies the need for adequate caring guarantees as well.

We are also back to straightforward efficiency issues. Citizens need to accept risks if we aim for a more dynamic and vibrant future economy, and they will have to do so in a context of widespread uncertainty. The prospect of, perhaps, twenty years of old age poverty is not conducive to risk-taking when you, as a 25-year old, know that you have to complete 35–40 employment years in order to qualify for a decent pension.

Population ageing incorporates efficiency and social justice issues into one at the moment we must decide on how to allocate the additional expenditure burdens of ageing. If we continue with a purely benefit-defined PAYGO system, the main additional burden will fall on those in working age. This means an even higher tax on employment and, as a result, probably higher unemployment among youth and the less skilled. If we instead move towards a contribution-defined system, we would allocate the burden to the elderly themselves.

The Three Welfare Pillars

One basic issue for any aspiring welfare architect is how to allocate welfare production. This means deciding on the division of responsibilities between markets, families, and government. Markets are the main source of welfare for most citizens through most of their adult lives, both because most income comes from employment and because much of our welfare is purchased in the market. The reciprocity of kinship that families represent has traditionally been another chief source of welfare and security, in particular in terms of care services but also in terms of income pooling. Familial welfare production continues to be quite prominent, especially in Southern Europe. Government's role in welfare production is, of course, based neither on purchase, nor on reciprocity, but on a redistributive 'social contract' that reflects some form of collective solidarity. Each of these three welfare pillars is mutually interdependent.[8] The family, just like government, may in theory absorb market failures; similarly, the market (or government) may compensate for family failure. Where neither is capable of substituting for 'failure' in the two others, this is when we encounter an acute welfare deficit or crisis.

It can probably not be avoided that some citizens will face an acute situation of triple 'failure'. No welfare regime, however ambitious, can realistically safeguard against all misfortunes. However, what is cause for alarm is that present-day societies seem to combine triple failure for a large and growing mass of citizens. As a result, to paraphrase C.W. Mills (1956), private troubles are becoming public issues.

Any choice of where to concentrate welfare production must consider two fundamental aspects. The first, and simplest, involves an accurate diagnosis of 'pillar-failure'. Thanks to the economists, we have a long and established tradition of identifying market failures. But this is not the case for family failures, in great part because they frequently remain hidden. Yet, families' ability to absorb social problems and provide adequate care is being doubly impaired. On one hand, many emerging risks—like Alzheimer's disease— require a level of caring intensity that most families are unable to furnish. On the other hand, families are increasingly fragile and they also lack available caring capacity.

The second, and arguably more urgent, aspect has to do with the potential second-order effects of allocating welfare responsibilities to any given pillar. To be sure, we have a massive literature on the moral hazards and negative incentive effects that government welfare provision may provoke. Unfortunately, we know far less about the second-order effects of familial welfare responsibilities. But we are becoming increasingly aware that traditional caring obligations contradict women's employment abilities. There is also evidence that the familial solution to youth unemployment typical of Southern Europe may be problematic in so far as it delays independence, job insertion, and family formation.

Too often, our attention is myopically focused on government. Should it shrink, grow, or do things differently? This leads to poor policy analysis because any specification of government's obligations has second-order effects on markets and families. If, for example, we decide *not to* develop

---

[8] The 'third sector' is arguably a fourth pillar, but where its role is of decisive importance its functioning tends to resemble markets or government, all depending on its chief financial underpinnings. For a discussion, see Esping-Andersen (1999).

public care services for the elderly, will markets and/or families compensate adequately? The real world of welfare is the product of how the three welfare pillars interact. If one pillar 'fails', there is either the possibility that the responsibility is absorbed in the two remaining pillars or, alternatively, that unsolved welfare problems mount. When we design social policies we must ask ourselves: *can* the family, market or, alternatively, the state realistically absorb such responsibilities and, if so, would this be the most *desirable* option?

Neo-liberals advocate the primacy of markets (and usually ignore the family), while conservatives favour more family and local community social responsibility. And social democracy's long-standing preference for collective solutions is anchored in its fear that both the family and the market alternative offer insufficient security while fostering inegalitarian results. From this diversity we can learn a lot about which institutional option seems to perform well or poorly in the pursuit of any specified welfare goal. The choice of how to divide the responsibilities between the three cornerstones of the welfare triangle is what scholars term a choice between alternative *welfare regimes*. And it is this, in the final analysis, which we must decide upon.

Similar Challenges for Different Welfare Regimes

By and large, all European nations face similar risks, needs and trade-offs. There is everywhere a rise in inequalities coming from the market, and the manifestations of demographic change are similar. But it is equally true that the convergence of post-industrial challenges confronts very different national welfare systems. Hence, their ability to respond effectively to new risks will inevitably differ due both to their inherent strengths and weaknesses. These, in turn, depend on how the three pillars are configured but also on the institutional properties of welfare *state* programmes.

The Nordic Countries

The Scandinavian welfare model is internationally unique in its emphasis on the government pillar. It has actively 'de-familialized' welfare responsibilities with two aims in mind: one, to strengthen families (by unburdening them of obligations) and, two, to strive for greater individual independence. It has also actively 'de-commodified' citizens' welfare needs, thus seeking to minimize the degree to which individuals' welfare depends on their fortunes in the market. But, and this is decisive to note, the crowding out of markets in the pursuit of welfare is attached to a 'crowding in' policy of maximizing citizens' employability and productivity.

The Nordic welfare *states* are characteristic for their triple accent on universal income guarantees, 'activation', and highly developed services for children, the disabled, and for the frail elderly. The broad and quite generous income safety net is demonstrably an effective bulwark against poverty. It is also meant as a means for greater risk-taking and, hence, should promote labour market flexibility and adaptation. Activation policies do appear to diminish long-term unemployment, and care services to families have provided a double bonus: enabling women to have children and careers while also maximizing employment levels. The Nordic welfare regime is inevitably costly on the government revenue and expenditure ledger. But it can be demonstrated that it is *not* more costly if we adopt a complete 'regime' accounting system. What Scandinavians are compelled to pay in taxes, their US equivalents are compelled to pay out of their own pockets. Still, notwithstanding an unusually balanced revenue mix, heavy tax requirements undoubtedly constitute a potential Achilles heel of the model.[9] So far it has been able to sustain its taxation needs thanks to broad support from the middle classes. Still, the deterioration of Danish health care over the past decade bears witness to severe financial constraints. As the experience of Sweden during the 1990s economic slump suggests, the model relies ultimately on sustained full employment and growth. If growth remains sluggish and if market-driven inequalities and dualisms continue to strengthen, the Nordic model will be seriously tested.

No doubt, the Scandinavian model is comparatively well positioned to face the exigencies of post-industrial change. Via its 'de-familialization' of welfare responsibilities, it is undoubtedly well placed to activate the full potential of women's new role. Since it is also effective in mobilizing the more vulnerable, such as single parents with small children, older workers, or people with disabilities, it manages to maximize inclusion and minimize exclusion. Along with Belgium, the Nordic countries are among the few OECD countries able to minimize *both* aged and child poverty. They demonstrate thereby that generous old age security is not *per se* incompatible with an active *pro-family* policy. Near-maximum employment, in turn, coincides with less early retirement and fairly high fertility. Perhaps the most important lesson to be learned from Scandinavia is its quite successful investment in preventative measures.

---

[9] The total welfare resource allocation (as a percentage of GDP) in Scandinavia is not greater than in the United States. The difference is simply a matter of the public–private expenditure mix (Esping-Andersen, 1999).

The 'Liberal' Welfare Model

The welfare model of Ireland and the UK, like the American, seeks actively to sponsor market solutions. It pursues this via the double strategy of encouraging private welfare provision as the norm, and by limiting public responsibilities to acute market failures. With the notable exception of national health care, the dominant thrust is towards a residual public role of targeting benefits only to the demonstrably needy. Hence, the middle classes have been encouraged to opt into the private welfare market while government has sought to strengthen income testing. In parallel, the accent is shifting from conventional needs-tests towards work-conditional benefits. This is seen as a more effective response to two problems. First, to what is perceived to be a widespread lack of adequate work incentives and, second, to the growth of low wage employment. It can, in fact, be regarded as a necessary cushion within increasingly unregulated labour markets.

The accent on targeted in-work benefits may be regarded as a more effective way to address social exclusion than, say, conventional social insurance. But this is far from certain. If benefits are work-conditional, they do not help workless citizens. To qualify, mothers with small children will, to begin with, require cheap day care. If eligibility is subject to a needs test, benefits are most likely set at a low level and coverage gaps and welfare dependency are likely to be substantial. Also, work-conditional benefits may produce unwanted externalities, such as downward pressures on wages.

The stimulus of private welfare plans helps balance public budgets, but this easily provokes social dualisms and second-order consequences. One result may be to relegate lower income households to the status of second-rate welfare citizens. If equality remains a priority, targeted welfare performs poorly as revealed by internationally very high poverty rates. Moreover, poverty is especially evident among the fastest growing kinds of vulnerable households (such as lone mothers and young families with children). And it may be unrealistic to assume that buoyant markets effectively diminish welfare dependency. In the UK, for example, the decline in unemployment in the 1990s was not accompanied by a similar decline in workless households. Without comprehensive investments in family services, the low-wage trap that, in the first place makes assistance necessary, may not disappear.

If the overriding goal of targeting and privatization is to reduce public taxation and expenditure, this appears to have been accomplished in Britain to a degree, especially in terms of longer-term pension expenditure projections. But the secondary consequence is growing household outlays for private insurance coverage and it is doubtful whether there are any real total cost savings to be gained. The great Achilles heel here is that government's ability to raise more revenues, as well as its capacity to conduct an effective social policy, will be progressively impaired the more that citizens exit to the market. If the welfare state provides ever fewer benefits to the middle classes, their acquiescence to high taxation will gradually evaporate—if for no other reason, simply because they are locked into paying for private insurance. The model may, therefore, face severely limited policy options for dealing with pressing social problems in the future.

The Continental European Welfare Model

One characteristic that is common to most, but not all, Continental European countries is their sustained adherence to traditional familial welfare res-ponsibilities—most powerfully in Southern Europe, and by far the least in Belgium and France. Within this context, the security of the chief (male) breadwinner assumes fundamental importance. The familialist bias is addi-tionally reinforced by the dominance of social insurance.

Employment-linked social insurance protects well those with stable, lifelong employment. For this reason, countries that follow the insurance tradition have usually also introduced strong employment guarantees and regulations. It is not surprising that Continental European labour markets systematically score very high on most labour market 'rigidity' indicators (Esping-Andersen and Regini, 2000). The long-term viability of a social insurance dominated system is, however, increasingly questioned because it offers inadequate security for those with a tenuous connection to the labour market, such as women and for workers with irregular careers. Worse, social insurance responds poorly to the emerging demographic and employment structure. Since entry into stable employment is ever-more delayed, and since work histories are becoming more unstable, citizens will face difficulties accumulating sufficient pension credits. And to cover financial shortfalls in pensions, the tax on employment is rising and this helps price the young and the less productive job seekers out of the market. Passive income maintenance, combined with strong job guarantees for male breadwinners, becomes problematic with rising marital instability and non-conventional households. Strong protection for the stably employed combined with huge barriers to labour market entry has, in many countries, nurtured a deepening abyss bet-ween privileged 'insiders' and precarious 'outsiders'. If strong reliance on the family absorbs many of the risks of social exclusion, it simultaneously negatively affects women's search for economic independence. As will be examined in Chapter 2, familialist welfare is paradoxically a major cause of low fertility.

To deal with 'atypical' risks, Continental European welfare states have either relied on continued family support or they have added *ad hoc* non-contributory programmes, such as social pensions and various social minima to the system. An overly transfer-biased social policy is, arguably, an ineffective response to social exclusion. There is now a clear realization across Continental Europe that services, especially for small children and for the frail elderly, are an urgent priority. Yet, the fiscal capacity to respond is limited due to a narrow tax base combined with costly pension commitments. The model is unusually vulnerable to employment stagnation and to high inactivity rates. Hence, expanding employment among women and older workers becomes *sine qua non* for long-term sustainability.

Yet Continental European welfare states find themselves in a 'welfare without work' trap, from which it is difficult to escape. Job growth in the market economy is made difficult by high wage floors and contribution burdens, and in public services because of severe fiscal constraints. In the absence of jobs, the response has been to subsidize early retirement requiring additional increases in social contributions. A common characteristic is the narrow, or even non-existent, scope for investing in measures which might help people out of the 'welfare without work' trap (such as women-friendly benefits and services).

It is in this context that the 'Dutch miracle' assumes importance. In the 1980s the Netherlands epitomized the negative aspects of an overly passive, income maintenance biased approach with very low female employment and record high transfer dependency ratios. The Dutch labour market success story is based on a number of interrelated policies including, first of all, protracted wage moderation and a huge growth of part-time and temporary employment. This was combined with a fairly effective curtailment of prolonged welfare dependency but *not* with any significant erosion of social benefits. The result has been an impressive rise in female employment and in service jobs more generally.

From National Regimes towards a European Model?

As national interdependencies strengthen and as European integration moves ahead, the advocacy for a new welfare architecture inevitably becomes more global and pan-national. Indeed, the neo-liberal project presented itself as a universal panacea and the Third Way, even if originally meant for a British audience, swiftly mobilized disciples elsewhere. The mere fact that most, if not all, European nations are struggling to reform their social protection systems at the same time should help boost a co-ordinated, joint effort at finding solutions. Hence, the noticeable intensification of an EU-wide social debate in recent years.

To be sure, there is nothing especially new in this. During the first great 'Bismarckian' phase of social reform, the debate was as international as today. Countries as far apart as Italy and Sweden were intensely considering the pros and cons of the emerging German model. Many countries, including even Japan, consciously emulated Bismarck. The arena was equally, if not more, global when Gustav Moller, Franklin Roosevelt, and Lord Beveridge launched the second great reform wave. The historical moment at which we now find ourselves appears to be uniquely global. A quick glance at history shows us it is not.

The embrace of a common European social strategy for the twenty-first century is still decidedly timid, if not reluctant. Granted, a first step was taken during the Dutch presidency of the EU, during which the common employment strategy was launched in tandem with an invitation to reconsider 'social protection as a productive factor'. A further, and more daring, impulse came from the Lisbon Summit in March 2000, where social protection was placed at the top of the political agenda. As a follow-up, point 7 of the EU Council's communication to the Nice European Council states that

the European social model, with its developed systems of social protection, must underpin the transformation to the knowledge economy. People are Europe's main asset and should be the focal point of the Union's policies. Investing in people and developing an active and dynamic welfare state will be crucial both to Europe's place in the knowledge economy and for ensuring that the emergence of this new economy does not compound the existing social problems of unemployment, social exclusion and poverty.[10]

A full-fledged, synchronized European reform policy, especially if it aims at harmonization, remains out of the question. But the pursuit of common objectives under the umbrella of the so-called 'open method of co-ordination' constitutes an acceptable—and possibly promising—avenue for Member States to move from 'negative' to 'positive' integration (Scharpf, 1999). Unsurprisingly, the search for commonly acceptable and realistic policy objectives has been intensifying over the past years.

The above-cited quote gives us a first, if utterly generic, glimpse at what Europeans might agree upon, namely that the promotion of economic competitiveness is conditional upon the preservation of accustomed social entitlements and a fight against social exclusion. Here the Rawlsian underpinnings

---

[10] The Council of the European Union. Document 14011/00, SOC 462 (Annex).

of political decision making are evident. Moving to the more concrete, so far the common employment guidelines remain the only real success. But we can identify a host of 'proto-objectives' being sponsored and debated across the EU. The Social Affairs and Employment Council has endorsed the pursuit of gender equalization, making work pay, safe and sustainable pensions, the promotion of social inclusion, and the pursuit of high quality and sustainable health care. Also, in the context of the Portuguese presidency, the Belgian–British call for benchmarks to combat poverty and social exclusion was adopted by the EU Council (where children were singled out for special concern). But with few exceptions, such as the 60 per cent female employment target for 2010, good intentions far exceed the number of concrete policies adopted.

Whether reform will remain predominantly a national or a common European affair should depend in large measure on two circumstances. First, do individual nations actually face the same set of challenges? Second, would it be realistic and advantageous to adopt similar targets considering extraordinarily diverse welfare constructions? The following chapters address four policy arenas that are key to any fundamental welfare model reconstruction: children and families, gender relations, work-life, and retirement. They are fundamental in a double sense. First, they represent the main cornerstones of citizens' life chances. Second, they represent four of the most pressing challenges from the point of view of post-industrial adaptation.[11]

The question this book poses is whether a new 'social contract' is necessary, and if so, what should it encompass? Let me conclude this first chapter with a brief overview of the issues.

Rewriting the Social Contract

A New Family Policy

The main objective of post-war family policy was to safeguard the male breadwinner and provide relief to families with large numbers of children. On five grounds the conditions are now almost the opposite.

1. The family structure that underpinned post-war policy is no longer dominant.
2. The employment of mothers requires new caring institutions for small children.

[11] Health policy is arguably a fifth area of key importance, one which we cannot examine in this study.

3. Widespread youth unemployment and huge entry-barriers to housing markets inhibit young peoples' ability to form families.
4. Families are increasingly unstable and this often goes hand-in-hand with poverty.
5. The quality of childhood matters ever more for subsequent life chances.

It is in childhood that citizens acquire most of the capital that they, later, will activate in the pursuit of a good life. Investments in education and abilities are becoming increasingly indispensable for peoples' life chances, but they must be undertaken in a context in which families are ever more fragile. The resources of parents are becoming ever more important as they themselves are becoming ever more vulnerable. Chapter 2 proposes a new child-centred social investment strategy based on a combined policy of income guarantees against child poverty and maximizing mothers' employment.

A New Gender Contract

Everywhere the post-war social contract was built on the then realistic assumption that women would, once married, withdraw into housewifery. But over the past twenty years women's educational attainment has come to surpass men's and the male wage advantage is in decline. In as much as the new service economy favours women, the welfare calculus of households should lead to an increase in female labour supply. Additionally, women themselves increasingly insist on greater economic autonomy and professional development.

The ongoing gender revolution is both irreversible and desirable. To fully reap its advantages, we must recast the nexus between work, welfare, and the family. Women's employment improves family welfare and at the same time helps to sustain future welfare state finances. But it also creates new social risks, such as greater family instability and new 'atypical', often vulnerable, households. If the 'incompatibility' problem is not resolved, it may lock European societies into a long-term low fertility equilibrium. This sharply contrasts with European citizens' own stated preferences regarding their desired number of children. There is clearly a strong case for a new 'women-friendly' social contract because improving the welfare of women means improving the collective welfare of society at large.

The policy challenge boils down to two principal issues. First, how to make parenthood compatible with a life dedicated to work and careers as well. This is usually identified as the question of 'women-friendly policy'. Second, how to create a new and more egalitarian equilibrium between men's and women's lives—the gender equality issue.

A handful of European welfare states have been vanguards in harmonizing motherhood and careers. Most others have, if not actively then at least verbally, begun to advocate similar 'women friendly' policy. The sheer force of women's claims may drive this, but it also gains urgency from pragmatic concerns. In Italy and Spain, for example, where female activity rates remain half that of Northern Europe, there is an evident need to raise participation levels; partly to meet commonly agreed employment targets and partly as a necessary component of any longer-term sustainability strategy. Most European nations have been far less responsive to the gender-equality challenge. It is clearly difficult to reverse centuries of acquired behaviour, and the search for an immediate patent solution would probably be futile. Yet, Scandinavian experience suggests that fathers' contribution to unpaid domestic work and childcare can be augmented by welfare incentives. Hence, the ongoing 'masculinization' of women's biographies may, via policy, find a parallel in a more 'feminized' male biography.

Social Inclusion through Employment

Paid employment remains, as always, the basic foundation of household welfare and it is hardly surprising that more jobs are seen as a *sine qua non* in the pursuit of an inclusive society. As far as this goes, little has changed since the post-war years. Yet, the challenge we face today differs considerably. When Lord Beveridge and his political contemporaries launched their commitment to full employment, they were explicitly referring to men only. Any meaningful twenty-first century commitment must now also include women. In the past, a nation's employment performance was related to expanding manufacturing jobs with steady productivity—and hence wage—growth and considerable career stability. Today we must depend mainly on services which are far more dualistic, and very uneven productivity growth poses the likelihood of growing earnings gaps. The transformation of work is, on the positive side, dominated by skilled jobs but, on the negative side, accompanied by an erosion of job security, more wage inequality, and a substantial number of low-end jobs. All this, in turn, affects people's career prospects and capacity to adapt to change, generating new forms of insecurity.

It is by now well documented that the overall thrust is towards rising skill levels. Industrial decline affects predominantly lower-skilled jobs; the most dynamic services, like finance, business, and social services are skill-biased. But the upgrading of employment easily produces polarization because labour intensive, routine services nurture a sizeable number of low-qualified jobs (the so-called MacJobs). If these are concentrated in the private sector, they are likely to offer low wages and poor working conditions.[12]

The European employment strategy aims to fight social exclusion through job expansion. In most EU Member States, fiscal constraints appear to preclude a major growth of public service jobs and, hence, such *quantitative* expansion may be accompanied by an expansion of less secure, *poor quality* jobs. The threat of job polarization is real because investment in new skills is concentrated in higher occupational classes, while low-skilled jobs offer few opportunities for training, skill enhancement, or personal development. High employment levels may nourish a low-end labour market with a class of workers locked into inferior jobs and poor life chances.

The transformation of work also affects employees' health. Physical dangers were the main risk in the 'old economy' whereas stress-related risks come to the fore in the 'new economy'. This is exacerbated by firms' competitive strategies, in particular by increasing workforce productivity through decentralizing responsibilities, intensifying work processes, and favouring non-standard forms of employment. The new forms of worker insecurity are a contributing factor. Skill change is doing away with the tradition of jobs for life and the chances of a stable career depend on one's ability to constantly adapt and acquire new competencies. In this context, traditional health regulation systems are losing their effectiveness. Yet those who fall victim to such new health risks face high chances of labour-market marginalization.

The employment chances of households are another source of polarization. On one hand, we see the rise of resourceful, work and income-rich households and, on the other hand, a similar rise in vulnerable households, such as lone parents and work-poor couples. Such polarization is additionally probable due to marital instability and marital homogamy. The challenge is how to co-ordinate employment and family policy to strengthen families' employment prospects and effectively attack household poverty.

Household vulnerabilities and inferior employment are likely to coincide and, in this case, the chances of social exclusion increase dramatically. Also here, we must distinguish between temporary and persistent deprivation. Individuals' life chances are not *per se* affected by a short stint of low pay or 'MacJobs' employment. But they are if it persists and, especially, if it bundles in the form of multiple deprivation. Any serious pursuit of social integration must include guarantees against entrapment in deprivation.

---

[12] For the most up-to-date survey, see OECD (2001c). See also Scharpf and Schmidt (2000) for an excellent synthetic analysis.

The duration of poverty increases substantially when overall poverty *levels* are high (Duncan *et al.*, 1993; Bradbury *et al.*, 2001; OECD, 2001c). This empirical relationship is absolutely critical because it suggests that lowering poverty *per se* is a first and necessary ingredient in any strategy for social inclusion. As will be examined in Chapters 2 and 3, persistent social exclusion and under-privilege constitute a growing risk and, for this reason, it is urgent to develop effective guarantees against entrapment.

Since it is abundantly clear that a negative spiral of social exclusion is primarily caused by lack of access to stable, well-paid employment, it is hardly surprising that policy is focused on either 'making work pay' or on activation and learning. The weakness of either is that it typically comes too late. A first and necessary policy must be to invest in improving the quality of jobs. Since it is realistic to expect that our future labour markets will include a fair number of low-end jobs, mobility measures such as lifelong learning and training become crucial so as to avoid entrapment. We know that even the best designed activation policies work poorly if they are primarily remedial. Active training and mobility policies can only be effective if they complement a strategy of prevention and this means, once again, the need for major social investments in childhood and youth. Or, to put it differently, our employment policies need to join hands with our family policies.

The Generational Contract

The post-war retirement contract was based on favourable demographics and robust economic growth. Generous pay-as-you-go pensions were financially viable because real wages and the number of contributors both increased. Neither is the case now and thus we face the problem of how to sustain our pension commitments.[13] Failure to reform existing pension systems may, in many countries, produce negative secondary consequences. This is especially so in countries where financing is contribution based because rising fixed labour costs jeopardize job growth, especially in low-productivity, labour intensive, private services.

Rolling back public pensions might improve upon public finances but this is unlikely to affect total GDP use. Privatization would, for most countries, imply both injustice (double payment), more inequality among pensioners, and heightened insecurity. Compensating for negative demographics with 'fertility incentives' is an inadequate avenue in the medium term and immigration will only realistically cover the shortfall if immigration rates become

---

[13] Of course, a return to strong real wage growth would diminish the problem substantially.

enormous. As a consequence, there is almost universal agreement that a viable new retirement contract must combine two elements. First, it must ensure retirement security for both today's and tomorrow's citizens. Second, it must produce a reallocation of work and retirement time. In part, this can be done by raising employment rates in active ages; in part, by delaying employment exit.

The great challenge is how to ensure at the same time *intergenerational equity* (a sustainable fair distribution of the costs of future retirement between workers and retirees) and *intragenerational justice* (safeguarding the welfare of the weakest, both in working life and in retirement). As we examine in Chapter 5, one solution to the transition cost issue might be to adopt the Musgrave principle of proportional sharing among the generations. And, in addressing intragenerational justice, we need to place greater emphasis on general revenue financing—both to protect the least advantaged and to meet additional retirement costs. A minimum guaranteed retirement income above the poverty line is not only affordable but must also be considered a precondition for any commitment to the well-being of future generations.

Still, the urgency of a new generational social contract does not stop here. Increased life expectancy means also a major challenge to health care systems and growing demand for services to the frail and disabled. A new generational contract necessitates both a renegotiation of the work–pension nexus and of the caring nexus. Since the EU is committed to gender equality and to raising women's employment rates (and since this is fundamental for sustaining welfare commitments in the first place) the traditional option of the elderly being cared for by (mostly female) family members is naturally precluded.

Conclusion

To reiterate, this book will not deliver policy *panacea*, solutions for all our problems, once and for all. A first, more modest, aim is to outline some of the ingredients that are necessary for a more comprehensive redesign. A second aim is to sound a warning note against some of the sweeping policy formulae that characterize contemporary debate. Take pension policy: delaying retirement is surely a sound objective, but will it work for all? Or, take social inclusion policy: activation seems an appealing alternative to passive income support, but can it adequately substitute for basic welfare guarantees? It is now fashionable to downplay passive and advocate active policy. This may be misguided if, as evidence suggests, activation is a costly, second-best alternative to prevention. Or, once again, take gender policy. The catchword everywhere is a 'women-friendly' policy of care services—plus—parental leave schemes. But this alone will probably not resolve the difficulties facing most working mothers.

In light of the diversity of national welfare systems, it is additionally fruitless to contemplate a single design for all nations even if they do face rather similar problems. Just as no EU Member State is likely to privatize its welfare state, neither is a radical welfare regime change likely to occur. The institutional framework of national welfare systems are historically 'locked in' and any realistic move towards common objectives must presume that such, if accepted, will be adapted to national practice.

Identifying broad policy objectives with no regard for their practical political relevance and implementation within diverse European welfare models would easily end up as a sterile academic exercise. For this reason our study includes a fourth 'problematic': the preconditions that make reform both necessary and feasible within nations as well as at the EU level. As discussed in Chapter 6, the challenges may be very similar, from Finland to Greece, but each Member State has its own welfare policy legacy, distinct system of interest organizations, and democratic polity. It is within such diversity that actual, concrete welfare reform will be undertaken.

A final thread in our book is the need to rethink policy boundaries and, in particular, the public–private welfare dichotomy. There are two issues at stake here. The first is that social welfare policy cannot be pursued distinctly from employment policy. To take an example from Chapter 2, an effective anti-poverty strategy must combine female employment, quality of work improvements, social care, and income maintenance. The second is that our point of reference for cost efficiency and viability should not be government revenues and outlays, but GDP use. Diminishing public health, pension, or social care expenditure is unlikely to produce any real cost savings since households will compensate with market purchase or with self-servicing. If welfare is externalized to markets, this will not result in appreciably lower net household money outlays. It will, however, result in more accentuated inequalities. If welfare is internalized in the family, this will probably result in more unpaid and less paid work—in other words, in a lower GDP (*and* less tax revenue). It will prove counter-productive for gender equality, and will seriously impair our capacity to generate new employment. Put differently, when we discuss what government should or should not do, we need to simultaneously consider its consequences for markets and for families.

2

A Child-Centred Social Investment Strategy

Gøsta Esping-Andersen

Introduction

Europe was a youthful continent in the post-war decades and, yet, its social welfare policies came to focus very much on the elderly. Now that our societies are ageing it is becoming quite urgent that we invest far more in the welfare of children. This would all appear a bit paradoxical.

The paradox disappears once we consider historical context. The average post-war male breadwinner enjoyed good job prospects and rising wages. This, in turn, secured adequate welfare for most families, and it allowed even working-class households the luxury of full-time housewifery. In brief, welfare capitalism gave rise to both income security and ample caring capacity within what we now regard as the traditional family. Add to this considerable marital stability and it is quite understandable that social policy could assume that children and, more generally, families were not the most urgent issue on the political agenda.

The same could not be said for the elderly. As the idea of mandatory retirement spread, older workers and especially widows often moved into old age poverty. In part because the traditional three-generation household was in eclipse and, in part, because those retiring in the post-war decades had been an historically unlucky generation. They were young during World War I, their adult careers spanned the deep depression and World War II. Having accumulated few resources, adequate pension provision was the main guarantee against poverty in old age.

Young families today face a wholly new and, yet again, historically bounded paradox. In the new economy, the fundamental requisites for a good life are rising ever more. This implies that life chances depend increasingly on the cultural, social, and cognitive capital that citizens can amass. The fundamental life phase is in childhood, and the crucial issue lies in the inter-play between parental and societal investments in children's development. The new paradox, then, is that strong families are becoming ever more detrimental for our well-being even as they are themselves becoming more vulnerable, fragile, and threatened.

The combined onslaught of employment and demographic transformation has particularly adverse consequences for youth and for young parents. Or, to be more precise, we see ominous signs of rising welfare polarization between income- and work-poor families on one side, and resource-strong families on the other side. And changing marital patterns imply not only a proliferation of new household forms, but also of vulnerability and insecurity. This alone is cause for policy concern. It is, however, from a life course perspective that we can identify the real importance of investing in the well-being and resources of children.

The new risks that young families face have both welfare and efficiency consequences of potentially major proportions. If we are concerned with equality and social justice, we must take note of one basic social fact: opportunities and life chances in today's society remain as powerfully rooted in social inheritance as in the past. Twentieth-century welfare reforms succeeded by and large in creating more income security, a less unequal distribution of incomes, and universal access to education. But contrary to expectations, the expansion of education failed to weaken the impact of social inheritance. Educational and occupational attainment remain as stratified today as in the past.[1] Table 2.1 helps illustrate the problem. As is evident, the parental effect on their children's cognitive abilities remains strong. There is clearly substantial variation in the strength of this impact across nations, a variation that seems to be related to overall levels of social inequality. The effect is systematically weaker in Scandinavia than elsewhere, considerably stronger in the US. A basic presupposition in this chapter is that the lower Nordic inheritance effect is a derivative of these countries' extraordinary commitment to investing in children and families.

The key problem, as noted, is that the society that is unfolding 'penalizes' ever more socially inherited under-privilege. To be a post-industrial 'winner', strong cognitive abilities and social skills are becoming a must; those without will likely find themselves trapped in a lifetime of low wages and precarious

---

[1] The most authoritative recent studies which demonstrate the historical (and comparative) constancy of opportunity structures are Erikson and Goldthorpe (1992) and Shavit and Blossfeld (1992). Interestingly, both studies find one key exception to the rule, namely Sweden, in the sense that the inheritance effect does appear to have declined. Although Denmark was included in neither of these studies, it is tempting to hypothesize that here, too, it has weakened. As Erikson and Goldthorpe suggest, Sweden's extraordinarily strong investment in the welfare of children and families may be the key explanation. This chapter will seek to substantiate this argument further.

Table 2.1 The relationship between parents' education and children's (aged 16–25, and 25–65) cognitive abilities. Standardized OLS regression coefficients

	Coefficient for 16–25 year olds	Coefficient for 25–65 year olds
Denmark	0.29	0.31
Norway	0.24	0.34
Sweden	0.23	0.39
Belgium (Flanders)	0.39	0.33
Germany	0.27	0.17
Netherlands	0.32	0.35
Portugal	0.32	0.48
Canada	0.34	0.47
USA	0.48	0.40

Explanation: Document literacy scores regressed on fathers' level of educational attainment.

Source: International Literacy Survey Data set.

employment. The 'ante' required to participate is constantly rising and, accordingly, we shall need to equalize life chances more than was ever before the case.

A concerted child-focus is, in the second place, *sine qua non* for a sustainable, efficient, and competitive knowledge-based production system. The coming working-age cohorts will be small, and they must sustain huge retirement populations. The income security of pensioners two or three decades down the line will in large measure depend on how much we can mobilize the productive potential of those who today are children. More generally, the only real asset that most advanced nations hold is the quality and skills of their people.

Those nations that do not manage to activate their full human potential are likely to fall behind in the productivity race. To dramatize the point, one may envision two future 'knowledge economy' scenarios. The first would result from an inegalitarian trajectory, nurturing 'islands of excellence in a sea of ignorance'. The United States may be heading in this direction when, on one hand, we consider its world dominance of centres of scientific excellence and, on the other hand, the shocking fact that about 20 per cent of adult Americans fall into the bottom, essentially dysfunctional, category of cognitive abilities.[2] The second, more egalitarian route, would look more like a 'tranquil pond with few ripples'. The Nordic countries (with no Harvard University but with less than 5 per cent in the dysfunctional category) appear closer to this scenario.

The islands-of-excellence formula may undoubtedly yield impressive growth dividends. But the open question is for how long can it remain dynamic? There may very well be a kind of Keynsian limit to the knowledge economy that will be reached when a large citizenry lacks the abilities to consume knowledge products. The functionally illiterate are unlikely participants in advanced internet communications.

Families: The Key to Social Inclusion and a Competitive Knowledge Economy

The mainsprings of people's life chances lie in the family conditions of their childhood. And, once adult, it is the household that gives meaning to the unfolding individual life course. It is here that social advantage and disadvantage are transmitted and activated; it is here that social risks and needs find primary expression; and it is also here that the primary social safety net is found. A person may be unemployed or a low wage worker. But its true ramifications depends on the household context. It is one thing if the only earner is low paid, another if the low paid worker is but one of several income recipients. If we set ourselves the goal of improving citizens' life chances, we need first to understand how ongoing transformation influences the distribution of well-being and security within households.

There are two ongoing trends that deeply affect contemporary family welfare. One emanates from the 'new demography', especially because of more unstable partnerships and the growing heterogeneity, and often also vulnerability, of households. Marital homogamy may, additionally, contribute to household welfare polarization. We see at once the formation of resource-strong, double earner households and of vulnerable, lone parent, and work-poor households. Since the life chances of most people will be powerfully dictated by the household setting, this is where policies aimed at social inclusion must be directed.

Social exclusion has emerged as a common policy objective throughout the European Union and, yet, its precise meaning is not altogether clear. As originally coined by the French, it refers to persons who are excluded from

---

[2] These estimates derive from the OECD's (2000b) international literacy study.

mainstream social protection, i.e. social insurance schemes. Its meaning is now far broader and may encompass many variant forms, ranging from social isolation through labour market marginality to income poverty. Probably all would concur that social exclusion occurs when citizens are trapped in inferior life chances. If this indeed is the core issue, then it is essential that we focus our lens on childhood and family welfare. As we shall see below, all available evidence indicates that (early) childhood is the critical point at which people's life courses are shaped. Remedial policies once people have reached adulthood are unlikely to be effective unless these adults started out with sufficient cognitive and social skills. A social investment strategy directed at children must be a centrepiece of any policy for social inclusion.

This chapter examines, first, how welfare risks concentrate across households, focusing both on child families generally, and on high-risk lone parent and work-poor households in particular. It then turns to the impact of family welfare on citizens' life chances, particularly during early childhood. Women's paid employment emerges as a key ingredient in any strategy to combat poverty in child families. This, as is well known, calls for a much more concerted strategy of equalizing women's opportunities—the theme of Chapter 3. It is nonetheless vital to note that any sustainable and effective policy to combat social exclusion must combine child, family, and women-friendly policies within an integrated strategy. The social quality and economic efficiency of twenty-first-century Europe will largely depend on whether we can successfully forge such a strategy.

The New Risk Structure of Households

If we are narrowly concerned with living standards, then we hardly need to be nostalgic about the past. Since the late 1960s, OECD member countries have seen their per capita GDP rise by 50–75 per cent, and this has brought about a dramatic improvement in the living standards of just about all citizens. But if we additionally prioritize equality, we seem headed for less golden times.

The contemporary welfare state is, in fact, confronting a double tide of inequality because the share of vulnerable households is growing for both demographic and labour market reasons. As Table 2.2. shows, primary income inequality has grown by 10 to 30 per cent in just about all advanced countries over the past decades. Some welfare states, like the Danish, Norwegian, French and Dutch, have kept the inegalitarian impulse at bay

Table 2.2 Changes in income inequality and government redistribution, 1980s to mid-1990s. Working age households only[a]

	Per cent change of Gini: market income	Per cent change of Gini: disposable income	Per cent change in government redistribution effort
Belgium (1985/96)	+2	+5	−6
France (1984/94)	−1	−2	+3
Germany (W) (1984/94)	+25	+33	−19
Italy (1986/95)	+17	+15	+22
Netherlands (1987/94)	−5	−2	−7
Denmark (1987/97)	+12	+4	+17
Finland (1987/95)	+29	+16	+18
Norway (1986/95)	+23	+4	+50
Sweden (1987/95)	+25	+1	+32
UK (1986/95)	+9	+14	−11
USA (1986/95)	+11	+10	+4

[a] Inequality measures based on household Gini coefficients for early 1980s and mid-1990s. Includes only households with head aged 24–55. Modified OECD equivalence scale used (1 for head, 0.5 for other adults, 0.3 for children). Calculations from LIS data.

through redistribution, while the opposite is true for Britain and Germany. In most cases, the welfare state has only partially offset the trend.[3]

This 'big picture' gives some support to those who fear a more polarized future, driven by long-term and overpowering structural forces. It is theoretically conceivable that the new inequalities are consistent with broadly shared principles of just rewards, in which case they would be perfectly acceptable, perhaps even welcomed. The gulf between the post-industrial 'winners' and 'losers' is no doubt widening. And this may simply reflect the fact that skills, motivation, and excellence is being rewarded while the lack thereof is being punished.

But any yardstick of justice must include at least two additional variables: whether the preconditions for success are equal for all; and, whether initial advantage or disadvantage is reinforced by inegalitarian social arrangements. The answer to both is, unfortunately, biased towards the no side. One core problem, to which this chapter is dedicated, is that social selection starts

[3] The dramatic increase in Italy must be considered in terms of the very low starting point. In terms of working age households, Italy still remains one of the least redistributive.

way before the age at which citizens are even remotely aware of what is happening to them. Another, widely documented, problem is that marriage behaviour remains highly homogamous. The weak bundle together with the weak, the strong with the strong. Therefore, we are far more likely to see a concentration of vulnerability and of success as individuals form partnerships and households. And this will reinforce not only the individual's life chances but also those of their offspring.

The basic requisite for a good life is *increasingly* strong cognitive skills and professional qualifications. For example, those with low cognitive abilities and/or less than secondary education face unemployment risks that are twice the average (OECD, 2000*b*). Likewise, family instability places mothers at great risk of poverty and welfare dependency unless they can also find well-paid jobs. Employment remains as always the *sine qua non* for good life chances, but the requirements for access to quality jobs are rising and are likely to continue to do so.

The social protection systems that were built in the post-war decades may, perversely, magnify rather than diminish such new risks. Most Continental European countries are almost entirely premised on social insurance schemes. They presume, in the first place, long and stable employment records—an arrangement that worked well for male breadwinners in an era of pervasive job security. It works poorly however for women with more unstable careers and—what is new—males too now face career instability and precarious employment. Moreover, it takes ever longer to get youths settled into employment while at the same time workers are being eased out of the labour market at an ever younger age. Under current conditions, a huge share of those now starting their careers will be hard put to accumulate sufficient pension credits.

The social insurance model is also inadequate in meeting the new risk structure because, almost by definition, it secures those who already enjoy security—the stably employed—while excluding those at the fringes. It deepens, in other words, the divide between insiders and outsiders. In Europe, unemployment is concentrated among youth who often have no social entitlements. The tragedy of European youth is that it can easily face the double 'failure' of market and welfare state. In Southern Europe, the main solution remains familial. In Italy, among the unemployed 20–30 year-olds, 90 per cent depend totally on parental support. As a remedy to the social risks of youth, this solution clearly has problematic secondary effects such as delayed independence, family formation and job insertion.

Aside from familial solutions, in most of contemporary Europe the emerging 'a-typical' risks are mainly addressed by needs-tested assistance programmes. Their efficacy depends on actual take-up rates and whether they create welfare traps. Targeted assistance is often set at a low level. As a result, unemployed youths on assistance benefits display very high poverty rates in some countries, such as France and the UK (Bison and Esping-Andersen, 2000a). As we shall see, the same holds for lone mothers. And, returning to Table 2.1, nations that favour targeting, like the British and American, perform quite poorly in terms of offsetting new inequalities. We may therefore require a new policy approach to deal effectively with the rising number of individuals and households that find themselves distanced from the regular employment relationship.

The rising preoccupation with social exclusion across Europe is warranted for many reasons. First, as inequalities mount so does poverty. And, as we shall see, the *duration* of poverty is intimately linked to overall *levels* of poverty. In other words, we can identify not only individual, but also *societal* downward, self-reinforcing spirals. Second, poverty risks are increasingly concentrated within families with children. An ominous sign is the pervasive upward trend in assistance dependency, especially among lone mothers. Third, and perhaps most tellingly, we are witnessing a growth in the number of work-poor and workless households which does not appear to abate even when unemployment rates decline (European Commission, 1999b). This indicates that some population groups are being progressively more detached from the labour market.

The process of exclusion can unfold very rapidly. Here we can draw lessons from Sweden during the troubled 1990s. Most would agree that Sweden boasts one of the world's most comprehensive social and employment policies, yet the business downturn, 1990–7, was accompanied by sharp welfare erosion among the more vulnerable. Poverty rose especially among immigrants and in households with children, reflecting the high concentration of unemployment among the unskilled, youths, and lone mothers. The percentage of households with a weak labour market connection almost doubled during this period, as did the share reporting severe economic difficulties (SOU, 2000).

The true extent of polarization emerges when exclusion becomes permanent. Citizens' life chances are not at stake if low pay, unemployment, or job precariousness is mainly a transient spell for young people leaving school, newly arrived immigrants or, perhaps mothers returning to the labour market. The real danger is that a sizeable minority becomes entrapped in inferior life trajectories. Hence, we must above all understand the mechanisms that turn a deficiency into a vicious circle of long-term exclusion.

Table 2.3 Household poverty: rates and trends[a]

	All (mid-1990s)	Trend (1980s–1990s)	With children (mid-1990s)	Trend (1980s–1990s)	Trend in extreme poverty (1980s–1990s)
Denmark (1987/97)	8.4	−1.3	6.9	+2.6	−0.1
Finland (1987/95)	4.5	−0.2	3.7	+1.2	−0.1
Sweden (1987/95)	6.2	−1.0	2.2	−1.3	+0.4
Netherlands (1987/94)	8.1	+2.9	7.8	+2.4	+4.1
France (1984/94)	7.5	0.0	7.0	−0.4	−1.9
Germany (W) (1984/94)	12.0	+6.4	14.1	+10.0	+3.3
Italy (1986/95)	14.1	+3.6	18.6	+7.4	+6.0
UK (1986/95)	11.7	+3.5	14.3	+3.8	+2.7
US (1986/97)	18.7	+0.5	21.4	+2.5	+1.1

[a] The data refer to final, disposable income utilizing the 50 per cent of median income poverty line (extreme poverty is 33 per cent of median), and the modified OECD equivalence scale (as in Table 2.2).[4]

Source: LIS Data.

The Hard and Soft Core of Social Exclusion

When we examine *all* households, poverty has remained fairly stable (with Germany being a main exception) in most countries over the 1980s–1990s. But this disguises two opposite trends. Poverty has fallen significantly among the elderly while rising among families with children. An overview centred on families with children is provided in Table 2.3.

Clearly, the trend is not perfectly uniform when we look at disposable income poverty. In Scandinavia and in France, families with children have fared rather better than average; in Germany, Italy, the Netherlands, the UK, and the US much worse—especially when we consider the rise in 'extreme

[4] Here and in all the following tables we use the 50 per cent poverty line, despite the fact that the EU has recently moved in favour of a 60 per cent line. Our principal motivation is that this makes our data more readily comparable with existing research.

poverty'. When we hold these trends up against the 'big-picture' inequalities previously shown in Table 2.2, it would appear quite clear that the driving forces of aggregate inequality are selectively hitting child families worse than others. When we consider that these underlying forces concentrate in labour market and demographic change, this should come as no surprise. In most nations, it is young adults who are mainly affected by unemployment, eroding wage levels, and by new and more vulnerable household arrangements—such as lone motherhood.

The unemployed and single mothers face, as the European Commission (1999b) has shown, the highest poverty risks of all—in each case almost 40 per cent are poor at the EU level.[5] But the reality is more complicated due to interactions. For example, since unemployment and low earnings concentrate among younger workers there is a spill-over effect on young families more generally. We know that young families have experienced both relative income decline and rising poverty rates over the past 10–15 years in many countries (Oxley *et al.*, 1999). And we also know that younger workers and the low-skilled are especially vulnerable to adverse business cycles.[6] The coincidence of household and child poverty is high and this means that social exclusion now will have problematic consequences for future adults as well.

This is especially the case if income poverty is persistent. Long-term poverty is far more likely to run down a family's resources and to gradually distance it from the consumption norms of society. From available data we know that countries with high *levels* of poverty also produce far more poverty persistence. Within Europe, Greek, Italian, Spanish, and British poverty rates are fairly high among families with children. If we define persistence as being poor in every single year, 1993–6, it is in these very same countries that we detect unusually high persistency (between 4 and 6 per cent of all families with children remain poor four years in a row). At the other extreme, persistency is exceptionally low in Denmark (0.1 per cent) and France (1.7 per cent).[7] If we extend the comparison to the US, the relationship is even clearer. Based on OECD (2001c) data, the total US poverty rate is a little more than three times the Danish and twice the Dutch. But the US persistency rate is ten times the Danish and six times the Dutch. Among those most likely to experience long-term poverty, there is a massive over-representation of heads

[5] A third group are couples with 3+ children, but this is a very small population. The EU study uses a 60 per cent poverty line, whereas we utilize the conventional 50 per cent line.

[6] Over the 1990s economic crisis in Sweden, employment decline was concentrated among youth (<25), immigrants, and the unskilled. Immigrant employment rates dropped by 18 percentage points, and youth rates by 24 points (SOU, vol. 41, 2000).

[7] Estimated from the 1994–6 waves of the ECHP.

of households with low education, of workless households (everywhere), and of lone parent families (in some countries).

Lone Parent Families

Lone parent households (almost all of which are lone mothers) have grown rapidly and now account for 15–20 per cent of all families with children. The rate is lower in Southern Europe, but shows signs of catching up. If by exclusion we mean poverty and/or joblessness, lone parents are an acute risk group, especially when they are not employed.[8] Lone mother employment is very high in the Nordic countries, in Belgium, France and even substantial in Italy and Spain. But it remains low in Germany, Ireland, the Netherlands, and in the UK (Bradshaw *et al.*, 1996). These differences are clearly related to day care provision and access to part-time employment. High activity rates in Italy and Spain are due more to family solutions: co-residence with family makes lone mother employment possible.[9]

Lone mother poverty is not only higher but also far more persistent than the average, especially in the US (Bradbury *et al.*, 2000). Some of the variation can be attributed to social transfer generosity, but whether the mother is employed is undoubtedly the single most decisive factor. An overview is provided in Table 2.4. In some cases, lone mothers' employment has a very powerful effect, reducing the chances of poverty by a factor of almost 8 (in France and Denmark).[10] The work-effect is more modest elsewhere, perhaps connected to the nature and pay of part-time or more sporadic employment. In many countries, there is also an over-representation of the low-educated among lone mothers and, hence, low wages may also play a role. An illustrative example of lone mothers' vulnerability to economic cycles comes, yet again, from Sweden in the 1990s (SOU, 2000). While the Swedish welfare state succeeded in avoiding a rise in lone mother poverty, their higher unemployment translated into a 50 per cent increase in social assistance dependency.[11]

---

[8] Although poverty and deprivation are multi-dimensional phenomena, in this study I limit the analysis to the income and employment dimensions. In any case, the correlation between alternative welfare indicators (such as housing) and income is very high.

[9] The surprisingly high rate of lone mother employment in Mediteranean countries is also due to selectivity: divorce and separations are most common among highly educated and resourceful women.

[10] The poverty odds we present here derive from logistic regressions. The extremely high Swedish odds-ratio is due to the fact that very few do not work in the first place, and those few are undoubtedly very unrepresentative.

[11] Another telling sign of lone mothers' vulnerability to business cycles is that their average number of days in unemployment jumped from 28 to 44, 1992–7.

Table 2.4 Lone parent poverty, and the impact of social benefits and mothers' employment, mid-1990s

	Poverty rate		Increase in poverty odds if mother does not work[a]	Per cent poverty reduction by social transfers[b]
	Mother works	Mother inactive		
Belgium	11	23	n.a.	n.a.
France	13	45	7.6	−31.3
Germany[c]	33	62	2.3	−20.2
Italy	25	79	4.6	−13.9
NL	17	41		
Spain (1990)	------------24------------		3.3	−20.6
Denmark	10	34	7.8	—
Finland	------------ 5------------			−38.2
Sweden	4	24	117.6	−49.9
UK	26	69	6.6	−36.4
US	39	73	4.6	−12.1

[a] Compared to mothers who work, holding number of children constant.
[b] Percentage point reduction of lone mother poverty (for *all* lone mothers) after taxes and transfers. Poverty is <50 per cent of median equivalent disposable income.
[c] West Germany only.

Source: Estimations from LIS data bases.

The 'work-strategy' is no doubt very effective, but for lone mothers only conditionally so. If they work, they are more likely to be in part-time or precarious employment and earn low wages. All in all, any realistic social inclusion policy for lone mothers must inevitably combine subsidized (or more realistically free) day care with income guarantees (whether or not they work).

It is for the latter reason that cross-national differences in lone mother poverty reflect differences in the generosity of countries' family welfare packages: Germany, Italy, Spain, and the US are far less effective in closing the poverty gap, while the Nordic countries are more so. Perhaps the best way to illustrate the point is to compare both pre- and post-transfer poverty across different countries. There is, for example, a surprising degree of convergence in pre-transfer poverty between Sweden, France, and Germany (at 50–55 per cent), but massive divergence in post-transfer poverty (5, 21, and 38 per cent, respectively).

There is ample room for the promotion of lone mothers' employment in most countries. While their activity rates are near universal in Scandinavia, Austria, and Portugal (between 70 and 80 per cent) they are extremely low (30–35 per cent) in Ireland, the UK, and the Netherlands (see also OECD, 2001c: Table 4.2). Access to affordable day care is obviously a first precondition but only in Scandinavia and the Netherlands are lone mothers guaranteed basically free access to care for the under-threes. The UK has an alternative approach with the new 'Working Families Tax Credit', which includes a subsidy of 70 per cent of childcare cost for lone mothers. However, this may be insufficient given typically low incomes and the high cost of private day care in Britain.

We note from Table 2.4 that, notwithstanding near-universal employment, government redistribution plays a vital role also for lone mothers' income in the Nordic countries. Due to their typically limited earnings capacity, lone mothers will usually need additional income support in order to escape poverty. Income transfers to lone mothers consist typically of three kinds of benefits: normal (in some cases with lone parent supplements) family cash benefits; maintenance advances; and social assistance. To these we should add tax deductions, which still constitute a major ingredient in family policy in some countries but which, of course, are a very ineffective tool in the case of lone mothers (or low income families more generally). There is a very strong case in favour of abolishing tax deductions and shifting resources to direct family cash transfers.

Using the most recent (2000) MISSOC data, child benefits are insufficient to eradicate poverty. Denmark and Sweden provide unusually generous benefits, but for a mother with two small children they amount to only 20 per cent of the average wage (roughly 340 Euros per month). If the lone parent has work income equivalent to, say, half the standard wage these benefits are probably sufficient to guarantee against poverty. If not, the need for additional assistance benefits arises. In fact, the modest poverty rates among Belgian and Danish lone mothers, even when not working, are no doubt related to generous social transfers: the combination of child allowances and social assistance would, for a lone parent with two children, arrive at 1,200 Euro (Belgium) and 1,639 Euro (Denmark). In both cases this is a sufficient guarantee against poverty. At the other extreme lie Spain and Italy, where the combined benefit package hardly reaches 200 Euro (far below the poverty line). We shall show below that the additional cost to the exchequer of ensuring sufficient income guarantees is minimal.

Income-tested assistance may trap mothers in welfare dependency. This, no doubt, was very much the case in traditional American and British social assistance but it generally depends on the design rather than the generosity of assistance and additionally, on the composition of the clientele. Gustafsson *et al.* (2000) compare assistance durations across eight European cities and find much longer durations among lone mothers in Spain, Portugal, and Italy (where benefits are very meagre), than in Sweden. One explanation is that lone mothers in Southern Europe may have fewer labour market skills and experience. Another lies in the far lower opportunity cost of moving to a job in Sweden than elsewhere (due, undoubtedly, to free day care and better earnings). The welfare trap may lie buried in day care and employment opportunities rather than in the protestant ethic.

These data alone speak in favour of the double strategy of supporting mothers' employment plus effective income assurance. Employment obviously presumes subsidized day care. But it also presumes access to jobs that are compatible with lone motherhood of small children, such as part-time jobs that offer sufficient flexibility and job security. The cash-benefit guarantee is necessary, first, because it is unrealistic to rely on absent fathers' maintenance payments. Many absent fathers are also economically weak and the monitoring costs of compliance can be excessively high. Second, it is necessary because lone mothers' job security can be very fragile (as we now witness in Sweden). Hence, an exaggerated bias in favour of 'make-work-pay' policy has substantial risks.

Work-Poor Households

Households are polarizing in terms of employment intensity. Part of the story lies in higher unemployment among prime age males, another part lies in women's employment profiles. Everywhere, the rise of married women's employment began among the more educated. In Scandinavia and North America this was followed by a surge of employment among the less educated as well. The far lower female activity rates in most of Europe, and especially in Southern Europe, reflect the fact that a similar surge is still pending.[12]

In some countries, the signs of household work polarization are strong. In the UK, for example, two-earner households grew from 54 to 62 per cent (1983–94) while workless households grew from 6 to 19 per cent, and we detect similar trends in Belgium, France, and Germany (OECD, 1995; Gregg *et al.*, 2000; Cantillon and Van den Bosch, 2001). But, polarization is not inevitable. In Denmark, almost all couples with children (81 per cent) have

---

[12] Employment rates of highly educated mothers hover around 80 per cent in North America, Scandinavia, and Belgium, declining to 60–70 per cent in France, Germany, and Southern Europe. Among the low-educated, rates are about 40–50 per cent in North America and Northern Europe, but drop to 20–25 per cent in countries like Italy and Spain (OECD, 2001c: Table 4.1).

double incomes; the incidence of workless households has declined sharply, to 4 per cent, over the 1990s (Andersen and Hestbaek, 1999). Once again, it is women's (and mainly lower educated women's) employment that makes the difference.[13]

Within the working-age population, workless households account for 10–15 per cent of all in the EU. Their numbers continue to grow in some countries and the persons affected are increasingly young.[14] A large share of the unemployed (ranging from 30 to 50 per cent) belong to workless households, an indicator of how unemployment concentrates in couples. An overview of the scope of the problem and associated poverty risks is presented in Table 2.4.

Workless households are the extreme case in a broader distribution. Although they are especially vulnerable, the changing nature of our economy and society also implies that the traditional one-earner family is increasingly at risk. We might preferably examine households along a band that stretches from fully workless through work-poor to work-rich.

Much suggests that the 'no-work household' concept itself is confused, simply because it covers too much diversity. It includes non-employed lone parents, but their share is often quite modest; in Scandinavia because the lion's share of lone mothers work; in Southern Europe because lone mothers tend to move in with relatives. More generally, it combines a hard core that exhibits unmistakable signs of long-term, if not chronic, exclusion and a softer element that appears more temporarily detached from the labour market. In an attempt to map out the prototypical European workless household, the following attributes are strongly over-represented:[15]

- very low education (at EU level, 45 per cent have less than secondary school)
- single, never-married persons (at EU level, 55 per cent)
- never-employed women (at EU level, 49 per cent of women)
- unemployed men (at EU level, 50 per cent of men)
- one adult with chronic disabilities or ill health (at EU level, 33 per cent)
- persons not looking for work (at EU level, 65 per cent)

[13] Two-earner households with full-time jobs constitute the vast majority (61 per cent), compared to one at full-time with the partner at half-time (20 per cent).

[14] In relation to the population aged 20–59. If, as OECD figures do, we include heads 60–65, the share is almost 5 points higher. The surprisingly high number of Danish (and Finnish) no-work households that derive from LIS data is due to conjunctural causes. Danish data refer to 1992 which was the trough of a recession. OECD's (1999b) data show a decline between 1986 and 1996.

[15] The following data derive from the European Community Household Panel, 1996 wave. Note that we exclude households with head aged 60+. Note also that these figures synthesize the European mean and thus disguise considerable national diversity. Due to substantial overlaps, these means should not be added.

Such numbers suggest important heterogeneity. A very large group are women who simply never worked. Another group (predominantly men) has been distanced from the labour market. Two-thirds of those who are unemployed are long-term (1 year+) and a third for more than three years. Poor health is clearly also prevalent. Since also two thirds do not even seek employment, it is difficult to automatically view them as simply 'excluded'.[16] All these indicators seem to point to older persons, but this is not so. Just about half of all persons in workless households are 39 years of age or younger and 33 per cent are between 25 and 39.[17] Although single person households are frequent (32 per cent), 18 per cent of all households have children. This therefore indicates that there are several factors involved:

1. There is one large group (mainly of women) who probably never had any real attachment to the labour market.
2. There is a second group that is clearly outside the labour force due to illness and disabilities.
3. There is a third group (made up more of men and generally low-skilled workers) that appears genuinely excluded in the sense of long-term unemployment. Twenty per cent among those reporting having worked once, have not worked for the past 5 years.
4. And there is a fourth group, also reporting unemployment, which must be regarded as more 'soft-core' since they have held a job during part of the year.

In short, those who are fully inactive constitute about two-thirds of all and slightly fewer than 30 per cent are unemployed and seeking work. But, the diversity among European countries is enormous. There are very few women who never worked in Scandinavia but many in Southern Europe. There are an abundance of single person households in Northern Europe while, in Southern Europe, single people typically live with others (usually family).

One would expect high poverty among workless households. But this varies by type and by nation, due to welfare state generosity and coverage. Table 2.5 presents poverty estimates for households with varying levels of work intensity. The growth and decline of workless households is only partly related to unemployment. In Denmark they rose to 12 per cent during the early 1990s, fell to 8 per cent by 1995 and continued to decline in the

---

[16] Ten per cent of these are women who care for others; about 25 per cent are ill or retired (on disability mainly); 17 per cent are in some form of education; and 39 per cent are apparently women who never held a job (estimates from 1996 wave of the ECHP).

[17] And, as indicated, there are signs that the risk of living in no-work households is rising among the young.

Table 2.5 Poverty rates within households according to employment intensity, mid-1990s

	All no-work households			2 Parents/ 1 Worker Poverty rate	2 Parents/ 2 Workers Poverty rate
	Share (% of all)	Poverty Rate	-of which extreme poverty		
Belgium	13	24	18	3	1
Denmark	8	25	27	4	0
Finland	15	13	17	4	2
France	9	34	24	7	2
Germany (W)	8	46	45	6	1
Italy	10	35	52	21	6
NL	14			5	1
Spain (1990)	9	38	44		
UK	18	38	20	19	3

Notes: Poverty is <50 per cent of adjusted median income.
Extreme poverty is <33 per cent of adjusted median income.

Source: LIS data bases for no-work households, and Oxley *et al.* (2001: Table 25.5) for one- and two-earner families.

late 1990s. This suggests a household composition that is fairly easy to re-integrate as the economy improves.[18] In contrast, the UK not only has a high rate of workless households, but here we see more 'hysteresis'. There has been a fairly constant growth between 1980 and 1995, with a less significant decline during the recent boom years. The composition here is likely to be more 'hard-core' (in 1996, indeed, 71 per cent were discouraged workers or fully inactive).[19]

The phenomenon has been growing over the long term in just about all countries, pointing to a possible hardening of labour market exclusion. In terms of income, the data suggest it is better being workless in Northern Europe and Belgium. The 'extreme poverty' indicator captures the income gap and in some cases (like Italy, Germany, and Spain), the workless households

---

[18] It may also reflect Denmark's strong accent on 'activation'. Largely due to activation, the number of persons receiving long-term social assistance fell by 37 per cent, 1994–1999 (Socialministeriet, 2001: 10).

[19] Analyses from the 1996 wave of the European Community Household Panel.

in poverty tend to be exceptionally poor—an indication that the basic social safety of public *and* family support is weak. This instance of 'family failure' is important to note. If family support of young unemployed people by and large averts youth poverty in Southern Europe, it does not do so for those adults who are more 'excluded'. Workless households may lack resources also in the sense that they may not have access to family support.

Work-poor households rely heavily on income-tested benefits and this means that poverty is related to the generosity and take-up rate of assistance schemes. If we again revert to MISSOC data, now for couples with two children, the lower poverty rates in Scandinavia and in Belgium are clearly linked to higher social assistance benefit rates. In Denmark, assistance puts the household fairly near an average worker's wage. In France and Germany, the same assisted family would arrive at roughly 40 per cent.[20] As one would expect, poverty declines with the intensity of employment to almost nil among dual-earner families. This confirms the fact that women's employment is becoming more indispensable for any anti-poverty strategy.

It would be impossible, given the information available, to identify with any precision the size of the hard-core or soft-core; in part because it all depends on what we imply by 'hard-core'. If we adopt the broadest possible definition and view it as persons who more or less certainly will not respond to activation or employment incentives, the hard-core might include, say, 50–60 per cent of the total. This comprises mainly the chronically ill and disabled and women who never have held a job. We should also clearly eliminate those who simply 'do not belong', such as students and apprentices (only 5 per cent of all). This leaves us with about 40 per cent of the workless households that can realistically be 'integrated'.[21]

With such heterogeneity, a workable social inclusion strategy needs to be multifaceted. A huge segment no doubt represents a long-term historical legacy. Especially in Southern Europe there exists a large reservoir of women with little education or employment experience. There may also exist a large segment of males that are difficult to reactivate, especially if they display multiple problems, such as low education, poor health, or alcoholism. This group is unlikely to become stably employed either by 'in-work' incentive policy or by activation and, consequently, an adequate income guarantee may be the only humane and cost-effective option. The high poverty rates in Germany and the UK suggest that the basic safety net may be too ungenerous.

---

[20] Calculations based on income data from *Eurostat Yearbook* (1988–98: 162).

[21] One explanation for why reintegration in Denmark during economic upswings appears superior is that very few women have never held a job.

Exclusion from the labour market may easily be compounded if such households do not have enough money to participate adequately in the society within which they live.

It is clear that workless households combine legacies from the past (low educated, never-employed women) with victims of new social dynamics. Demographic change will produce rising numbers of single persons and lone parents. Most worrisome of all is the rapidly deteriorating position of low educated people. When we also consider marital homogamy, precariousness in the labour market will concentrate in couples. However, there are reasons to believe that the 'hard-core' of exclusion may diminish on its own over time. The number of never-employed women will naturally decrease and the more that policy supports working mothers, the more this decline should accelerate.

Women's employment levels, as noted, are no doubt the *sine qua non* if we wish to minimize household polarization around the work-intensity axis. The key issue is how to mobilize labour supply among the less educated women. In countries like the Nordic, which actively pursue universal female employment, the activity rates among low educated women are very high (62–68 per cent), followed by the UK and the US (59 per cent), dropping to 46–50 per cent in France, Germany, and the Netherlands, and hitting rock bottom in Italy and Spain (20–22 per cent). If we were to apply the 'acid test' of focusing only on low educated *mothers* with small children, the employment gap widens hugely—but not everywhere. In Belgium, Denmark, Sweden, and the US, motherhood makes no significant difference; everywhere else, it does. In the UK employment rates drop by 20 percentage points and in Germany by a dramatic 30 percentage points. In Southern Europe, their employment rates fall to 15 per cent.[22]

Since the employment chances of both men and women depend on skills, clearly the most effective remedy against chronic non-employability would be to prevent young people from leaving education prematurely. At the EU level, 22 per cent of today's young cohorts do not complete any form of secondary education. This share rises to 30 per cent in Ireland, Italy, Spain, and the UK, but is only half in the Nordic countries. Furthermore, young cohorts with low schooling face especially steep hurdles during the transition from school to employment. Among 25–29 year olds, those with less than secondary education have twice as high unemployment rates as the average. Even worse, they are much more likely to become trapped in prolonged exclusion. In France,

---

[22] These estimates derive from Cantillon *et al.* (2000: Tables 4 and 5). Chapter 3 provides a more detailed treatment of issues related to the harmonization of motherhood and labour supply.

for example, 20 per cent of men with less than secondary education remain unemployed five years after leaving school (OECD, 1999b: Tables 7 and 16). In Denmark, persistent welfare dependency is overwhelmingly concentrated among those with no professional qualifications (Socialministeriet, 2001: 14).

We have some comparative evidence on longer-term entrapment in both low pay and in unskilled work. One alarming finding is that the youngest cohorts are more likely to remain trapped in unskilled jobs than was the case for earlier cohorts in Germany, Sweden and the UK. At the same time, the chances of moving out of low skilled jobs are greater in Sweden (about a third who began as unskilled eventually leave, compared to 20 per cent in the UK). A similar comparative scenario is evident for low wage entrapment. Among the continuously employed, aged 25–34, those who in 1986 were low wage workers could expect 4 years more of low wage employment over the next five years in the UK and the US, about 2.5 years in Germany, France, and Italy, but a much lower 1.7 years in Denmark.[23] Scandinavia appears better able to stem entrapment and the unusually high rates in Britain and America suggest that unregulated labour markets do not guarantee greater mobility.

The most realistic short-term policy for the hard-core workless is probably adequate 'passive' income maintenance combined with training, or sheltered employment for people with disabilities who have difficulties in entering the open labour market. The most effective long-term strategy would be to invest in prevention, which, as will be argued in the following section, must start in early childhood. Table 2.6 provides a broader picture of how different factors affect poverty in workless households.

The table presents estimates for the EU as a whole and for four representative welfare models. The analyses are limited to ages 20–55 in order to exclude those in early retirement. The results summarize quite well our earlier findings. The risk of poverty rises among the young and less educated, but above all when the head of the household is long-term unemployed and when there is no earner (throughout the entire year). The poverty risk is especially severe when the head of the household is long-term unemployed in Spain and the UK while this implies no significant risk in Denmark—implying that Danish income support is quite effective.

The fact that chronic illness does not influence poverty suggests that welfare states protect those *medically* unable to work quite effectively.[24]

---

[23] For unskilled entrapment, see Allmendinger and Hinz (1996); for wage mobility, see OECD (1999b).

[24] However, this may be offset by the potentially high costs to households when a member is disabled or seriously ill. Obviously, the cost structure of health care becomes decisive for whether adequate incomes are genuinely 'adequate'.

Table 2.6 The odds of poverty among workless households. Logistic regressions for select countries, and for the European Union as a whole, 1996 (includes only head of household aged 20–55)

	Denmark	Germany	Spain	UK	European Union
Age of head	0.95***	0.97***	0.99	0.97*	0.98***
Education	1.29	0.86	0.40***	0.76*	0.54***
Head chronic illness	1.73	0.77	1.33	0.91	0.84**
Head long-term unemployed	0.30	1.57	4.64***	3.21***	1.74***
No work income	5.14***	9.77***	4.74***	5.34***	7.70***
Children present	0.44*	1.05	1.62**	1.52**	1.03
Lone mother	0.93	1.37	0.70	2.05**	1.04

Explanation: Odds less than 1.0 imply that the risk of poverty diminishes; odds greater than 1.0 imply that this factor raises the probability of poverty.
    *** Significant at 0.001 level.
    ** Significant at 0.01 level.
    * Significant at 0.05 level.
Source: ECHP, wave 1996.

The presence of children in the household raises poverty risks significantly in Spain and the UK, while in Denmark the effect is to reduce poverty. This indicates that the generosity of family support can be decisive. Lone motherhood contributes to poverty only in the UK. The single most overwhelming effect everywhere comes from 'no income from work' over the whole year, an indication of where the core problem is buried: households become very vulnerable everywhere when they drop out of the labour market.

In the immediate future, managing social exclusion for workless households will necessarily imply income support for the 'hard-core', but what can realistically be done for the 'softer-core'? Here contemporary policy promotes two, not mutually exclusive, remedies: 'make-work-pay' and activation.

Make-Work-Pay

Make-work-pay policy is directed at work incentives. These may express themselves in poverty traps or as unacceptably high opportunity costs of taking paid employment (as in the case of the day care 'tax' on mothers' labour). Can we identify clear supply-side disincentives across the EU?

Overall, there is little scientific evidence that social benefits reduce work incentives *per se*.[25] In most EU countries, unemployment or social assistance benefits are simply too low to affect work motivation among all but the lowest paid workers. Interestingly, countries with unusually generous unemployment benefits often have much lower long-term unemployment *and*, at least in the Danish case, one of Europe's highest flow-rates out of unemployment (Esping-Andersen and Regini, 2000).[26] Vice versa, long-term unemployment is especially pronounced in Italy where the majority of all unemployed (mainly youth) have absolutely no entitlement to any social benefit.[27] If we examine the economic situation of the unemployed in workless households we find that poverty rates are generally high and, in some countries, extremely high.

This is not to say that work incentive problems do not exist. It often depends on policy interactions. High social benefits may not reduce work incentives if, as in Denmark, they are combined with activation policies. Vice versa, if social benefits are reduced when partners work there may be a negative effect on spouses' labour supply. During the 1990s, EU Member States have taken some steps to remedy such dependency traps. Belgium and Germany, for example, now permit some work income in combination with assistance receipt. In the Nordic countries, where unemployment benefits are individualized, the negative spousal effect disappears. Ireland and the UK, following other Anglo countries, favour the tax credit approach to supplement incomes from low-wage employment.

Such measures may reduce the number of working-poor households at the margin, but 'in-work benefits' are unlikely to be an effective solution if half of all workless households are *de facto* impossible to integrate in the labour market.

Activation

Activation refers to any policy that enhances the capabilities of citizens. In this sense, providing day care to mothers is activation. Its legacy stems from

[25] See also Chapter 4.

[26] The drastic decline in unemployment *and* in no-work households in Denmark after 1992 is, in part due to the recovery of full employment, but also to the new employment activation policies.

[27] Hence they continue to live with parents (and thus avoid poverty). Indeed, this very fact may indirectly provoke incentive effects since the reservation wage among unemployed youth equals the living standard they maintain in the parental home. Accordingly, unemployed youth are generally unwilling to move geographically even when offered a job. For an overview of the income situation among young unemployed in Europe, see Bison and Esping-Andersen (2000*a*).

the long Swedish tradition of 'active labour market policies'. Activation policy has changed philosophy in recent years. Now it typically combines a work-motivational element with individually tailored re-integration plans. Remedial policy is believed to be effective only if it takes a long-term perspective and if it focuses on developing broad skills. Hence, it is unavoidably very costly. Except for the Nordic countries (and especially Denmark), most EU Member States pursue less comprehensive activation measures. We may distinguish three broad approaches. One group favours targeted (especially youth) job subsidies with some training content attached to the subsidy. In France, a third of young workers with low education find their first employment in a subsidized job (OECD, 1999b: Table 25). In Italy, subsidized training jobs account for 60–65 per cent of all first youth entries into the labour market. It is not clear how much training is provided, but the policy can claim one success, namely that the rate of passage from temporary training to permanent contracts is very high. Unfortunately, it also demonstrates a basic failure in lowering (youth) unemployment (Samek Lodovici, 2000). A second group, already discussed, puts the emphasis on changing work incentives via work-conditional benefits.

The third approach, epitomized by recent Danish policy, invests heavily in across-the-board (but youth biased) reintegration. Briefly, it aims to avert prolonged exclusion by stipulating a maximum of six months' unemployment or assistance benefits for the under-29s (longer for older workers), upon which continued benefits are conditional on either accepting a job or education. Job assignments are often in sheltered or subsidized employment. Education offers depend on the candidate and may involve prolonged schooling (up to eighteen months as a norm). The key is that integration is tailored to the profile, needs, and prospects of the individual, and that it involves intensive and continuous follow-up. This is unavoidably expensive, but it is regarded as an investment in future productivity and self-reliance.

Does activation pay off? That question is almost impossible to answer because we will never know whether 'activated' persons would have succeeded (or failed) without such help. Follow-up analyses of Danish activation produce mixed results. There is first the interesting finding that the 'activated' are systematically more satisfied when they move from passive welfare support to activation. This may be more important than it sounds: it suggests not only that welfare dependency is not an incentive problem, but also that inclusion in an educational or job-insertion programme arguably heightens clients' sense of belonging and participating in society. Additionally, there is some evidence that activation (and the 6-month ceiling on unemployment benefits) spurs the unemployed to seek employment more energetically.

There is also solid evidence that activation has brought down long-term assistance dependency. But more global assessments of its effectiveness are more hedged. Most studies arrive at a very similar '30-30-30' conclusion, namely that about one-third of cases are clear successes in the sense that they escape fully from welfare dependency; a second third escape only partially or temporarily; and a final third remain dependent on benefits. The important addendum here is that success is substantially greater among young people (under 25).[28]

Towards a Preventive Strategy

There is one basic finding that overshadows all others, namely that remedial policies for adults are a poor (and costly) substitute for interventions in childhood (Heckman and Lochner, 2000). Since a person's job and career prospects depend increasingly on his or her cognitive abilities, this is where it all begins. Activating or retraining adults is profitable and realistic if these same adults already come with a sufficient ability to learn. Households with limited resources can probably never be eradicated entirely, but their relative proportion can be minimized and this is our single greatest policy challenge. With this aim in mind, what does the scientific evidence tell us?

First and foremost, it all begins in early childhood. At this point, three factors are of crucial importance: health, income poverty, and 'developmental priming mechanisms' such as reading to children, social stimuli, and guidance.[29] Families with limited resources are likely to fall short on all three counts. A strong welfare state in the conventional sense can avert the first two factors, but if cognitive stimulation is key we must rethink policy. We cannot pass laws that force parents to read to their children, but we can compensate. One option, further examined in Chapter 4, is to ensure that parents of small children are given the possibility of low-stress employment and adequate time with their children.[30] A second, perhaps more effective option, is to promote universal, high-quality day care.

---

[28] For an overview, see Ploug and Sondergaard (1999) and Socialministeriet (2001). These results seem to confirm the idea that there exists (and possibly always will) a hard-core group of citizens for whom the only realistic welfare policy is adequate (passive) income support.

[29] For an overview of existing scientific research, see Karoly *et al.* (1998) and Danziger and Waldvogel (2000). For more detail, see below.

[30] As discussed below there is ample evidence that mothers' employment *per se* does not affect negatively children's welfare or development, but there is also strong evidence that it will *if* mothers have stressful working conditions.

Here is a case for giving priority access to quality day care for children from vulnerable families.[31] The challenge then continues at school age. Here the evidence points to two key factors. First, that family poverty (and instability) remains decisive, especially in dictating school attendance, motivation and drop-out risks. Second, the quality of schools and the nature of the local community interact heavily (this is especially an American problem, but it may very well transplant itself to Europe as segregated immigrant communities proliferate). The situation to avoid is that schools are inferior in deprived neighbourhoods. Education experts advocate the development of after-school programmes that yield the double advantage of supporting the intellectual development of children while alleviating pressure on working mothers.

Even if many of the roots of social exclusion emanate from childhood, there is strong evidence that the experience of poverty *per se* has a compounding, self-reinforcing effect on marginalization. Whelan *et al.* (2001) show that persistent income poverty accelerates the erosion of resources which, in turn, hardens deprivation.[32] Poverty, as we have seen, is generally triggered by lack of income from work so this is where policy should naturally focus. But we must also recognize that a work strategy alone is far from being a sufficient measure. In other words, any serious social inclusion policy cannot avoid income guarantees that, minimally, avert cumulative resource depletion.

A social inclusion strategy for Europe depends, in the immediate sense, on a combined work and income support policy. The need for income support will obviously decline massively if women's employment levels rise. And this 'strategy', as we have seen, would be especially effective among less-educated women and mothers. Since they are likely to be married to low-educated men, and since the latter are losing terrain very rapidly, the mobilization of the less educated female labour reservoir is quite urgent. If we shift our sight further into the future, the obviously most effective preventive strategy is to invest heavily in the resources of our children today. Most contemporary welfare states fail to do this and, if uncorrected, they will pay a heavy price tomorrow.

---

[31] As will be clear further on, we strongly advocate a *universal* child care policy, but within such a framework one might contemplate special measures (such as subsidies) in favour of those most at risk. Additionally, the establishment of a comprehensive system of childcare will take years, even decades, and one might therefore pursue some selectivity in favour of the most needy in the meanwhile.

[32] Their deprivation measure is a multi-indicator composite of need and social integration.

Investing in Children

There is cause for optimism *and* worry about the epoch we are entering. We shall benefit from substantial upskilling of our job structure overall, although this will undoubtedly occur in tandem with a sizeable low-skilled labour market in areas such as personal services or retail. The seminal increase in skill requirements implies that the preconditions for good life chances will rise as well. Those with inadequate skills or resources risk sliding into a life of precariousness and exclusion. The concentration of welfare problems within contemporary families with children and young people are accordingly of major concern. If we aim for a productive and socially integrated future society, our policy priorities should centre on today's children and youths. Solid investments in children now will diminish welfare problems among future adults.

Many believe we face a naked generational clash so that greater social allocations to children will be at the expense of the elderly or vice versa. This is, generically speaking, a fallacy. To begin with, there is no golden rule that dictates that the welfare of one implies misery for the other. On the contrary, poverty among the elderly *and* child poverty is simultaneously very low in the Nordic countries and Belgium; simultaneously very high in the US and Britain. This is even more evident when we examine long-term trends. The decline in elderly poverty is internationally convergent, but long-run (1970–1990s) trends in child poverty diverge: declining steadily in the Nordic countries, fairly stable in most of Continental Europe and rising significantly in Italy, the UK, and in the United States. Spending on the elderly may, of course, crowd out resources for the young but such a scenario can be avoided by the adoption of the kinds of decision rules advocated in Chapter 5.

Also, we must not forget the continued importance of the intergenerational social contract *within* families. Traditionally, resource flows were more likely to go from children to their elderly parents, whereas the flow is now largely reversed. Income-rich pensioners transfer large amounts of excess retirement income to their children and grandchildren (Esping-Andersen, 1999; Kohli, 1999). The conventional intergenerational contract is becoming problematic for two reasons. On the monetary side, the timing of inheritance is being delayed due to increased life expectancy. Hence, rather than arriving when the offspring most need it (as young families), it is now more likely to arrive when the children are already in their prime. More generally, we see the emergence of a distorted life cycle redistribution. If excess retirement income is redistributed downward within families, the redistributive effect will be regressive: the children of rich pensioners will be favoured. Indeed, here we confront a rather problematic example of socially inherited privilege partly sponsored by the welfare state. Any future welfare architecture must include stronger investments in children and youth, but this cannot be undertaken without placing it in the context of a just and viable model of intergenerational solidarity.

With some notable exceptions, contemporary welfare states give rather low priority to families with children. This is historically rooted. Traditional family policy was more indirect, focusing on upholding the earning power of the male breadwinner. As long as marriages were stable and breadwinners enjoyed secure, well-paid employment, governments could assume the self-reliance of families in terms of both income and caring needs. Married male workers were also often paid an additional marriage supplement, which typically added 5-10 per cent to men's wages (Montanari, 2000). Child allowances and other transfers mainly addressed households with large numbers of children (a large percentage had 3+ children until the 1960s).

Furthermore, family support policies entered a long era of decline in tandem with falling fertility and rising real wages (Gauthier, 1996; Wennemo, 1994; Kamerman and Kahn, 1997).[33] A small group of nations began, since the 1970s, to pursue more active family policies and during the 1990s we see a broader pan-European attempt to respond to the needs of families. See Table 2.7.[34]

It can be seen that the income position of families with children continues to decline in many countries regardless of a rise in *per child* transfers. As discussed, this is related to the proliferation of high-risk households and the often problematic labour market conditions among young adults. For example, the share of children who live in a workless household has increased by 32 per cent in the EU since the mid-1980s (Micklewright and Stewart, 2000: Table A4). The growth in child poverty is related to widening overall inequalities.[35]

The question is whether policy can make a difference. Scandinavia is an obvious benchmark for comparison. Nordic child poverty rates are systematically low and, more tellingly, continue to decline; not so much because of

---

[33] The mean EU fertility rate in 1960 was 2.61; in 1990 it had dropped to 1.54. Kamerman and Kahn's (1997: Table 4.9) data show that the value of family cash benefits (as a percentage of disposable income for a one-earner married couple, with two children) declined in 14 out of 18 countries, 1975-90.

[34] As Table 2.6 suggests, welfare state allocations *per child* began to increase during the 1990s in several countries, most notably in Australia and in Scandinavia. Yet, as we shall see ahead the rise in child poverty continues regardless. Trends in aged poverty are discussed in Chapter 5.

[35] The bi-variate correlation between changes (1985-95) in primary income Gini and child poverty rates is +0.691 for 15 OECD countries. In OLS regressions, every one point increase in Gini raises child poverty by 1.1 points (estimated on the basis of data furnished by Oxley *et al.* (1999)).

Table 2.7 Trends in incomes and social transfers among families with children, mid-1980s to mid-1990s (Adjusted for changes in population shares)

	Trend in disposable income	Trend in transfers
Australia	−3.4	+6.3
Canada	+1.5	+2.9
UK	−3.4	+1.3
USA	+2.4	+1.3
Denmark	−0.6	+2.0
Finland	+1.6	+5.5
Norway	−0.3	+3.5
Sweden	−1.9	+2.0
France	+3.6	−0.4
Germany	−1.8	−3.5
Italy	+0.6	0.0
Netherlands	+2.4	+0.3

Source: Data from Oxley *et al.* (1999). Estimates based on equivalence scale (e = 0.5).

social transfers, but primarily because fathers *and* mothers are gainfully employed and adequately paid.

This combination does not exist anywhere else. The Anglo-Saxon nations favour targeted support, currently through work-conditional tax credits. The Australian and Canadian approach is more generous and, hence, child poverty has declined far more than in the UK or in the US.[36] The worrisome increase in child poverty in several Continental European nations must, likewise, be linked to social policy. The Continental social insurance tradition is ill-equipped to offer more than residual assistance benefits to needy households without established work records. With few exceptions child allowance schemes are undeveloped and ungenerous and public provision of childcare virtually non-existent. Nowhere is the youth concentration of unemployment as severe as in Continental and Southern Europe. Even if

[36] Britain has recently improved these benefits, but we lack up-to-date data to gauge its effects on poverty.

Mediterranean families remain far more stable, market inequalities none-theless generate poverty.[37]

The Case for Abolishing Child Poverty

We have seen that in some nations the relative position of families with children is deteriorating, both when compared with their own income position a decade earlier, as well as when compared against others. In little more than one decade, child poverty has risen in 6 out of the 10 countries we examine, and in the UK, Germany, and in Italy (at about 7 percentage points), alarmingly so.

Families with children are vulnerable to unemployment and it is not easy to disentangle the separate effects of income poverty from the experience of unemployment on children's well-being. There is strong evidence that unemployment, even if not accompanied by poverty, has serious secondary effects. A recent Danish study shows that it doubles the chances of family break-ups and, much later, of unemployment among the children. It is also highly correlated with parental alcoholism, violence, and incarceration (Christoffersen, 1996). Similar long-term consequences for life chances and family welfare also spring from child poverty. As research documents, these consequences spill over to society. We know from American research that childhood poverty is strongly associated with less schooling (two years less), more criminal behaviour, various psychological pathologies and with lower earnings in adulthood (30 per cent less). Children from poor families are also much more likely to become poor parents later and, thus, to repro-duce the poverty syndrome across generations (Haveman and Wolfe, 1994; 1995; Duncan and Brooks-Gunn, 1997; Danziger and Waldvogel, 2000). European research (Gregg and Machin, 2001) comes to similar if, perhaps, less dramatic conclusions.[38] To the extent that child poverty is indeed asso-ciated with inferior life chances, fighting child poverty should be considered a priority.

---

[37] In Spain, however, child poverty has remained basically stable at 10–12 per cent between 1980 and 1990. Note that our estimates (from LIS data) refer only to households with head aged 25–55.

[38] American data show that children (aged 16–24) from the poorest quintile are three times as likely to drop out of high school (Cornia and Danziger, 1997: 201). Buchel et al.'s (2001) data for Germany suggest that children from the bottom two quintiles (i.e. poor families) are half as likely to go to Gymnasium as the mean. For Britain, Gregg and Machin (2001) find that poor economic conditions in childhood are 5 per cent more likely to lead to unemployment or to provoke problems with the police (if men) and 9 per cent more (if women). Also in their study, the negative impact of childhood poverty on schooling is the key mechanism.

If childhood poverty translates into less education, inferior cognitive skills, more criminality, and inferior lives, the secondary effect is a mass of low-productivity workers, highly vulnerable to unemployment and low pay in the 'new economy'. They will yield less revenue to tax authorities and probably require more public aid during their active years. In short, here we can identify the basis for social exclusion in tomorrow's Europe. There is mounting evidence that the harm done in childhood is very difficult to undo later. Remedial 'second-chance' policies are much more costly and far less effective than policies aimed at improving especially *early childhood* welfare (Heckman and Lochner, 2000). If the parental environment has an overpowering effect on subsequent learning and cognitive acquisition, clearly a major objective of social policy must be to lessen this potential effect.

Cognitive inequalities are strongly correlated with poverty and income inequalities more generally.[39] Regression analysis suggests that a 10 per cent rise in child poverty implies a 8.5 per cent increase in the share of adults that fall into the lowest (basically dysfunctional) level of cognitive abilities.[40] In turn, low cognitive abilities, like low educational attainment, are powerful predictors of unemployment.

If poverty harms children's life chances *and* if it also creates negative externalities, we see the contours of a positive-sum strategy: minimizing child poverty now will yield an individual and social dividend in the future. And in the far-off future, it should diminish the risks of old age poverty (and possibly also the need for early retirement).

It is clear that there is a strong case in favour of activation and lifelong learning strategies. But, and this is a crucial point, *such strategies are unlikely to work if not accompanied by a broader attack on childhood deprivation.* Unless we intervene in the mechanisms that transmit inferior resources, such as cognitive abilities, from parents to children, it will probably not be effective. Some countries have succeeded in reducing the parental impact on children's cognitive abilities, others far less (OECD, 2000*b*). In the first group we find the Nordic countries with Australia. Here the impact of parents' educational level on their children's cognitive abilities is comparatively weak and,

[39] This is also a key finding in Gottschalk *et al.* (1994) and in the Gregg and Machin (2001) study. For a more comprehensive treatment, see Huston (1991).

[40] OECD's literacy studies distinguish 5 cognitive levels. The lowest (1) must be considered inherently dysfunctional, reflecting a level so poor that people are generically untrainable and able to perform only the most routine unskilled work. T-statistic in estimation = 4.38, and R^2 = 0.635 (N = 12). A similar equation predicting low cognitive abilities with overall inequality (Gini coefficient for the working age population) yields even stronger elasticities: for each Gini-point increase, the percentage in cognitive level 1 increases by 1.3 points. (T = 5.81, and R^2 = 0.772).

more importantly, in marked decline. In the second group we find Belgium, Germany, and the US. Here the parental impact is very strong and, worse, increasing.

It is not possible to isolate all the relevant factors involved in intergenerational cognitive inheritance, but some are clear and eminently subject to policy. First and foremost, the inequality of educational attainment among parents is all-important and policy must therefore concentrate on closing educational gaps among contemporary youth cohorts. This means minimizing secondary school drop-out rates, perhaps via special incentive schemes and more diversified (and integrated) secondary-level educational menus. If, as occurs in several European countries, a third of youths leave school without a secondary-level diploma, this is likely to translate into a two-thirds society two decades hence. A concrete step one might consider is to apply the logic of 'in-work' benefits to diminish school drop-out rates, i.e. introduce *'in-school benefit schemes'* to parents. One might, for example, introduce supplementary social benefits to families that are conditional on the verified school attendance of their children.[41]

A second well-documented factor has to do with family instability. Lone parent families can be especially problematic since they combine low income with less parental attention to children (if mothers work). The problem is that mothers' employment—especially in lone mother households—is a key to reducing poverty risks. What is important to note, however, is that (lone) mothers' employment is not *per se* a source of childhood disadvantage. The effects are positive if mothers have rewarding jobs, but become negative if their jobs produce stress and fatigue (Lynch, 2000; Haveman and Wolfe, 1995; Duncan and Brooks-Gunn, 1997). An approach to combat childhood deprivation may therefore have to follow a combined strategy that: (*a*) assures adequate family income, (*b*) helps weaken the direct impact of parents on children's cognitive development, and (*c*) improves the work environment of employed mothers—a point also emphasized in Chapter 4.

Strategies to Minimize Child Poverty

Poverty may be brief, sporadic, or lasting.[42] It may occur when children are small (and parental earnings generally lower), or later in childhood (due to

---

[41] Here Europe can draw lessons from Brazil where the Cardoso government has sought to diminish child vagrancy by subsidies to parents whose children attend school.

[42] The duration of child poverty is clearly detrimental to the dynamics of welfare. From the rather limited studies available on comparative poverty dynamics, there are pretty clear indications that persistence is positively related to overall poverty levels. The likelihood of remaining

family break-ups, unemployment, or mothers' inability to work). Equally, the longer it lasts, the more harmful it is. There is a growing consensus that *early* childhood is key for subsequent development. Moreover, the household context of deprivation may be influential. As noted, divorce is very problematic and lone mother poverty may have substantially worse consequences than similar poverty within a stable two-parent family (Haveman and Wolfe, 1995; Duncan and Brooks-Gunn, 1997). On the other hand, children's well-being improves dramatically when (and if) lone mothers remarry or cohabit—in either case, this almost doubles household income (Morrison and Ritualo, 2000).[43]

Today, as always, work income remains the single most powerful bulwark against poverty. But, at the lower end of the earnings scale and especially when households are excluded from employment, transfer dependency is intensifying. Yet, transfer dependency can and is being effectively reduced in some countries by the provision of childcare services. Unaffordable childcare can be a serious poverty trap for low income families. If, as is typical across much of Europe, the cost of full-time, quality care *per child* exceeds a third of mothers' expected earnings, the resulting real tax on her employment becomes prohibitive. The outcome may be undesirable: educated women with high wages will be able to afford care; low educated women and women on low incomes will not be able to afford care, notwithstanding that the urgency of affordable care is greater among the latter.

Let us, for analytical purposes, reduce the issue to two basic factors: the earnings capacity of households with children (which is related to affordable day care) and the level of social transfers to which they are entitled (which may help offset the cost of children). In order to isolate the relative salience of either, we should examine two-parent and one-parent households separately. As in the previous section, we can estimate the odds ratios of child poverty given parental employment status and the size of social transfers. Table 2.8 repeats the analysis provided earlier for lone parent families, now for two-parent households with children.

The table groups countries by their general social protection characteristics, as discussed earlier. The number of children has a fairly strong effect on poverty, in particular where the family benefit package is ungenerous,

poor in 3 out of 3 years (and 5 out of 5 years) is substantially higher in the US than in Europe (Duncan and Brooks-Gunn, 1997; Duncan *et al.*, 1998; Bradbury *et al.*, 2000). Correspondingly, the likelihood of exiting poverty is lower in any given year in the US than in Europe.

[43] Although information is totally lacking, the general practice of single mothers in Southern Europe to co-reside with other relatives may have a positive effect on the children's welfare.

Table 2.8 The odds of being poor. The impact of parental employment and social transfers on poverty in two-parent families with children. Logistic odds-ratios, mid-1990s

	Father does not work	Mother does not work	Impact of social transfers	
			All	Only pre-poor families[a]
Denmark	2.3	3.0	0.7	0.07
Sweden	4.2	20.3	0.4	0.05
France	8.3	4.1	0.9	0.18
Germany	12.0	3.0	1.0[n.s]	0.23
Italy	9.1	5.5	0.9	0.05
Spain	6.2	3.0	1.0[n.s]	0.12
UK	8.8	2.1	0.8	0.07
US	1.3	3.1	1.7	0.42

[a] Estimates for households poor before taxes and transfer.
[n.s] Denotes statistically non-significant effect.

Note: All estimates control for number children.

Source: LIS data.

i.e. falling below the Ditch *et al.* (1998) country mean (estimates not shown in Table). But the impact of number of children basically disappears among pre-transfer poor families, an indication that support to low income families is more in tune with the size of the household.[44]

Also, there are important variations in the degree of male-breadwinner dependency. The relative importance of fathers' earnings is pronounced in the UK, Germany, Italy, and France, but far weaker in Scandinavia and the US. Generally speaking, there is no single country in which mothers' employment (controlling for fathers') would not reduce poverty substantially, typically by a factor of 4 or 5. For two-parent families, the conventional male breadwinner model raises poverty risks considerably and we arrive at a conclusion very similar to the earlier analysis of lone mothers. Mothers' employment is a key factor in any policy approach to fight child poverty.

[44] Bradshaw (2000) shows that even in Italy (one of Europe's least 'child-friendly' transfer systems) social assistance benefits to large child families assume a standard comparable to France or the UK.

But this does not imply that social transfers become unimportant. When we examine 'all families', the majority of which are not poor before transfer incomes, the transfer effect is only noticeable in the Nordic countries.[45] It becomes key in 'pre-poor' families, and here we have a good indicator of the efficiency of the family transfer package: very effective in all cases, except the United States and, to a lesser degree, Germany.[46] It is telling that the impact of mothers' work in pre-poor families is by far the strongest in Sweden, and not at all significant in the UK, France, Germany, and Italy. This suggests that Sweden secures minimal child poverty by its *combined strategy* of generous transfers and support for working mothers. In Continental Europe (and the UK) families depend far more on either the male breadwinner or on transfers.

The Cost of Eliminating Child Poverty

What is the cost of a child? First, there are the direct costs of feeding and clothing an additional member of the family. Such costs may have a marginal effect for low income families. What has changed dramatically are the opportunity costs involved. These are best measured by the (cumulative) wage penalty that motherhood incurs. It is this part of the cost burden that contemporary families are increasingly unwilling to internalize. Policy makers seem to assume that the opportunity cost is simply a matter of more day care and paid leave. This is not true for countries where employers impose huge costs on motherhood.[47] If 'getting started' for a woman necessitates renouncing motherhood, the cost of children comes close to being equal to the benefits of female economic independence. This aspect of the 'cost of children' will be examined in Chapter 3.

A policy paradox of our times is that while the costs of childhood deprivation can be very high the costs of eliminating the problem can be quite modest. As an experiment, let us for the moment ignore the contribution of fathers to family welfare and simply focus on the two main alternatives: lowering poverty via mothers' employment and/or via more generous family transfers. Which policy might most efficiently ensure zero child poverty—regardless of number of children?

Spain is arguably an excellent illustrative case because it combines very low female employment, exceptionally undeveloped economic support to

---

[45] In the US, the tax–transfer combination actually contributes to poverty.

[46] Note, however, that Germany has recently upgraded its child allowance scheme.

[47] In Italy and Spain, employers routinely force female employees to contractually agree to dismissal in the case of pregnancy. Perhaps this happens rarely in Sweden but then competitive sector Swedish employers rarely employ women in the first place.

Table 2.9 The cost of eliminating child poverty. National
Accounts estimates, 1990[a]

	Number poor child-HH's (000's)	Poverty gap (PPP in 1995 US $ Currency)	Extra cost as percentage of GDP
Denmark (1992)	19	3952	0.01
Sweden (1995)	25	3403	0.01
France (1994)	315	1460	0.08
Italy (1995)	1033	2497	0.29
Spain (1990)	531	1319	0.16
UK (1995)	1210	1927	0.26
USA (1997)	6665	3481	0.30

[a] Estimates are based on the objective of bringing poor child families above
50 per cent of the median adjusted disposable income line. The exercise ignores the
fact that this, in itself, will alter the overall distribution and, thus, also the median.

Source: LIS Databases and OECD National Accounts.

families, and fairly high child poverty rates: in brief, a worst-case benchmark
for comparison. Regression simulations for Spain indicate that mothers'
employment would reduce, but not eliminate, poverty. If all mothers actually
worked, Spanish child poverty would drop to approximately 3–4 per cent.
Hence, a mother-employment strategy based on subsidized childcare and
the usual 'women-friendly' welfare package would be very, but not fully,
effective. A second, and complementary, policy would be to raise family
transfers to the rate necessary to bring families above the poverty line.

If we were to rely entirely on public transfers to attain a zero-poverty
rate, the cost calculus would be a simple arithmetic function of [(#poor
households × poverty gap)/GDP]. The cost of bringing all child families
above the standard poverty line would, in most countries, be cheap.[48] Since
Nordic poverty rates are already close to zero, obviously the additional cost
would be minute. At the other extreme, high poverty rates combined
with large poverty gaps (as in the US) require more substantial spending
requirements. In any case, the transfer expenditures needed are, everywhere,
surprisingly modest (see Table 2.9).

[48] Of course, by doing so we will have altered the whole distribution, including the median used
for our calculations.

The cash strategy would be cheaper and less urgent the more that mothers work but this, in turn, implies expenditures elsewhere—namely the need to subsidize day care. What would be the public cost related to the employment-based strategy? The first step is to define a benchmark for 'affordability'. Without any subsidies, day care costs are a purely regressive tax on mothers' employment. Since mothers' employment is almost universal in Denmark and Sweden, the cost structure in these countries may provide a good benchmark for a realistic affordability calculus. The parental share of total is about one-third in Denmark (and also Belgium and France), corresponding to between 6 and 11 per cent of family income (Meyers and Gornick, 2001).[49] In other words, one might adopt the norm that public subsidies cover two-thirds of the cost.

With this benchmark, what would be the comparable public outlay elsewhere? Across Europe, private day care costs appear surprisingly similar. In licensed urban centres, the annual, full-time per child (ages 0–3) cost is 8–9 million Lira in Italy, 5–600.000 Pts in Spain, and £4,000 in Britain.[50] This would eat up about one-third of a mother's expected *net* earnings. To reach the Danish 66 per cent public subsidy benchmark, a rough national accounts based calculation (again using Spain) suggests an additional treasury outlay of roughly 3.5–4 billion Pesetas—under the assumption of two children per mother. Fairly similar costs would be expected in other countries that, like Spain, rely almost exclusively on private care provision. The actual net cost can, of course, be reduced by eliminating existing tax deductions.

If the aim is to eliminate poverty in child families, the 'servicing strategy' is clearly more costly (and seemingly less effective) than the 'transfer strategy'. But it is vital to note that the two are interdependent. Family benefits add to household disposable income. The more generous they are, the lower the childcare subsidy will need to be. Conversely, the more that mothers work, the less subsidies will be needed. The obvious strategy is to combine both, but it is vital to note that the two policies represent distinct philosophies with distinct secondary effects. Our 'transfer strategy' was targeted exclusively to households with less than 50 per cent of median disposable income (with the modest aim of bringing families above the 50 per cent line). Such targeting could be based on negative income tax methods or, as in some countries, on direct, universal transfers. There are two strong arguments in favour of the latter. First, it solidifies public support for family benefits. Second, by asking

[49] The parental co-payment share is about half that in Sweden.
[50] Costs based on telephone interviews with day care centres in one or two larger cities in each country.

childless households to finance part of the cost of children, it implicitly recognizes that children contribute value to all citizens. On a life cycle basis, childless citizens are free-riders. If government is concerned with *re*-distribution in favour of the neediest households, supplements could be paid to low income households.[51]

At present, the norms governing child benefits differ widely. Predictably, Scandinavia (with Austria, Belgium and recently also Germany) is generous, granting roughly 2,400–3,000 Euros (per annum) to a family with two children. At the other extreme lie Greece, Italy, and Spain where benefits are extremely low and/or subject to an income test. If we return to the earlier Spanish example, a Nordic-level child allowance would offset half of the childcare supplement needed among average income families.

The 'servicing strategy' was premised on explicit universalism, providing a subsidy to rich and poor alike. One might of course prefer to target childcare subsidies and this would lower public outlays.[52] Besides the standard repertoire of externalities and moral hazards associated with targeting, there is actually a strong investment-based case to be made in favour of universalism. First, affordable childcare will reduce the cumulative wage penalty that mothers incur by interrupting their careers. Second, society needs to mobilize female labour reserves to the maximum. And, third, working mothers will quite likely reimburse the subsidy via higher tax payments throughout their working life. If day care minimizes women's employment interruptions, their cumulative lifetime earnings will be substantially higher and this means substantially higher future tax revenues.[53]

European countries with low female employment hardly even need 'actuarial' justifications for a universalistic childcare policy. To meet the new EU guideline of a 60 per cent female employment rate by 2010, countries like Italy and Spain must attain close to a 25 percentage point growth over the next ten years. Regression simulation suggests that each 10 percentage point increase in day care provision results in an increase in mothers' employment

[51] Some countries provide extra benefits to single mothers, either in the form of additional allowances (Denmark, Finland, France, Ireland) or by guaranteed maintenance allowances (Finland, Germany, Norway, and Sweden).

[52] Although in this case, administrative costs are high, fraud possibly widespread and, worse of all, it may create poverty traps. A targeted servicing strategy also runs the risk of reinforcing class dualisms among families. One very strong argument in favour of universal day care systems is that they help neutralize unequal social capital among children. Note though that earlier, a case for selective policy started from the premise that it was a short-term measure, needed in order to let the most vulnerable groups 'catch up' as childcare consumers.

[53] I have tried to cash out this effect for Denmark with the result that the treasury obtains a (small) net revenue gain in the long run (Esping-Andersen, 2000).

rate of about 5.3 percentage points (controlling for family transfers and fertility). Hence, Italy and Spain might reach the 60 per cent goal with a ten-fold increase in day care coverage (from a current 3–5 per cent to approximately 40–45 per cent). When we consider that the Danish 57 per cent day care coverage rate was attained over three decades, countries like Italy or Spain would need to produce annual growth rates three times as high as the Danish.

The two-pronged strategy would suit the current policy scenario in much of Europe in the sense that the 'mother-employment' strategy is already on the agenda and will, according to our analyses, help reduce child family poverty substantially in its own right. The residual poverty that surely will remain would prove very inexpensive to eradicate.

Fertility and Family Welfare

We have so far concentrated on the monetary dimensions of family well-being. Yet, the ability of citizens, in the first place, to form families according to their true aspirations must be regarded as the bottom-line measure of any society's welfare performance. It is evident that adults are opting for new and more variegated household arrangements, and the rise of one-person households and less marital stability testify also to greater individualism. Nonetheless, there is strong evidence that people's desire for children has not waned. European men and women (in the 25–34 age group) exhibit a striking convergence in what number of children they would consider optimal. The EU average is 2.4 children with virtually no variation—the sole exception is Ireland where the ideal is 2.8 children (Bien, 2000; Hank and Kohler, 2000). Examining actual fertility rates (for 1998), we can only conclude that most nations exhibit a substantial welfare deficit. The 'child gap' is enormous in Southern Europe (exactly half of the number desired) and hardly smaller in the rest of Continental Europe. In only two cases, Denmark and the UK, do we see reality approaching aspirations. For an overview, see Table 2.10.

What concerns us here is not the long historical decline in fertility, nor pro-natalistic objectives, but simply families' apparent inability to arrive at desired welfare levels. Hence, we must be concerned with the obstacles that citizens face in forming families of their choosing. Recent research points to three key factors. The first refers to the basic 'cost' that children impose. It can be expensive to have children and prospective parents with low incomes may simply find it unaffordable. Blau *et al.* (1998), for example, estimate that a child runs to $136.320 from age 0 to 18 in the US. Naturally, where generous family allowances exist, the net cost is lower. Hoem and Hoem (1997) argue

Table 2.10 Family welfare deficits: the 'child gap'

	Ratio of actual over desired number of children
EU average	0.6
Denmark	0.8
Finland	0.7
Sweden	0.7
Belgium	0.7
France	0.7
Germany	0.7
Netherlands	0.6
Greece	0.5
Italy	0.5
Spain	0.5
Ireland	0.7
UK	0.8

Source: preference data are from the International Social Survey Programme (Bien, 2000), actual fertility data (for 1998) are from Brewster and Rindfuss (2000: Table 2).

that births in Sweden rose in response to improved financial incentives in the 1980s, only to fall with cut-backs in the 1990s. But the sudden drop in Swedish fertility during the 1990s is probably due to a different complex of issues, such as heightened unemployment and insecurity. In fact, the fertility decline was concentrated among second and third births, and the number of women with no child did not increase. Generally speaking, there is no systematic evidence that family benefits (nor paid parental leave provision for that matter) influence fertility (Brewster and Rindfuss, 2000; Gauthier, 1996). Income may affect fertility decisions but this is mainly a symptom of other factors.

A second, and far more weighty factor lies in the increased difficulties young adults face in 'getting started'. In the Golden Age, family formation began quite early because women expected to move straight into housewifery and males usually went straight from school to a career. Today's young people spend far more years in education and then in search of stable employment. In Northern Europe and America, youths establish independent living during the transition, usually on the basis of transitional jobs and low incomes. In Southern Europe, the norm is prolonged job search and continued dependence on parents, often until age 30. In either case, the transition is ever more protracted due to youth unemployment, job precariousness and the difficulty of entering the housing market, all producing what Livi Bacci (1997) calls the 'postponement syndrome'. The mean age of marriage and, hence, first childbirths has moved upwards by 2–3 years in the past decades in most EU countries.[54] The postponement syndrome is, no doubt, far stronger among educated youth.[55] As Peter McDonald (2000: 21) concludes in his synthesis of the issues: 'a range of brilliant gender equity policies will be ineffective if unemployment rates for young people of child bearing age are high. Work-family policies can only work if there is work.'

We can also, as does McDonald, turn the issue on its head and argue that even if there are plenty of jobs, young prospective parents may shun children if they are seen as incompatible with career preferences. This leads us to the third and, what most agree upon, fundamental factor behind the emerging low fertility equilibrium: the incompatibilities between motherhood and work which young women face in today's society.

The traditional negative correlation between female participation and fertility has now turned positive. It would seem paradoxical that higher fertility goes together with high female employment. It is the mechanism that drives this that we need to understand in order to develop a family and gender policy, which corresponds to the twenty-first century. One clue comes from those nations that managed to reverse fertility decline. Beginning in the 1960s–1970s, we see everywhere a steady fall in birth rates, hitting all-time lows (1.4) in Northern Europe in the late 1970s, a little later elsewhere. The great international bifurcation begins at this point. One group of countries, mainly the Scandinavian, experience a resurgence of fertility in tandem with women's employment; most other European countries remain caught in a low fertility equilibrium even if female participation remains low. Most telling is the sharp drop in Swedish fertility during the 1990s, which

[54] There is a much higher rate of births among young Danes than elsewhere. This is probably because even unemployed youths enjoy an unusual high level of income security. Thus, Bison and Esping-Andersen (2000a) found that 40 per cent of unemployed Danes, aged 20–30, are parents, compared to less than 5 per cent in Italy and Spain.

[55] In an unpublished study, Bison and Esping-Andersen (2000b) estimate that educated Italian women are equally likely to have their first child at age 25 as at age 35. Nahn and Mira (2001) show that the extraordinarily difficult problems of gaining stable employment in Italy and Spain— especially among educated women—is the principal reason of postponement. In Spain, 80 per cent of educated women would renounce on children in order to establish themselves in a career.

coincides with a 7 percentage point decline in female employment. The core issue, obviously, has to do with how women succeed in combining paid work and children. We have now awakened to the fact that a rewritten gender contract is an indispensable ingredient in any credible post-industrial welfare formula.

Conclusion

There is a fatal disease among academics to complicate matters. But there are good reasons involved because current policy fashion has a tendency to embrace patent solutions for all ills. In addressing social exclusion, there is a tendency to rely too much on activation, make-work-pay and lifelong learning.

A first conclusion that emerges is that credible solutions to the challenges families face necessitate *combined strategies*. Social exclusion is driven by multiple factors, among which labour market precariousness is one. If more than half of workless households include the chronically ill or persons who have never held a job, clearly the problem will not disappear with even the best designed activation plan. Here, a more effective response is income maintenance and, in the long term, a far stronger accent on social prevention so that the share of 'unemployable' citizens in the future will be far smaller. Since the long-term prevention strategy will work best when children are protected from poverty and insecurity, one basic conclusion emerges: adequate income maintenance is a first *precondition* for either preventive or remedial longer-term strategies.

All evidence shows that the root cause of lack of resources and sub-optimal life chances lies in childhood and this is where a social investment strategy should focus. The mechanisms at work are fairly clear but not all can be influenced by public policy. Yet, we do know that poverty in childhood is a crucial factor, as is unemployment among parents and marital break-ups. Examining the data, we arrive again at the necessity of *combined strategies*. Without doubt, adequate income guarantees for families with children are *sine qua non* and there is a very good case for promoting a broad European goal of— simply—abolishing child poverty altogether. This goal can be achieved by supporting mothers' employment, which lowers poverty risks dramatically and by an adequate family benefit package. Neither can substitute for the other and the policy approach must therefore be two-pronged. Mothers are often vulnerable in labour markets. This increases the importance of an adequate basic income guarantee for families with children.

There is also a case to be made for some creative 'affirmative action' policy to help children. The key to a good life in the decades to come lies in solid cognitive abilities and 'social capital'. It is therefore paramount that we minimize school drop-out rates and ensure that children continue in education for as long as possible. This is not the place to discuss education policy. However, if children receive inadequate schooling and insufficient intellectual stimulation from their parents, we urgently need to promote compensatory measures so as to weaken the impact of inherited under-privilege. A first step is to ensure that children have access to good quality pre-school and day care. This is especially important for underprivileged children. Here there is a case for affirmative action. A second step is to ensure that children complete at least secondary level education. Pre-secondary level drop-out rates are hugely concentrated among poor families. One possible response might be to emulate the 'make-work-pay' principle and peg family transfers to children's verifiable school attendance.

Policy-wise, social exclusion, family poverty, and gender equality are closely linked. The links all boil down to women's employment. There are two major conclusions that emerge. First, improving the resources of women is indispensable for improving the welfare of families and of society at large. Second, we should therefore rethink gender equality policy as societal policy. The implications are more than rhetorical because, as we have seen, gender inequalities can probably not be effectively dealt with unless we simultaneously rethink employment policy. These are the key issues in Chapter 3.

There exists no evidence that mothers' work as such is harmful to children's development. On the contrary, the better that mothers do in the labour market, the more positive is the psychological spill-over within the family. Overworked mothers can have a negative impact on children, especially if combined with insecure or stressful jobs, but far worse is unemployment. Indeed, to conclude with a finding from Danish child research, when asked, children themselves strongly prefer that both parents work (Christoffersen, 1997).

3

A New Gender Contract

Gøsta Esping-Andersen

Social scientists are too easily persuaded that the real cause of change is some exogenous force which lies far beyond their conceptual grasp. Whether we call this force modernization or globalization, we are nevertheless hiding behind an umbrella term for those macroscopic developments that other disciplines study and we only vaguely understand. Technological change and heightened global integration have, no doubt, a causal impact on wages, employment, welfare states, or culture. But good social science is always 'dialectic', able to recognize two-way causalities, and there exists hardly a better example of this than the changing role of women.

It is not difficult to see that rising female employment is triggered by the emergence of the service economy and that this, in turn, reverberates through family life, politics, and the economy. Yet, the changing social behaviour of women, once in motion, also has powerful reverse causal effects. A huge part of the service economy owes its existence directly to the disappearance of housewifery. Population ageing is one of the great 'macroscopic' changes, but this is merely the by-product of novel fertility patterns driven by the kinds of choices that women prefer to, or are compelled to, make. Men were the indisputable protagonists of high industrialism; women may occupy centre-stage in post-industrial society.[1]

The institutional underpinnings of welfare capitalism, from its full employment commitment to collective bargaining, labour market regulation, and social protection, aimed to safeguard the standard male production worker and breadwinner. It was he who constituted the nexus between economy and family, between production and consumption. His security, it was assumed, implied universal security. In the 1950s and 1960s, women's economic dependence on men was near absolute (Sorensen and McLanahan, 1987). The

---

[1] Rather similar women-focused treatments of post-industrial change have been developed by Block (1990), Clement and Myles (1994), and by Gershuny (2000).

great welfare *lacunae* of the post-war decades occurred where there was no male provider and, hence, widows and orphans were unusually vulnerable.

In North America and Scandinavia this reality has for all purposes passed into the annals of history. It is in rapid decline elsewhere. As male breadwinner hegemony fades, women gradually emerge as the lynchpin of any new equilibrium between households and the economy. In the Nordic countries, where the housewife has all but disappeared, women's earnings now account for almost 50 per cent of all household income.[2] This would indicate that a good many Scandinavian couple-households would find themselves in dire economic straits were it not for her contribution. Indeed, all across the advanced world, families increasingly require women's work income in order to uphold living standards.

The service economy is certainly the result of new technologies and changing business practices, and these are what fuel financial, marketing, design, and consultancy services. But its vitality is equally ignited by the changes in household behaviour that stem from the disappearing homeworker and the emerging reality of regularly employed mothers and wives. Like modern firms, families also outsource their servicing needs and this is what promotes jobs in social and consumer services. The move of women into paid employment implies a double job multiplier, visible on both the consumption and production side of the national accounts ledger.[3] Their earnings add to households' purchasing power; their employment reduces households' available time to service their own needs.

Many regard the fight for gender equality as largely a 'women's affair', requiring perhaps some concessions here and there. If women are emerging as a key axial principle in the new socio-economic equilibrium, it follows that the quality of our future society hinges on how we respond to their new claims on men, the welfare state, and on society at large. For good or bad, gender equality becomes therefore a 'societal affair', a precondition for making the clockwork of post-industrial societies tick. Gender equality is one of the key ingredients that must go into our blueprints for a workable new welfare architecture. The questions we raise in this chapter are, simply, what kind of equality and how?

The promotion of gender equality provokes confusion because it often embraces two distinct objectives. There is, first, the issue of harmonizing the dual aims of careers and motherhood that most women now pursue. Strictly

---

[2] In Denmark, women's share is 46 per cent. Estimated from ECHP, 1996 wave.

[3] Some, albeit shaky, statistical estimates suggest that an additional fifteen service jobs are created for every 100 women who move from housewifery to paid work (Esping-Andersen, 1999: 118).

speaking, this seems more a question of *equity* than of egalitarianism, a matter of resolving inherent trade-offs created by the new reality of gender prefer- ences. It has become a fact of life that women insist on being economically independent, and only the genuinely thick-headed will have failed to realize that their employment is fundamental for household welfare as well as for the collective good. Long-term pension commitments, to cite an example, will be hard to sustain if women remain housewives. It is an equity issue if the trade-offs involved incur costs that, in the first instance, are unfairly allocated to women. In current political debate 'women-friendly' policy is pretty much the consensual solution to such trade-offs.

The second objective is far more ambitiously (and far less precisely) aimed at full gender neutrality in the allocation of opportunities, life chances, and welfare outcomes. In its most radical formulation, any demonstrable inequality that correlates with gender (and not with, say, educational levels) implies sex-discrimination. This objective encounters scepticism from those who insist that the fight against, for example, class inequalities should be prioritized. It is also a difficult objective to manage in practice simply because it is frequently very difficult to ascertain whether an apparent gender inequality is genuinely so or, perhaps, a manifestation of something else. In contemporary debate, the equality objectives usually pertain to job-segregation, unequal pay for equal work, and the asymmetric distribution of domestic burdens.

The first (and major) section of this chapter is dedicated to the compatibil- ity question; the second to the broader 'equality' challenge. What complic- ates matters is that the twain turn out to be closely interwoven. To pre-empt the main conclusion, ongoing change in gender behaviour is producing an increasingly 'masculine' profile of female biographies. As a matter of fact, it is fairly clear that changes and adaptations in social behaviour have been pretty much limited to the female side of the gender coin. The egalitarian challenge is unlikely to find resolution unless, simultaneously, the male life course becomes more 'feminine'. In other words, if we want more gender equality our policies may have to concentrate on men's behaviour.

The Multi-dimensional Compatibility Problem

The gender dynamics of past decades might lead some to wonder whether the incompatibility of careers and motherhood is as intractable as we think. Consider for example the correlation between fertility rates and levels of female employment. Traditionally the cross-national correlation was strongly negative, but it has now become strongly positive. Where women's activity rates are high, this is also where we register above-average birth rates (Nahn and Mira, 2001). Or, to take another clear trend, women have been making tremendous employment progress within the higher occupational echelons and have, in some countries, successfully penetrated privileged, convention-ally male bastions within professional and managerial hierarchies. Moreover, the typical woman increasingly commands sufficient resources so as to ensure an autonomous choice of living arrangements and life goals. Marriage is being transformed from an economic necessity to a personal option. These changes may seem to indicate that gender policies are becoming less pressing. The problem, however, is that such positive signs mask problematic second-order trade-offs.

Let us begin with the positive correlation between births and women's employment levels, an empirical regularity that would appear counterintu-itive for many. At one end, this cross-national correlation is driven by the Nordic countries' unique ability to maximize female activity and birth rates. At the other end, the correlation is being driven by a totally different reality, namely that women in large parts of Europe postpone having children as long as they cannot find affordable day care or remain stuck in seemingly endless job queues. All this suggests that the compatibility of motherhood and careers is contingent on the nature of institutional support. This becomes even clearer when we examine the number of children. With few exceptions, women in Europe are compelled to settle for fewer children than desired.[4] In other words, the new and positive cross-national work–fertility correlation camouflages a derivative, negative trade-off. Or let us consider the double burden issue. Women's life course is becoming more 'masculine' in terms of their lifelong career behaviour, but their ability to remain employed when children arrive incurs, once again, second-order costs. The issue is not so much that women are prohibited from embracing goals of lifetime careers. The issue is that if they do so they pay a high price if, that is, they also prior-itize motherhood.

This multifaceted opportunity cost structure expressed itself dramatically in the astonishing Swedish fertility drop during the 1990s: from almost 2.1 to 1.6 in the matter of 7 years. True, the Swedish government reduced maternity and parental leave benefits, but these cuts were fairly modest. The fall was, by all accounts, a reaction to sudden unemployment, falling incomes, and far greater uncertainty about the future. Considering that the Swedish govern-ment's crisis strategy included the elimination of almost 100.000 welfare

---

[4] For an overview of these issues, see Blossfeld (1995).

state jobs, clearly the conventional sheltered female labour market began to appear less mother-friendly. Swedish fertility has always been exceptionally high among women in public service jobs and this is exactly where the single sharpest job decline occurred (Bernhardt, 2000; Hoem, 2000; SOU, 2000).

As Hakim (1996) reminds us, the intensity of the trade-offs that contemporary women face will depend on their life course preferences.

The Heterogeneity of Women's Preference Sets

The share of women who prefer to forego motherhood entirely remains small and we can assume the majority does not. It is additionally safe to assume that most women are no longer inclined to internalize the full cost of having children. But it all depends very much on the individual woman. As Bernhardt (2000) and Hakim (1996) suggest, policy making should be tailored to three distinct female preference sets.

For *family-centred* women, the main life course priority centres on marriage and motherhood and if they work it will mainly be out of necessity. For such women gender equalization policy will generally hold little relevance. They often represent a large proportion of older women, but are rapidly disappearing—even in Southern Europe. At the other extreme we find the *career-centred* women who invest heavily in their human capital and who have children only if they do not interfere with careers. These women will not respond much to the incentives provided by 'women-friendly social policy'. They remain a minority representing, according to Hakim, maybe a fifth of all women (ranging from 10–30 per cent, with the highest share in North America and the UK).

The vast majority of contemporary women opt for the *dual-role* model, intent on lifetime employment, but unwilling to sacrifice motherhood. Hakim (op.cit) argues that they typically pursue conventionally female educational choices and jobs (like teaching, nursing, or social work). They are likely to concentrate in part-time and 'soft economy' jobs, like public sector services. This group should be the most responsive to public policy incentives, to opportunity costs, tax/income penalties, and to employment fluctuations. In other words, 'women-friendly' policies would be most directly relevant for this group. It is clearly the largest of all groups and probably also the most expanding considering trends in female educational attainment.

In current debate most attention has focused on public support to working mothers. If the goal is to make women's new roles and preferences more compatible, a generous 'women-friendly' policy package is certainly indispensable, but hardly adequate. Any serious and realistic compatibility policy must address the combined (and interactive) effects of public support, employment structure, and wage expectations.

Public Support for Working Mothers

Alva and Gunnar Myrdal, writing in the 1930s, were pioneers of 'women-friendly' policy. The Myrdals were principally guided by pro-natalist concerns and hence defined the challenge in terms of 'how to ensure that working mothers can also have children'. In their times, Swedish mothers *had to* work. From the 1960s onwards, we see the first reversal of the housewife model as educated women began to seek careers. In its wake, the trade-off underwent a reformulation: 'how to ensure that mothers might also be able to work'. We are now entering a third phase which, ironically, implies a return to the original Myrdal formulation. But now the meaning is completely different because most young women *demand* to work, and a growing minority even puts careers before motherhood.

To be sure, governments have, with varied commitment, begun to address women's new claims. Where female employment, economic independence, and political participation is most advanced, the pressure for 'women-friendly' policy is undoubtedly strongest. Yet, even a mere glance at actual policy across the high-participation countries suggests that: (*a*) there is no direct relationship between pressure and policy results, and (*b*) very different policy measures are being applied to address, ostensibly, identical demands. North America has shunned public responsibility for paid child leaves and day care provision, favouring instead indirect market regulation, such as affirmative action programmes and tax incentives. Scandinavia and, to a lesser extent, Belgium and France, have followed exactly the opposite course.[5]

Most countries have strengthened entitlements to child leaves, but the crucial issues of day care provision for children and servicing the elderly have not been addressed seriously in the vast majority of welfare states. If we restrict our horizon to the EU area there undoubtedly exists, if more in word than deed, a consensus in favour of what might be called a basic 'women-friendly' policy package: adequate child leave entitlements plus day care. We begin, in Table 3.1, with an overview of nations' performance on the

---

[5] This juxtaposition is admittedly too crude. The Nordic countries have, for example, begun to apply affirmative action style policy in order to promote greater gender equality in firms' personnel management (Rubery *et al.*, 1999: 53). US legislation now stipulates the right to (unpaid) child leave.

Table 3.1 A comparison of the basic women-friendly policy package, 1990s

	Publicly guaranteed day care for ages 0–3 (per cent of all covered)	Weeks of paid child leave entitlement
Denmark	48	30
Sweden	29	36
Austria	2	24
Belgium	20	27
France	22	36
Germany	3	36
Italy	5	9
Netherlands	2	16
Spain	3	16
UK	2	7
US	1	0

Sources: Esping-Andersen (1999: Table 4A); OECD (2001c: Table 4.7).

basic 'women-friendly' policy package which includes (*a*) guaranteed child-care for small children (aged 0–3), and (*b*) length of *paid* maternity and parental leave.

While necessary, even the best policy package is unfortunately not sufficient to stave off the broader set of trade-offs. In a stylized way, the Scandinavian–American contrast spells out one of the key dilemmas. We can, as in the Nordic countries, combine high female participation with high birth rates but at the cost of extraordinarily gender segregated employment. Using the dissimilarity index of sector-gender concentration, the Nordic countries invariably rank among the OECD's most segregated labour markets.[6] Explicitly dedicated to gender equality, they pursued a massive expansion of public social services and produced, inadvertently, new inequalities. The welfare state became a female labour market, providing good pay and the kind of job security and flexibility that makes careers compatible with

[6] The least segregated Nordic country is Denmark with an index score of 18.6; Finland and Norway both score 21.1, and Sweden scores 20.6. Indeed, Finland and Norway are the third most segregated labour markets in the OECD (next to Turkey and Switzerland). See OECD (2000c: Table 3.5).

having children. This is especially the case with the two dimensions of motherhood that are most difficult to harmonize, namely having pre-school age and/or more than two children. The creation of a cushioned 'soft economy' in the Nordic countries helped women realize their preferred fertility level but at the expense of a virtual female employment ghetto.

At the other extreme, as exemplified by the US, we cannot preclude that a market-driven model may harmonize births and work with far less job-segregation. Indeed, the US scores the third lowest (15.3) among all nations on the gender segregation index. Opting for the American way would inevitably necessitate a degree of labour market deregulation that is unrealistic to expect in most European economies. But we must recognize that it does not preclude day care. According to OECD (2001c: Table 4.7) figures, half of the under-threes in the US use (private) day care arrangements, but of very uneven standards. Still, the American way is almost certainly *not* an optimal Paretian solution to the trade-offs. One problem is that childcare arrangements reflect women's ability to pay. Gornick *et al.* (1997) and also official US statistics indicate that only a quarter are licensed, quality care centres. A large number of families must make do with low quality or *ad hoc* care (from a lady down the street to the TV set). Moreover, educated American career women are far more likely to work in the competitive 'hard' economy where reduced productivity will penalize professional ambitions. Hence, fertility is low among highly educated women. Finally, strong inequalities in childcare and in wages double up and spill over to the welfare status of families and children in the form of poverty. In other words, the market approach to gender equality catapults second-order inequalities, too.

The Supply of Jobs

Working conditions are of paramount importance for the great majority of 'dual role' women. As Hoem (2000) and Bernhardt (2000) show, Swedish fertility is *curvilinear*: significantly lower among the least and most educated, and highest among women with a semi-professional education, almost invariably working in the public sector. These are the women with 3+ children. The key here is that 'dual role' women selectively opt for educational trajectories that are targeted towards public sector service jobs. The rising birth rates in Scandinavia since the 1970s were closely related to public sector expansion of welfare, health, and education services. During the 1990s Danish and Swedish leave schemes and day care provision were very similar, notwithstanding marginal cutbacks in Sweden. In Sweden births dropped dramatically but not in Denmark. The most credible explanation for this divergence lies in the substantial reduction in Swedish public service jobs and, no doubt, the heightened economic uncertainties facing Swedish families.

Patterns of female labour supply are beginning to converge among younger cohort women across all of Europe, but actual employment rates and fertility are not. The kind of social service labour market which exists in Scandinavia has failed to grow in most of Europe due to financially strained welfare states and to unaffordable prices in the market economy.[7] This means less job growth, particularly in 'soft economy' labour markets. In most countries, female unemployment is far higher than male; in Southern Europe, dramatically so. This is especially accentuated among the young.

One additional compatibility problem, then, is that the desire for work is thwarted by the lack of access to jobs in general and to 'mother-friendly jobs' in particular. Since the work–child trade-off is demonstrably weaker in Denmark than in most other countries, this should offer a good benchmark for comparison. What then is the relative shortfall (or possibly surplus) of 'mother-friendly' job opportunities in other countries compared to Denmark? Table 3.2 presents an overview based on the entire service economy and on three conventionally 'soft-economy' sectors: education, health, and social work, and community and personal services.[8]

One severe handicap for most European women is that they live in severely undeveloped service economies. Lagging service growth has little to do with economic development, and much to do with institutional factors. In fact, the data support almost perfectly a three-, or maybe four-worlds distinction in welfare capitalism (Esping-Andersen, 1990; 1999). The Swedish 'soft economy' job levels are almost identical to the Danish; in the Anglo-Saxon countries there is a noticeable deficit of social services but this is compensated for by more developed private personal and community services. The Continental and especially Southern European countries exhibit substantial overall service job deficits and, especially, huge gaps in the key health, social, and educational sectors.

If we apply the more restrictive definition of protected jobs, namely public sector employment, the differences are even sharper. In Denmark, the public sector accounts for 53 per cent of all female employment while in virtually all Continental European countries the share lies around 34–35 per cent (Spain

---

[7] For a discussion of the Continental European service-employment impasse, see Scharpf and Schmidt (2000).

[8] Women are hugely over-represented in the education, health, and social services sector. The OECD average is a female/male ratio of 1.8 (in Sweden it is 3.0 and in Finland, 3.5). Women are also very concentrated in personal services (the OECD ratio is 1.4).

Table 3.2 The comparative employment rate gap in mother-friendly sectors (Percentage point deviations from Denmark, 1999)[a]

	Education	Health, social Work	Community and personal services	All services
Sweden	+0.2	+0.4	+0.2	+1.9
Austria	−1.2	−8.0	−0.1	−9.1
Belgium	+0.1	−6.8	−0.3	−11.1
France	−0.7	−7.1	+0.7	−11.8
Germany	−1.8	−7.1	+0.4	−12.2
Italy	−1.5	−10.1	−0.5	−20.5
Netherlands	−0.4	−3.5	+0.2	−0.4
Spain	−2.2	−10.7	+0.2	−21.0
UK	+0.4	−5.6	+0.9	−1.2
US	+0.8	−4.9	+3.4	+3.3

[a] Plus/minus values indicate that a country's employment rate within a sector is superior/inferior to Denmark's. The measure used is percentage point deviations.

Source: Recalculations from OECD (2001c: Table 3.C.4).

is the lowest with 27 per cent). And almost 60 per cent of Danish mothers with two or more children work in public employment.[9]

Besides its generally greater adaptation to women's double burden, the public sector is also far more likely to offer quality part-time options. The potential trade-offs toughen when women have young or several children, and this is where day care provision and the part-time option become detrimental if a woman seeks to avoid punitive career breaks (Blossfeld, 1995; Henz and Sundstrom, 2001; Stier *et al.*, 2001). A comparison of full-time, part-time, and non-employment rates among young women with two or more children should furnish a strong test of how different labour markets help resolve potential trade-offs (see Table 3.3).

Considering that the majority of (youngish) mothers with two-plus young children are outside the labour force, the EU as such would hardly appear 'mother-friendly'. This is especially evident when we compare with the inactivity rate among non-mothers (41 per cent) or even mothers with only one child (48 per cent). But Europe presents itself very bi-modally. In Denmark, two-child mothers only rarely need to interrupt employment and, indeed,

---

[9] Data from the 1995 wave of the ECHP.

Table 3.3 The employment status of mothers with two-plus children in Europe, 1995 (Percentage Distributions)[a]

	Per cent of all outside the labour force	Per cent of all part-time employed	Per cent of all full-time employed
EU average	56	13	31
Denmark	26	14	60
Belgium	36	24	40
France	44	13	43
Germany	63	18	19
Italy	60	4	36
Spain	70	5	25
UK	49	29	22

[a] Table includes only women aged 20–45 with children aged less than 12. Note that the table excludes unemployed mothers.

Source: ECHP, 1995 wave.

they typically remain in full-time jobs.[10] At the other extreme, we find Germany, Italy and Spain where mothers with several children are clearly discouraged from working. Yet, also in Italy we see the importance of 'soft economy' employment. As Bernardi (2001) shows, working in the public sector lowers the probability of leaving employment substantially. In Italy and Spain, especially, the trade-offs are additionally heightened by the scarcity of a part-time option.

The Role of Wages

Recent research has re-examined the wage and job penalties that women face by marriage and motherhood (Waldvogel, 1998; Davies and Joshi, 2001). No doubt, the best way to estimate the penalty is to examine the lifelong, cumulative earnings effects of employment interruptions.[11] As a rule of thumb, if a full-time worker interrupts her career for a 5-year interim she will forego 1.5–2 percentage points *per annum* in potential life-time earnings.

---

[10] Among the 26 per cent non-working Danish mothers, a little less than half are actually unemployed. As Henz and Sundstrom (2001) show, the story is fairly similar in Sweden.

[11] See Mincer and Polachek (1974). For a recent overview, see Blau *et al.* (1998: chapter 6).

This massive loss would, however, decline to only 0.5 per cent per year if the same woman were to remain employed on a part-time basis for the same 5 years.[12]

Full, life-time earnings estimations are difficult to come by for national comparisons. Bernhardt (2000) provides a simpler, illustrative measure of the 'child penalty' by comparing work-years lost for women. In fact, what emerges is pretty much the same bi-modal distribution we encountered in Table 3.3. The estimated work-years lost over the life course for an average woman range from 14–15 years in Italy and Spain to only one year in Finland and Sweden (4 in Denmark and 5 in the UK). In between, we find Continental Europe (Belgium, France, Germany, and the Netherlands) with 8–10 years lost.[13]

We are often told that women are concentrated in low-paid and irregular jobs. It would be equally true to say that women are also concentrated in well-paid and stable jobs. The variation is huge among women and between nations. The incidence of low pay among full-time women workers is quite high in most European countries, hovering between 15 and 20 per cent, but rather insignificant in Scandinavia (OECD, 1996).[14] It is often believed that women are also hugely over-represented in precarious jobs. The lion's share of part-time jobs are of course female, and these have often been the catapult of female employment growth, first in Scandinavia and more recently in the Netherlands (Blossfeld and Hakim, 1997; Rubery et al., 1999). But they do not automatically imply precariousness; in many countries not at all. And with few exceptions, rates of involuntary part-time work are modest. The female bias in temporary jobs is, moreover, insignificant except in a handful of countries like Belgium, France, the Netherlands, and Spain (Rubery et al., 1999: 278). Wages in typical female sectors such as social, educational, and health services are above average, part-time jobs are prevalent, and levels of job tenure are high. Distributive and personal services are also female and part-time biased, but exhibit very high levels of job instability and, at least in personal services, low pay (OECD, 2001d: 106 ff.).

To a great extent these differences simply reflect concentrations of educational qualifications. When we make comparisons across broad occupational strata, we discover that the distribution of women looks fairly similar to the

---

[12] See e.g. Bruyn-Hundt (1996) and Joshi (2000).

[13] The measure is expected years of employment for men *minus* expected years for women. These data should be considered a proxy for the cost of children to women since the comparison assumes that all women do have children (Bernhardt, 2000: Table 3).

[14] Germany and Austria are here the extreme cases with about one woman in four working in low-paid jobs. The OECD definition of low paid (full-time) is less than two-thirds of median earnings.

distribution of men. Among women *and* among men, a quarter to a third are in the managerial—professional occupations (the EU average is exactly 33 per cent among males and 34 per cent among females). Similarly, another third of women are concentrated in typically female, lower-end service occupations which is more or less true also for men—albeit in lower-end, typically male jobs.[15] Since, traditionally, menial male jobs offer better pay and job security, and since women generally earn less than men in similar kinds of jobs, there is nothing especially surprising about the fact that a large share of presumably less-qualified women are in low-paid employment.

The trade-offs between motherhood and employment are invariably *class-specific*, and one of the main arguments in favour of strong 'women-friendly' policy is that it will reduce such inequalities. Gender-based wage discrimination or not, women's labour supply should be guided by two kinds of opportunity costs. One, following straight from Becker's (1991) model, has to do with prospective earnings, relative to their husbands'. A second has to do with the implicit tax on mothers' earnings that childcare incurs. Less-educated women face much steeper barriers to employment if, as in most countries, day care is uniformly expensive. This regressive incidence can be diminished by government subsidies and/or by relative pay compression. Scandinavia is doubly advantageous to less-qualified women because day care is very available and affordable, and because the wage structure is unusually egalitarian. This, combined with an ample labour market, explains why female participation *and* fertility rates in Scandinavia (and France) are high even among low-qualified women. A similar rise in lower-skilled female employment may also occur if, as in the United States, wages among less educated *males* decline. See Table 3.4.

We can highlight the multifaceted compatibility issue by juxtaposing what emerges as two directly opposed trajectories. The Nordic countries represent a positive-sum scenario in which public support for working mothers coincides with an ample 'mother-friendly' labour market and a wage structure that encourages near universal female employment. In direct contrast, Southern Europe's low fertility rates are testimony to the fact that *all* factors influencing compatibility combine negatively: an almost complete lack of affordable child- and eldercare, unusually limited part-time options, a very undeveloped service labour market, pervasive job precariousness, and also fairly pronounced gender wage inequalities.

[15] Estimates based on Rubery *et al.* (1999: Table 5.5) and on Esping-Andersen (1990: ch. 8). If we use the ISCO system's definition of menial jobs ('elementary occupations'), there is female over-representation in some countries (Spain, Germany, and France stand out), but not in others (like Denmark and the UK).

Table 3.4 Participation rates and relative
Earnings levels for women (Aged 30–44) with
low education, 1997–8[a]

	Earnings of low-educated women (% of males)	Activity rate of low-educated women[b]
Denmark	74	56
Sweden	72	67
France	68	57
Germany	60	46
Italy	69	33
Netherlands	47	44
Spain	62	39
UK	45	52
US	53	50

[a] Low education is less than upper secondary education.
Earnings are annual and expressed as a per cent of males'
with equivalent education.
[b] Ages 25–64.

Source: OECD, 2000d.

Motherhood

Children are, of course, the other side of the incompatibility coin. It is often believed that modern women are losing interest in family and children. This, of course, is not true as we saw in Chapter 2. What no doubt has changed is the relative ordering of women's biographical priorities. Recent Spanish data, for example, show that 40+ per cent of young women now prioritize jobs over children.[16] All available evidence suggests that marriage and birth decisions are increasingly woven into a simultaneous pursuit of education and gaining a foothold in the labour market. The average age at first birth is now almost 30 in Europe. The share of women with zero children is rising in some countries, but not by very much. Rock-bottom fertility occurs primarily

[16] Which, oddly enough is the highest level in Europe (the EU average is 25 per cent). See Fernandez Cordon and Sgritta (2000: 14). This extraordinarily high Spanish rate is, no doubt, a mirror image of the difficulties which Spanish women face: the necessity to prioritise clearly is thrust upon them by the simple absence of support for motherhood. For a broader discussion of the changing biographical priority structure, see Goldin (1997) and Hakim (1996).

Table 3.5 Women with two or more children by educational and employment status, 1995

	Denmark	Germany	Italy	Spain	UK
Share of mothers with					
Low education	22	30	52	62	40
Secondary level	37	53	39	20	40
High education	41	17	9	18	20
Share					
Inactive	10	53	53	56	50
Employed	77	41	42	32	48
Share employed in					
Private sector	39	59	49	63	66
Public sector	61	41	51	37	34

Source: European Community Household Panel (ECHP), 1995 wave.

because women shun having two-plus children. It is chiefly this (together with having pre-school age children) that lies at the heart of the incompatibility problem. One clue emerges when we note that the share of women (aged 20–55) with two-plus children is 50 per cent higher in Denmark than in Italy (and 20 per cent higher than in Spain).[17] When we compare by education and employment status, the contrast is even more dramatic (see Table 3.5).

Having two or more children is easy to reconcile only in Denmark and evidently very difficult in Spain. More generally, the data suggest an international bifurcation. In most countries, and here the US is no exception, high fertility is concentrated among the least educated (with less than secondary education). In Scandinavia almost the opposite is true.

We begin with the motherhood side of the coin. Table 3.6 estimates the probability of having two-plus young children, conditional on marital status, educational attainment, and employment, controlling for age. I prefer to examine the compatibility issue in terms of two-plus children because this corresponds to average self-declared preferences, and because this unquestionably poses more difficulties for working mothers than only one child.

The statistical analyses include regressions for all EU Member States combined, and for a few countries representing the European welfare regime

---

[17] Estimated from 1995 wave of the ECHP.

Table 3.6 The likelihood of having 2+ young children among women Aged 25–45 by age, education, employment, and marital status, 1995 (Logistic odds ratios)[a]

	All EU	Denmark	Germany	France	Italy	Spain	UK
Age	0.93***	0.95***	0.91***	0.92***	0.92***	0.95***	0.94***
Secondary education	1.21***	n.s.	0.74*	n.s.	n.s.	n.s.	n.s.
Tertiary education	1.39***	n.s.	n.s.	n.s.	n.s.	n.s.	n.s.
Employed	0.47***	n.s.	0.18***	0.47***	0.65***	0.57***	0.28***
Married	36.37***	33.56***	59.26***	277.03***	58.31***	34.79***	64.35***
N	24664	1137	1883	2526	3375	2999	1688
Chi2	3596.46	96.26	298.16	485.86	416.72	402.05	366.77

[a] reference group for dependent variable = zero or one child, for both education variables = primary education only, for employed = inactive. Married includes also cohabiting partners. Note that the analyses are limited to having children less than 12 years of age.

Note: n.s. = non-significant coefficient. *** = $P > 0.001$; ** = $P > 0.01$; * = $P > 0.05$.

Data Source: ECHP, 1995 wave.

variations. The key question is the extent to which employment inhibits family formation. That the effect of age is (slightly) negative is hardly surprising since women are less likely to have two small children as they get older. The influence of higher educational levels is generally not significant which, unsurprisingly, suggests that it is being in paid employment which really matters. On this count, most European women face severe obstacles. At the pan-European level, the odds are roughly twice as low for employed as for inactive women to have two-plus children, and in Germany and the UK the likelihood is far lower (five times as unlikely in Germany and three times as unlikely in the UK). Denmark is the sole example of apparently perfect compatibility: being employed has no effect whatsoever on being also a mother of two-plus children.

Marital status (or better, the *strength* of the marital variable) may, with considerable caution, be interpreted as a proxy for the degree to which women's ability to harmonize children and work includes also a dependency on the presence of a male.[18] If we are willing to interpret it as such, we find

---

[18] Note that 'being married' includes also cohabitation.

exceptionally strong dependencies in France, Italy, and in the UK. The main reason for caution is that the causality may be quite different in some circumstances, namely that divorced or widowed mothers may be more compelled to seek paid employment. Hence, the coefficient of marital status may very well reflect national divorce patterns.[19]

Turning to the other side of the incompatibility coin, namely the likelihood of being employed given motherhood, we are compelled to conduct a somewhat more complicated analysis. We need, first, to distinguish between part-time and full-time work. The latter obviously constitutes the 'acid-test' of compatibility. Consequently, we conduct multinomial logit regressions. It is also necessary to consider two potentially distinct obstacles that are associated with motherhood: one lies in the *number*, another in the *age*, of children. The analyses concentrate on the 'tough' scenarios: having more than two children aged less than 16, and whether there are children aged less than 3. The analyses control, as before, for age, educational attainment and marital status and also a dummy variable for availability of day care (see Table 3.7).[20]

In the table the following findings stand out. First, the incompatibilities of motherhood and work are greatly reduced when women work in part-time jobs. Except for Germany, the number of children appears to be no impediment for those opting for part-time work. Having infant children does imply a major obstacle in Spain, the UK, and, surprisingly, also in France (where day care is widely available).[21] In the countries which we already know present more severe compatibility problems (such as Italy, Spain, and the UK), access to day care is crucial also for part-time employment.

If we now turn to the tougher case of full-time employment, the presence of children and the availability of day care become far more decisive. As is widely known, having one (non-infant) child is usually not incompatible with full-time employment. Having two clearly begins to pose severe obstacles, certainly in Spain and the UK. Nonetheless, the real barrier arrives when children are under 3 years old. Except for Denmark (and, again, surprisingly also Italy), the presence of infant children has a very powerful negative effect on full-time work in Germany, France, and the UK especially. It is also now of detrimental importance that mothers have access to day care.

---

[19] I thank Annemette Sorensen for this point.

[20] The age and education coefficients are not shown in Table 2.7. Age is almost invariably insignificant. Education effects conform to the well-known finding that employment is positively related to levels of educational attainment. Due to the wording of the ECHP questionnaire, day care can be either private or public.

[21] One explanation may lie in the peculiar French practice of school-free Wednesdays.

Table 3.7 Harmonizing employment and children: the probabilities of
part-time or full-time employment among mothers aged 25–45
(multinomial logit analysis, 1995)

	EU total	Denmark	Germany	France	Italy	Spain	UK
Part-time employment							
1 child 2+	n.s.	n.s.	n.s.	n.s.	n.s.	n.s.	0.965*
children	n.s.	n.s.	−0.961***	n.s.	n.s.	n.s.	n.s.
Child <3	−0.307***	n.s.	n.s.	−1.25***	n.s.	−0.595*	−1.21***
Day care	1.342***	n.s.	n.s.	2.502***	1.822***	1.667***	1.210***
Married	n.s.	1.881*	n.s.	n.s.	n.s.	−0.930**	0.888**
Full-time employment							
1 child	0.318***	n.s.	n.s.	n.s.	n.s.	n.s.	0.843**
2+children	−0.264***	n.s.	−1.27***	n.s.	n.s.	−0.771**	n.s.
Child <3	−0.326***	n.s.	−1.34***	−1.16***	n.s.	−0.351**	−1.19***
Day care	1.622***	0.850***	0.412*	2.93***	2.430***	1.476***	1.613***
Married	n.s.	n.s.	n.s.	n.s.	−1.04***	−0.662**	0.870**
N	12140	653	931	1473	1548	1649	1012
Chi2	2498.82	138.68	172.19	564.91	384.63	365.92	269.07

Note: The estimates include only women with children. The regressions control for age and
educational attainment. The day care variable measures actual utilization by parents. For
explanations, see Table 3.6.

While marital status by and large matters little, one may note the strong
negative effect of being married on full-time employment in Spain and, especially, in Italy. Although we can do little more than speculate, this may signal
a particular kind of selection problem. Full-time working mothers are, to
begin with, a fairly rare species in Southern Europe. They often combine two
distinct groups that are uniquely able to cancel out the opportunity costs of
having children: on one side, highly resourceful and educated women; on
the other side, women working in family enterprises.[22]

If we were to sum up so far, only Denmark emerges as a case in which the
incompatibility problem seems to have been largely eradicated. Our data do
not include the other Nordic countries but it is quite certain that they devi-
ate little from the Danish norm (OECD, 2001c). But it is worth noting that

---

[22] This may also explain why there is no observable effect of children on full-time employment
in Italy. In fact, we know from Table 2.5 that employment and motherhood are quite incompatible
in Italy. The strong, positive effect of being married in the UK is probably a mirror-image of the
well-known labour supply difficulties that British lone mothers face.

the difficulties of harmonizing work with children are not homogeneous across Europe. Part-time employment seems to provide women with a functioning option where, that is, it is readily available and not associated with precariousness. It is obviously not a genuine solution in countries like Italy and Spain (where it hardly exists), nor perhaps in Great Britain (where it is widespread but also associated with poor-quality jobs).

A second source of international heterogeneity stems from the fact that the number and age of children often have a very different impact. There are certainly more severe incompatibility problems once mothers have two or more children, but the toughest obstacles no doubt arise when children are small. Hence, we are back where we began: the basic 'mother-friendly' policy package—and day care coverage in particular—is a first *sine qua non* in any strategy to harmonize employment and motherhood. As we saw in Table 3.7, access to day care raises the probability of being employed by a factor of 1.3 in part-time and 1.6 in full time jobs at the pan-European level.

Yet, as was argued, this will probably not provide *sufficient* conditions for maximal compatibility, mainly because wage differentials may influence the employment of the less educated women negatively and because access to sheltered, 'soft economy' jobs can be a crucial determinant for family formation, principally among the 'dual role' female majorities. The 'wage effect' cannot be tested but, in separate analyses (not shown), we test for the importance of public employment among mothers. Working in the public sector reduces the negative effects of having children substantially. Indeed, without including public employment in the model, the effect of having a small child reduces women's employment probability by 20 per cent; when included, the employment probability *rises* by 16 per cent.[23]

There is one basic point concerning the interactive effects between day care and labour market structure. As we discussed, the penalties of interrupting work for family reasons become most evident when we examine life cycle effects. The cumulative wage losses are potentially huge, not simply due to foregone earnings during interruptions, but also to skills erosion, less experience, and lost seniority. All this directly influences lifetime career opportunities. As most recently Stier *et al.* (2001) show, the real pay-off from day care provision is that it diminishes substantially the likelihood that mothers must interrupt employment careers.

We would conclude from the preceding that it is possible to resolve the incompatibility issue and, no doubt, Scandinavia presents us with a benchmark

---

[23] The underlying model is similar to that shown in Tables 2.6 and 2.7. As noted earlier, public sector employment is also key for compatibility among Italian women (Bernardi, 2001: Table 6.2).

model for how to do it. But the Nordic model appears less persuasive if we *simultaneously* aim for the more ambitious goal of gender equality.

Gender Equality across the Life Course

It is not difficult to see why 'women-friendly' policy may inadvertently produce heavy gender segregation in labour markets. Leaves, high wages, part-time and public sector jobs all help reduce incompatibilities, but the consequence may be to intensify other inequalities such as job segregation. Can we conceive of a model that optimizes not only women's ability to work and have children, but also one that lessens segregation? This will depend on the interaction of social policy, women's preferences, and employer incentives. Through 'women-friendly' programmes, the welfare state inadvertently increases the costs to employers of hiring women. Feminists have a persuasive argument when they advocate that this risk must be equalized between men and women.

Any snapshot view of society will elicit big gender differences in pay, employment, and professional career attainment. But the same can be said for age, class, ethnicity, or race differences. The key issue of gender equality (like *any* inequality) lies in life course dynamics.

Life chances, for women as for men, are the joint product of individual choice and encountered constraints. The menu of choice among men has traditionally been narrow; constraints, ample. The standard male of welfare capitalism would at, say, age 16 or 18, get a job and would then work his way through 40 or 50 years doing more or less what he did at age 25. Most men enjoyed limited opportunities for mobility, but their jobs were pretty secure and wages were generally good.[24] The 'Fordist' era working-class male epitomizes the standardized, homogeneous, linear life cycle.

Gender equality cannot be separated from social class differences. In fact, the norm of post-war housewifery sprang from the fact that average working-class women were able to cease working. But, at the same time, highly educated women were already beginning to abandon the model. There is no doubt that the 'Fordist' era working class female faced a wholly different system of constraints and that, in great part, this was truly gendered. The educational gap between the sexes remained huge until quite recently and so

---

[24] This is obviously an extremely stylised depiction, but one that broadly conforms to a now long tradition of social mobility research, from Lipset and Bendix (1959) to Erikson and Goldthorpe (1992).

working-class girls had far less schooling or apprenticeship than boys. Facing the alternative of a life in textiles, women got pregnant early and since men's earnings rose, couples could afford full-time motherhood. Hence the arrival of the traditional, orthogonal male and female lifetime participation curves.

We now live in an era in which women have control over their pregnancy, in which women's educational attainment more often than not surpasses that of males; an era in which women have largely abandoned Hakim's (1996) family-centred role. We also live in an era in which the constraints of industrial welfare capitalism are giving way to a very different order—within which the array of constraints are far less documented. In order to address the gender equality question, we are therefore faced with a double bind: on the one hand, citizens' (perhaps mainly women's) choice menu is being revolutionized; on the other hand, so also are the forces that limit citizens' ability to realize their dreams and aspirations.

In a growing number of countries, women's lifetime participation curves begin to resemble men's. Lifetime employment is now practically the norm among North American and Scandinavian women. And indications are that the same norm is now being embraced throughout the advanced countries. We are witnessing a 'masculinization' of the female life course, driven probably more by choice than by constraints. We also witness an erosion of the conventionally stable and linear male life course. Men face greater employment instability (especially in the younger ages) and ever more early exit (in the mature years). Heavy unemployment, especially among the less skilled (and erstwhile standard male workers), implies also risks of lengthy employment interruptions. In a sense, this puts males closer to the more interrupted character of women's work biographies. No doubt, if this makes men's life course appear more 'feminine', it is probably less a question of choice than of constraints. And it certainly has little to do with family obligations.

Life course convergence or not, gender-equality tensions remain *precisely because the forces that spur convergence also create or enhance second-order inequalities*. The latter are, following the literature, particularly acute in terms of the inbuilt obstacles to career advancement, in particular gender segregation in work, and in terms of the unequal division of domestic responsibilities. In respect of either, how do we disentangle the freedom of choice from the tyranny of constraint?

In countries with very low female participation, like Italy and Spain, the women who do work most of their lives are a very bi-modal group: either highly educated and very career oriented or low-educated and driven by necessity. 'Women-friendly' Scandinavia, but also 'market-clearing' America, stand out because, here, lifelong employment commitments are near universal

(Blossfeld and Drobnic, 2001). The lion's share of women who make up the Scandinavian–Spanish differential are, no doubt, representative of Hakim's 'dual role' model. In Scandinavia, they evidently make full use of their child leave entitlements, they obviously prefer sheltered public employment, they increasingly prefer full-time jobs but like the part-time option because they also desire to have several children. Hence, a blend of full- and part-time work with paid leaves is clearly in line with most Nordic women's preference sets.

More generally, the masculinization of female biographies that we see in educational attainment and in participation curves hides persistent feminine life choices. This becomes apparent when we examine sex-specific tertiary level education enrolments. Be it within academic or more professional training paths, women overwhelmingly cluster in health and welfare studies (84 per cent female within professional training) and humanities (69 per cent female in universities), and they literally shun engineering (only 15 per cent female in professional schools) and mathematics/computer studies (31 per cent female).[25] Most strikingly, these hugely gendered selection mechanisms remain unabated, and are equally strong in countries where women's incorporation has gone furthest, such as in Finland, Sweden, and the US.

Many feminists insist that this preference set is imposed upon women. This is empirically not evident. Petersen and Morgan (1995) has, for example, shown that in very specialized, high human capital occupations, men's and women's earnings are very similar. Hence, if women who want a career follow labour market signals, they should favour engineering over humanities studies. Still, even if it seems hard to believe, standard economic theory would lend some support to the alternative feminist interpretation.

If, for the moment, we were to assume that girls and boys are equally prone to select between humanities and engineering, gender inequalities would probably still remain. The final and least insurmountable barrier to gender equality probably lies more on the 'constraint' side than on the 'choice' side. Even if women are as skilled, clever, or talented as men, competitively placed employers will rationally prefer male to female workers if they expect that women, and not men, will experience a productivity decline due to births. And if the cost of interruptions is wholly or even partly allocated to employers, then the gender bias will obviously strengthen. We face the age-old question of statistical discrimination. Employers are rational when they expect that their investment in women workers will yield comparatively less as long as women do, indeed, take more time off for family reasons. Undoubtedly, the

---

[25] These are OECD member country averages for 1998 (OECD, 1998b: Table C4.4).

higher risk and lower comparative yield associated with women workers can be neutralized by wage differentials—i.e. by reverting to institutionalized gender inequalities of pay.

The gender pay-gap, although slowly closing, varies considerably from one country to the next. In Europe it ranges from 25–30 percentage points in Germany, Austria, and Spain to 10–15 percentage points in Belgium, Denmark, and France.[26] The general decline that we observe in most cases is a composite effect of women's rising educational credentials and a downward trend in lower-skilled male earnings. A large part of the remaining gap is simply a compositional effect: women are more concentrated in less paying jobs. The vast consensus is that horizontal (such as sector-level) segregation matters far less than vertical, or job-ladder segregation.[27] Additionally, as Blau and Kahn (2000) argue, the size of the gender pay gap is intimately connected to the *overall* degree of inequality within an economy. The wage profile in the UK and the US is far more polarized than in Scandinavia, and this amplifies also gender differentials. It is illustrative that the US gender wage gap is double the Danish, Belgian, and French even if female employment levels are rather similar.[28] Beyond compositional and national idiosyncratic factors, there undoubtedly remains a directly 'gender-inegalitarian' or discriminatory component. The chief problem that plagues the literature is that it is very difficult to identify precisely.

Gender pay inequalities mirror two sets of dynamics: women are systematically more prone to end up at the disadvantaged end of the 'compositional effect'; and women are likely to be paid less, 'all things equal'. The really thorny problem of gender equality is that the two are mutually and, possibly, negatively interconnected. In highly compressed earnings structures, women (and especially less skilled women) will have larger incentives to seek employment.

Well-informed statistical discriminators will know that the kind of women who respond positively to such wage incentives (mainly the 'dual role' women) are the very same who are more likely to prioritize also motherhood. This would predictably result in both horizontal and vertical segregation.

---

[26] The latest OECD figures suggest that the gender wage gap has declined by about 10 percentage points in Germany and 15+ points in France, the UK, and in the US (OECD, 2001d: Chart B42.). The gender pay gap measure used is the difference between male and female median full-time earnings as a percentage of male full-time earnings.

[27] Most important here is not so much sectoral (or horizontal) job segregation as vertical occupational segregation, namely that women are typically concentrated on the lower rungs of any job-hierarchy ladder (e.g. primary rather than secondary school teacher) or in less responsible positions within identical professions (Bielby and Baron, 1984; Goldin and Polacheck, 1987; Rosenfeld and Kalleberg, 1990; and Hakim, 1996; Rubery *et al.*, 1999).

[28] There is, of course, a greater female concentration in low paid jobs in the US.

The marginal preference of a competitively exposed firm would, if costs are equal, favour male workers. Hence, women would be more likely to concentrate in 'soft economy' jobs—if such exist. Everywhere, the greater risk associated with female employees would spur a rational manager to favour men when promoting employees to higher echelon functions. On the 'constraint' side, equality of career opportunities is being hampered by egalitarian pay policy and, no doubt, also by 'women-friendly' social entitlements.

Advanced 'women friendly' welfare states, like the Nordic, have inadvertently raised the relative risks and price of employing women. 'Women unfriendly' welfare states, be it the market driven American model or the average Continental European model, have extended far fewer rights to working mothers. In the former case, this has led to one form of 'supply-side' adaptation: women committed to a career opt for extremely short interruptions if and when they have children (Gustafsson, 1994). In the latter case, the dominant type of adaptation is to postpone family formation until one has become firmly anchored in the labour markets.

The Domestic Solution

Neither social nor labour market policy will, alone, solve the problem. In the last instance, the tyranny of constraints that employer strategies impose derives from the incarnated empirical fact that it is women, and not men, who abandon work when an acute family servicing need appears. At first glance, feminists' call for a more egalitarian distribution of domestic work may appear unrealistic. Even if there is evidence that husbands' unpaid hours increase when wives' decrease, they fall far short of compensating. Granted, the data do show that male partners of employed women contribute more (especially among the more educated), and that their share is rising in just about all countries.[29] But the kind of egalitarianism that feminists call for is hard to find. Should a more equal division of domestic tasks be a matter of policy? If so, can we envisage realistic means?

If we follow standard textbook economics, the answer would be, yes, public policy may be of relevance. The key here lies in career expectations. As long as women's expected earnings lag significantly behind their partners', households will adopt unequal specialization strategies, and women will continue to shoulder the lion's share of domestic work. It is possible to

---

[29] For an overview, see Bonke (1995) and Gershuny (2000). The substantially greater contribution among educated males may be due to cultural factors, or due to the fact that they are likely to be married to highly educated, professional women.

narrow the cumulative career differential, either by making women's life cycles even more masculine or, vice versa, by making males' even more feminine. As we know, women's employment careers have become substantially more like males', especially in North America and especially among highly educated women. But the masculinization of women's lives reaches limits if they want children, or prefer part-time employment, regardless of how 'women-friendly' is policy.

We notice, however, also a (much weaker, yet significant) feminization of male life cycles. In part this is due to unwanted factors, such as more unemployment. But, in part, it is also due to policy. All the Nordic countries now boast explicit incentives for fathers to take leaves during pregnancy and childbirths. The male share of total child leave days certainly remains modest, but it is rising. In the 1990s, the paternal share rose by 32 per cent in Denmark, 67 per cent in Finland, and 45 per cent in Sweden (NOSOCO, 2001: Table 4.6).

Sweden is undoubtedly a test-case for the 'specialization thesis'. To begin with, male paternity leaves are twice as frequent (13 per cent of total leave days) as in other Nordic countries. Additionally, Sweden holds the international record in terms of husbands' contribution to unpaid, domestic work: an average of 21 hours a week (Esping-Andersen, 1999). This is not only far ahead of other countries with comparable levels of female participation (in Denmark, as in the US, the male contribution averages around 13–15 hours a week), but it is also approaching female levels (working women's weekly domestic hours typically lie in the 25–30 hour range). Besides the doubtful possibility that Swedish males are genetically more disposed towards solidarity, this can be attributed to internationally very narrow gender earnings differentials and to welfare state incentives: full utilization of paid (post-birth) parental leave requires that also fathers take it. Fathers' actual use of the programme remains substantially less than mothers', but it has grown impressively over the past ten or so years (SOU, 2000).[30] The problem is that male propensity to take leave is mainly concentrated among those married to highly educated women and among those working in public sector jobs.

We can provide some rough figures on the gender distribution of unpaid, domestic work (see Table 3.8). Since we compare both part-time and full-time employed women with males, cross-national variations cannot be ascribed to overall female participation levels. The United States and Scandinavia begin

[30] This is equally true for Denmark. During the child's first year, fathers' leave days average 40–50, mothers' 250 (Christoffersen, 1997).

Table 3.8 Gender inequalities in time allocation to domestic work.[a] Female–male ratios

	Part-time (women : men)	Full-time (women : men)
Denmark	2.0	1.7
Finland	1.9	1.7
Sweden	1.9	1.6
Austria	3.0	2.7
Italy	n.a	3.6
Germany	2.1	1.8
UK	2.2	2.4
US	1.8	1.7

[a] The data refer to c.1990. Domestic work includes cleaning, cooking etc. and also caring for children.

Source: OECD (2001c: Table 4.5).

to approach a more egalitarian division of unpaid household work while, at the other extreme, Italy and Austria (and less so the UK) represent a traditional division of labour. Considering that the gender ratio is pretty similar in the United States and Scandinavia, one might question whether parental leave incentives for fathers actually make much of a difference.

If women desire to have children, there is an upper-limit to female life course 'masculinization'. Hence, the pursuit of gender equality will necessitate a substantial alteration of the male incentive structure, and it appears unlikely that even the most progressive parental leave policy, alone, will make a huge difference. Since data (and solid research) still are scarce, we cannot arrive at any clear conclusions, let alone policy guidelines: (1) intra-household time allocation decisions will depend a lot on what type of woman is involved and on the number of children; (2) it is very difficult to disentangle the effects of expected life-time earnings from the effects of welfare state incentives— huge paid leave incentives for fathers may have no effect whatsoever if gender earnings differentials remain significant; (3) the same time-allocation decisions will also depend on gender occupational segregation. If women are predominantly concentrated in 'soft economy' jobs, as in Scandinavia, and men in the competitive sector, males' ability to respond to welfare state incentives will remain limited due, simply, to 'constraints'.

Still, to the extent that fathers' lower propensity to take leave is partially motivated by the relatively larger income decline that they are likely to suffer with paid leave, policy might give a substantial boost to the feminization of male behaviour simply by neutralizing this effect, i.e. by guaranteeing *full* wage compensation (with no upper ceiling) during parental leaves.

Conclusions

It is uncontroversial to promote better opportunities for women, not only because they respond to women's demands but also because their employment may yield increasing social returns. In many countries women constitute a massive untapped labour reserve that can help narrow future age dependency rates and reduce associated financial pressures. Moreover as, women's educational attainment exceeds men's, clearly there exists an often large, untapped productive reservoir. We also know that female employment is one of the most effective means of combating social exclusion and poverty. All this implies that 'women-friendly' policy is, simultaneously, family- and society-friendly. If it yields a private return to individual women, it also yields a substantial collective return to society at large. It should, accordingly, be defined as a social investment.

There exists a broad consensus on what constitutes women-friendly policy. It includes:

1. Affordable day care (and we have tried to specify the level of subsidization required).
2. Paid maternity but, arguably much more importantly, also paid parental leave. A more equal division of family tasks may occur at the margin by encouraging fathers to make use of parental leave entitlements.
3. Provisions for work absence when children are ill.

It is well established that day care and school hours are fundamental for mothers' capacity to remain employed.[31] No one questions that such a woman-friendly policy approach is a fundamental precondition for a productive post-industrial society. But it is doubtful whether it is sufficient.

The central point is that public support for mothers will not alone resolve the incompatibility problem unless accompanied by jobs that allow mothers to combine careers and family. This is crucial not just for equity reasons but also for the goals discussed in Chapter 2, namely the well-being of children. Harmonizing motherhood with employment will help establish the

---

[31] As observed above in n. 21, the French practice of school-free Wednesdays is arguably a major impediment for working mothers.

preconditions for, but will not ensure, gender equality. If the overarching goal is, indeed, genuine equality between the sexes we need, as most would agree, to change both gendered choices and societal constraints.

On the choice side, most women probably belong to the 'dual role' category and hence place a strong priority on forming families. But this alone cannot be invoked as an argument *against* gender equalization. It may be that there is a sizeable group of dual role women who view careers as second to family on their priority scale. Even this is not a decisive argument if, that is, we entertain the basic counterfactual that some and, perhaps, a growing number of men prefer likewise. Or, to echo an earlier reasoning, girls may begin to match boys in their educational choices and, still, this would be insufficient if the goal remains true equality.

We can abstractly imagine a world in which women begin to embrace the typical male life cycle model, lock, stock, and barrel. In this world there would be almost no children. We do happen to know that men's and women's desire for children remains intact, so this leads us to conclude that there is, realistically, a limit to female life course masculinization. Remaining at the level of pure abstraction, we must conclude that true gender equality will not come about unless, somehow, men can be made to embrace a more feminine life course. Whether or not such a scenario would truly conform to the prevailing choice set of today's men and women is pretty unclear.

As far as tomorrow is concerned, there is one bit of evidence which speaks in favour of the egalitarian agenda, namely the vision of the 'good society' as today's children see it. In a Danish survey of children's opinions, the vast majority preferred that mother *and* father work part-time and stay home the 'other' part-time (Christoffersen, 1997). What, unfortunately, we do not know is whether this is merely an egoistic juvenile preference, or whether a new gender choice-set is simmering in the minds and hearts of the coming twenty-first-century adults.

4

The Quality of Working Life in Welfare Strategy

Duncan Gallie

Introduction

The central policy orientation for enhancing social inclusion is currently that of increasing the employment rate. Yet this can be at best a very partial solution. The extent to which employment offers opportunities for social participation depends crucially on the quality of jobs. At present, a substantial sector of the job market offers only a restricted possibility of social participation. Moreover, some current developments in the nature of employment are accentuating risks of labour market marginalization, as a result of skill polarization and a marked intensification of work. For work to provide social integration it must offer meaningful work tasks and conditions of work that allow sustained employability. This would require a more general improvement in the quality of lower-skilled jobs, in particular so that they provide the conditions for the long-term maintenance of learning skills.

The view that increasing the employment rate is the key to social inclusion is not just premised on the fact that a job provides a regular source of income, but also on the belief that it is a source of skill development and motivation. It provides opportunities for personal self-development, through enabling people to use their initiative and to develop decision-making skills. But a considerable proportion of jobs in the EU do not provide such opportunities; indeed, often they do not provide the level, or security, of income that would support full involvement in the life of the community. The people that occupy such jobs are condemned then to a very restricted form of social participation, especially if there are limited opportunities for mobility out of such positions.

Not only does much low-skilled employment provide rather limited life opportunities, but it enhances the risk of persistent labour market marginalization. The very rapid upskilling of the workforces of most countries of the EU over the last decade has tended to leave aside those in low-skilled jobs. The majority of people in such jobs do not experience skill development as part of their everyday work and they have been largely excluded from training programmes. This has made them highly vulnerable to unemployment in times of economic restructuring and poorly placed to find new work opportunities. At the same time, there has been a sharp intensification of work effort, posing serious risks of work stress and tension between work and family life. With economic modernization the health risks of work shift from those of physical injury to those of psychological strain. This could well accentuate the problem of increasing numbers withdrawing from the workforce early through disablement or early retirement.

Finally, improving the quality of work is crucial for ensuring that those made unemployed have a reasonable chance of finding work again afterwards. In the great majority of the EU countries, the principal emphasis in social policy has been on tackling the risk of social exclusion after people have entered unemployment. Typically there has been a mixture of short-term training and activation policies, together with a concern to ensure clear financial work incentives. These policies have proved inadequate for ensuring longer-term employability. The attempt to reskill the unemployed in a relatively short period of time can only have limited results in a context in which people have spent long periods of their working lives without learning new skills or maintaining their basic learning capacities. There is little evidence that the unemployed, who are usually highly committed to employment, are failing to get stable jobs because of lack of financial incentives. Rather the key factor is the constraint on job choice resulting from accumulated skill deficit. The orientation of European social policy needs to shift away from a primary reliance on short-term curative measures towards the development of a long-term preventative programme that will protect people from the risk of labour market marginalization by ensuring continuous skill enhancement over their working lives.

These issues are likely to become of even greater importance in the coming decades. Economic internationalization is placing increased pressures on the traditional skill and employment structures of the European Member States. The dismantling of capital exchange controls, the reduction of tariff protections, widespread privatization and the loss of the ability to offset cost disadvantage through devaluation have led to increased cost competition (Scharpf and Schmidt, 2000). Despite concern about the impact of competition from developing countries, it would appear to be the greater integration of the product and capital markets of the advanced societies that is (at least at present) generating the greatest pressure for change. In general, this has favoured an acceleration of technological change and a marked upward shift in the skill structure, heightening the vulnerability of those in low-skilled work. The main area in which there remains a potential for the expansion of low-skilled work (judging from comparisons with the US) is in areas of personal services, supplying the domestic market, where the dispersed nature of employment makes effective regulation particularly difficult.

In the late 1980s and 1990s, nation states developed very different policies for addressing the problem of the low-skilled. The 'neo-liberal' solution, followed in the UK, favoured increasing wage differentials and reducing collective bargaining controls on employers. The 'Scandinavian' solution involved an effort to improve the quality of work of the low-skilled and to provide more effective ladders for skill enhancement. Contrary to widespread belief, there is no evidence that the neo-liberal solution compensates for its higher personal costs with greater effectiveness in generating employment for the low-skilled in general (Nickell, 1996; Nickell and Bell, 1996; Morley, 1998). Even with respect to employment in personal and distributive services, the positive effects of higher wage differentiation are weak (Scharpf, 2000a: 82–4). 'Low' and 'high' welfare solutions can have broadly similar short-term consequences in terms both of economic competitiveness and effectiveness in combating unemployment—compare the cases of the UK and Denmark in the 1990s (Scharpf, 2000a). But they have radically different implications for the quality of life of those affected, both in terms of immediate well-being and of longer-term opportunities for self-development.

It is clear that economic constraints allow substantial scope for choice with respect to labour standards and welfare. An effective welfare strategy against employment risks requires (as in the areas considered by other chapters in this book) a reorientation to longer-term preventative strategies. To ensure the social integration of those in low-skilled employment, to minimize the processes within work that create risks of social exclusion and to ensure that the unemployed are more rapidly reintegrated into work, new policies are needed to enhance the quality of jobs. In combating social exclusion, a policy of employment expansion needs to be accompanied by a major programme of improvement in the quality of working life.

Dimensions of Employment Disadvantage

Work and Personal Development

There can be little doubt that generally employment, particularly where it provides scope for individual initiative, is a source of personal stability and development. This is well supported by the research of social psychologists. Marie Jahoda (Jahoda, 1982) argued that, quite apart from its importance in providing a source of income, employment provides an important source of psychological stability through providing a clear time structure to the day, a sense of participation in a collective purpose, a stronger sense of identity, and a stable pattern of required regular activity. Research consistently shows that where people exercise initiative in their jobs, they have particularly high levels of job satisfaction (Gallie *et al.*, 1998) and, indeed, there is some evidence that they develop their competencies in dealing with situations out of work (Kohn and Schooler, 1983). Certainly, in all the EU countries for which there is adequate evidence, people in employment have significantly higher levels of life satisfaction than those who are jobless (Gallie and Russell, 1998).

Yet, at the same time, it is important to remember that the quality of employment is highly stratified. There are sectors of employment, in which many of the assumed benefits for personal development are difficult to discern. A considerable proportion of jobs do not have the characteristics that are usually described by those who emphasise the integrative effects of employment (Table 4.1). Only about a third of the workforce are in jobs offering good opportunities for learning, while only a quarter have significant initiative in decision making on the job. Even taking those who report that such characteristics are either 'very' or 'quite' true of their jobs, only 60 per cent think that they can learn new things through the job, while just over half say they can influence what happens on the job. On these criteria, at least four out of ten jobs, then, would have to be regarded as of rather poor quality.[1]

There are several groups in the workforce that are particularly deprived in terms of the job characteristics associated with personal development. The

---

[1] There were significant proportions taking the extreme negative view of their jobs, saying that these features were 'not at all true' of their jobs. This was the case for 15 per cent for learning opportunities, 19 per cent for say over their job and 20 per cent for taking part in decisions. The Third European Survey on Working Conditions also found that, although job control had slightly increased over recent years, still one-third of all employees reported having no control over either work methods, speed or the order of tasks (European Commission, 2001c: 73).

Table 4.1 Work tasks characteristics: percentage saying characteristic is 'very true' of their jobs (EU employees)

	Job requires that keep learning new things	A lot of say over what happens in the job	Takes part in decisions that affect the work
All employees	31.2	23.4	26.0
Semi & non-skilled	18.5	17.7	18.7
Full-time employees	32.3	24.1	26.5
Part-time employees	22.7	15.6	20.8
Full-time semi- & non-skilled	19.6	18.6	18.4
Part-time semi- & non-skilled	12.2	10.7	15.9
Semi- & non-skilled <45 yrs	20.8	18.1	18.5
Semi- & non-skilled 45+ yrs	13.4	16.6	19.1
Ns (All employees)	6609	6613	6613

Source: Employment in Europe Survey, 1996.[2]

first is that of semi- and non-skilled workers, who represent approximately a third of all employees. These are in jobs of relatively low task complexity, where little is required in the way of qualifications or training.[3] Less than one in five of these employees are in jobs where they can definitely learn new things or exercise significant influence over the way the jobs are done. Even if one takes the broader group of those who consider it is either very or quite true of their jobs, only two out of five employees consider their jobs offer such opportunities.

Another sector of the workforce that is clearly heavily disadvantaged in terms of both regular opportunities to learn new things and the ability to exercise discretion over the job is that of part-time employees. This is not just a reflection of general occupational level. Part-time workers have less chance for self-development and control in the job than full-time employees within each occupational class. Part-timers in non-skilled work suffer from cumulative disadvantage with respect to job quality. Only 12 per cent of semi- and non-skilled part-timers are in jobs that give significant chances to learn through the work and only 11 per cent feel they have much say over what

[2] The survey (special Eurobarometer, 44.3) was commissioned by DG V and involved national representative samples in all of the EU member states.

[3] For details, see Gallie *et al.*, 1998: ch. 2. These categories are operationalized in terms of the Goldthorpe–Erikson class scheme (for details, see Erikson and Goldthorpe, 1992: 35–47).

happens in the job.[4] The proportions giving the extreme negative account of their job are notably higher: 37 per cent report that it is 'not at all true' that they have learning opportunities in their jobs and 34 per cent with respect to the say in the job.

Finally, a particularly sharply deprived group with respect to jobs that provide ongoing learning opportunities are older semi- and non-skilled employees. Whereas possibilities for self-development increase with age for professional/managerial employees and technicians and supervisors, they decrease with age for both skilled manual and non-skilled workers. Only 13 per cent of non-skilled workers over the age of 45 are in jobs where they regularly have to learn new things (indeed, among those aged 55 and over, the proportion is as low as 7.5 per cent).

Work and Poverty

The effectiveness of employment in ensuring social participation will also depend on the extent to which it protects people against poverty. Certainly in comparison with the US, the EU has been very successful in limiting poverty among people in work. Nonetheless in several EU countries a significant proportion of those in work are in poverty, defined as having less than half average household income (Marx and Verbist 1998). Taking those with some work attachment, the proportions among male workers rise to 7.4 per cent in Spain and 8.7 per cent in Italy (Table 4.2). In Germany, the Netherlands, Spain, Sweden, and the UK around 5 per cent of all female workers are in poverty. The risk of poverty in work is particularly high in certain household situations—for instance, where people are in single adult households or in two-adult households where there is only a single earner. More than 10 per cent of workers in single adult households are in poverty in Finland, Germany, the Netherlands, Norway, and Sweden.

The existence of a substantial sector of jobs in which people are still severely constrained by financial difficulties is also confirmed by people's own assessments of the difficulties they face (Table 4.3). Approximately 15 per cent of employees in the EU report that they have difficulty or great difficulty making ends meet. There is, however, a very strong contrast between Northern and Southern Europe. In the Northern countries, with the exception of Ireland, less than 10 per cent of employees are under severe financial constraint. However, in the Southern European countries, with the exception

---

[4] Again taking the broader category of those who said it was very true or quite true of their jobs, only 38 per cent thought they had opportunities to learn new things or that they had say in the job.

Table 4.2 Poverty rates among people in work

	Men	Women	Single adults in work
Belgium	0.9	0.5	1.3
Denmark	2.5	3.1	8.6
Finland	3.4	4.3	12.1
France	3.1	3.0	3.8
Germany	4.1	4.9	10.5
Italy	8.7	2.1	3.2
Netherlands	3.1	5.0	12.1
Norway	2.7	3.6	10.0
Spain	7.4	6.5	8.8
Sweden	4.8	5.6	13.5
UK	3.2	5.1	7.0
US	13.3	14.4	19.3

Source: Marx and Verbist, 1998. Poverty is defined as having equivalized household income less than 50 per cent of the mean.

of Italy, financial difficulty is very extensive, affecting 31 per cent of Spanish, 35 per cent of Portuguese and 49 per cent of Greek employees.

The existence of substantial sectors of low-paid employment is one contributor to such poverty. The extent and evolution of this sector clearly vary a great deal between European countries, reflecting institutional and policy differences. Taking as low-paid those who are working full-time (and full-year), but with gross earnings less than two-thirds of the median, the proportion affected varies from 6.7 per cent in Finland to 19.9 per cent in the UK (Nolan and Marx, 2000). Given that relatively high proportions of part-time and temporary workers are likely to be low-paid but are excluded from these figures, the prevalence of low-paid work is probably rather greater than is suggested by these estimates. There are wide variations in trends over time. Between 1976 and the early 1990s, the proportion of low-paid workers in France fell from 17 per cent to 14 per cent of full-time adult workers, while in the UK it rose from 14 per cent in 1977 to 20 per cent in the mid-1990s (Bazen *et al.*, 1998). Moreover the relative position of the low-paid (comparing lowest decile to median earnings) remained stable and possibly improved over this period in France and the Netherlands, while it deteriorated in the UK. The existence of a minimum wage system is clearly an important

Table 4.3 Financial difficulty among employees (% finding it difficult to make ends meet)

	1994	1995	1996	Average
Austria		16.1	12.8	14.5
Belgium	8.3	9.0	8.7	8.7
Denmark	10.7	6.8	7.7	8.4
Finland			15.6	15.6
France	16.3	15.7	15.4	15.8
Germany	6.5	5.3	5.7	5.8
Greece	51.1	47.6	47.3	48.7
Ireland	19.8	15.4	16.9	17.4
Italy	16.8	16.3	12.6	15.2
Netherlands	7.7	6.5	7.8	7.3
Portugal	34.6	35.7	33.7	34.7
Spain	33.5	30.9	29.7	31.4
UK	11.9	13.6	12.1	12.5
EU	15.4	14.9	14.2	14.8

Note: The figures are taken from the 1994, 1995, and 1996 waves. The two most extreme difficulty categories are taken from the six point response set i.e. 'great difficulty' and 'difficulty'. The country sample numbers (in 1994) ranged from 2,715 in Belgium to 5,618 in France. Sweden did not participate in the study and Austria did not participate in the first wave, nor Finland in the first two. Luxembourg data are excluded from the separate country results on the grounds of relatively small sample numbers, but are included in the overall EU figures. The overall EU figures (based on the countries for which data was available in the particular year) are weighted to reflect country shares to overall employment.

Source: European Community Household Panel.

factor in the protection of the low-paid, although there can be significant differences between countries in the efficacy of procedures for updating the minimum wage.

As will be seen in the next chapter, the implications for deprivation of sustained low pay may not only be for current income. It may have major consequences for people's lives long after they have left employment. In part, this will reflect differential ability to build up savings that can be drawn upon when there is no longer income from employment. But it is also due to the fact that disadvantage may roll on in the form of lower pension entitlements.

This will depend upon the characteristics of the particular pension system in a country. It will be particularly serious where systems are predominantly earnings related, and less in those based on a flat-rate pension.

A solution to the problem of the 'working poor' will clearly require much broader measures than those relating specifically to low pay. Low pay does not necessarily imply that a person is in poverty (as measured say by equivalized household income below 50 per cent of the mean). Poverty rates are defined in terms of household income, and the low pay of one household member can be offset in multi-person households by the income of others. Although a majority of employees who live in 'poor' households are low-paid, the majority of the low-paid are not 'poor'. Low pay is only one component of the broader problem of low household incomes among those in work. The relationship between low pay and poverty varies between groups: poverty rates are much higher for low-paid men than for low-paid women, for single earner than for multiple earner households, and for the prime-aged than for younger low-paid workers (Marx and Verbist, 1998; Nolan and Marx, 2000). The risk of poverty is particularly high for low-paid workers who live on their own.

It must be remembered that poverty estimates assume that resources are shared in the household. It is clear that particularly for women, low pay does not translate into poverty in good part because of the importance of their partner's income for the household's living standards. However, those low-paid who are currently protected by the income of a partner may experience heavy financial dependence as a result of their lack of independent resources, they may experience real financial deprivation if resources are not shared and they are at a much higher risk of poverty in the event of a breakdown in the relationship.

The Intensification of Work

A feature of the developing nature of work that is likely to generate increasing problems for low-skilled workers is the widespread intensification of work, with its potential implications for work-related stress and ill-health. Faced by increased economic internationalization, employers have emphasized higher standards of product quality, downsized their organizations, sought higher degrees of flexibility of working practices and devolved increased responsibilities on work teams. At the same time, organizations have been undergoing rapid technological change, with the problems this poses in terms of the disruption of established working practices and heightened insecurity. The growing centrality of this issue has been recognized in diverse national studies (Gallie *et al.*, 1998; Dejours, 1998; Green, 1999), although good comparative data are still rare.

Nearly half of all European employees (43 per cent) report that they work under a great deal of pressure, 36 per cent say that they always or often find their work stressful, and 35 per cent that they always or often come back from work exhausted. There is no evidence of systematic differences between men and women. If men are more likely to report pressure in work, women are just as likely to find the job stressful and are somewhat more likely to report that they are exhausted when they return home (Table 4.4).

Employees' reports also suggest a marked increase in work effort over recent years. Taking the EU as a whole, 48 per cent of employees (47 per cent of men, 48 per cent of women) say they had experienced a significant increase over the previous five years in the effort they had to put into their job. Less than 10 per cent report a significant decline in work effort. The proportion experiencing increased effort is highest among those aged between 20 and 54, peaking at 52 per cent among employees aged 35 to 44. But it is notable that even among older workers, aged 55 or more, 40 per cent have been affected by an increase in work effort.

The increase in work pressure has affected not just the low-skilled but all occupational classes. Indeed, there is some evidence that it may have increased most for those in higher skilled jobs. But there is now a wide body of research that points to the fact that the long-term health effects of increased pressure are likely to be particularly severe among the low-skilled. This is because the

Table 4.4 Work pressure among EU employees (%)

	Men	Women	All
Works under a great deal of pressure	46.0	39.5	43.1
Always or often finds work stressful	36.0	35.6	35.8
Always or often returns home from work exhausted	32.9	37.9	35.1
The effort required by the job has increased over the last 5 years	47.3	47.8	47.5
The stress involved in the job has increased in the last 5 years	45.4	46.4	45.8

Source: Employment in Europe Survey, 1996.

impact of work pressure is mediated by the degree of control that employees can exercise over the work task. Where people are allowed initiative to take decisions themselves about how to plan and carry out their work, they prove to be substantially more resilient in the face of high levels of work pressure (Karasek and Theorell, 1990; Johnson and Johansson, 1991; Marmot and Wilkinson, 1999). It is jobs that combine high demand with low control that pose the highest health risks. This has been shown with respect to self-reported stress, blood pressure levels, and risk of cardiovascular disease.

Insecure Work

A final factor that is likely to restrict opportunities for social participation is job insecurity. While more extreme visions of the growth of a large permanently insecure sector of the labour market are (with the exception of Spain) unsupported to date by evidence, there has been some increase in recent decades in temporary jobs, a widespread experience of unemployment, and a rise in perceived job insecurity.

By 1997 11 per cent of male and 13 per cent of female employees were in temporary jobs in the EU as a whole (European Commission, 1999a). In several EU countries there was a marked rise between the 1980s and 1990s in the proportion in temporary jobs: it was particularly spectacular in Spain, but it was also evident in France, Ireland, Italy, and the Netherlands (and among men in Denmark, Germany, and the UK).

Those sceptical of the view that there has been an increase in insecurity point to the fact that these contractual changes have not led to any overall change in the stability of jobs, as indicated by job tenure. Job tenure varies considerably between the EU countries (it is shortest in the UK and Denmark and longest in Italy, followed by Belgium, Portugal and France). But an analysis by the OECD (OECD, 1997: 140) of *changes* in job tenure between the mid 1980s and the mid 1990s found that there was little change in nine out of ten countries (the exception being Spain). Broadly similar findings were found for the EU countries between 1995 and 2000 (European Commission, 2001c). It must be borne in mind, however, that while often taken as a proxy of security, job tenure is a questionable indicator in this respect. It reflects employee choice in the form of voluntary departures as well as factors such as contract termination and redundancy. Similar patterns of job tenure may represent very different degrees of experienced labour market insecurity depending on how easy or difficult people find the transitions between jobs.

The main factor that has led to a marked rise in the experience of labour market insecurity in the last two decades has been the periodic return of levels of unemployment unprecedented since the interwar period. In 1996, among those who were currently employees, one in five had experienced a spell of unemployment in the previous five years (Employment in Europe Survey), and of these 56 per cent had had a spell of unemployment that lasted six months or more.

This helps account for the considerable rise in *perceived* job insecurity. While job tenures may have changed little, the transition between jobs was more likely to be associated with a spell of unemployment, leaving a lasting sense of anxiety about job stability. Satisfaction with job security fell in almost all countries in the first half of the 1990s (OECD, 1997). Security only rose clearly in two countries—Finland (which had exceptionally low levels in the early 90s) and Ireland (which had entered a phase of rapid improvement in its unemployment rate). Job security in the EU remained in general higher than in the US, although the levels were similar to the US in Germany and lower in both the UK and France. Again it was particularly those in less skilled occupational positions who suffer most from job insecurity (Table 4.5). Consistently, in most countries the low-skilled represent a disproportionately large share of the unemployed, with unemployment risks three or four times higher than those of the more skilled (Nickell and Bell, 1997). Even among those currently in jobs, the low-skilled are twice as likely as professional and managerial employees to have had an experience of unemployment in the previous five years (Table 4.5).

Table 4.5 Occupational class, average job tenure and satisfaction with job security

Occupational Class	Percentage 'highly satisfied' with job security	Percentage with experience of unemployment in previous 5 years
Professional/managerial	48.0	14.4
Lower non-manual	45.8	16.7
Tech/supervisory	44.9	16.6
Skilled manual	38.7	27.5
Non-skilled	34.9	27.9

Note: high satisfaction with job security is defined as points 6 and 7 on a 7-point scale in which point 7 is defined as 'completely satisfied'. The figures for both security and unemployment experience relate to people currently in employment.

Quality of Work and Non-Work Life

EU employees who are in poor jobs are more likely to experience deprivation not only in their work lives but also in their non-work lives (Table 4.6). Those who are in jobs that did not maintain learning skills not only enjoy their work less, but they also have less satisfactory experience of their out-of-work lives. They are less satisfied with their family lives, their leisure activities at home and their social lives. Financial constraints also have substantial implications for the quality of people's lives. Those who have difficulty making ends meet have lower levels of satisfaction with their family lives, with their home

Table 4.6 Job characteristics and satisfaction with life domains (Percentage very satisfied)

	Work	Family	Home leisure	Social life	Life in general
Job requires regular learning					
Not at all true	30.1	40.9	23.8	24.5	25.3
A little true	33.5	41.0	27.3	28.0	24.8
Quite true	38.8	48.0	31.1	32.7	34.9
Very true	54.2	55.9	36.7	38.0	41.7
Financial difficulty					
Not difficult	45.9	52.2	36.2	35.5	39.1
Quite difficult	31.0	38.4	21.9	20.7	20.2
Very difficult	29.7	36.8	23.8	18.9	17.7
Work stressful					
<always/often	42.2	44.3	28.2	29.0	29.5
Always/often	31.8	41.3	20.4	23.2	23.9
Job contract					
3 years +	40.3	46.7	26.4	28.6	28.9
1–3 years	32.8	36.9	24.5	26.7	26.6
<1 year	22.2	29.1	21.1	30.1	19.0
Chance of losing job in next 12 months					
Not likely	42.7	44.6	26.2	28.5	28.2
Quite/very likely	20.6	28.3	19.9	22.3	13.8

Source: Employment in Europe Survey, 1996.

leisure and social lives. Taking an overall measure of life satisfaction, only 18 per cent of those under severe financial constraints are 'very satisfied' compared to 39 per cent of those who are not in financial difficulty.

Work stress also clearly cuts into home life. As well as reducing satisfaction with the job, it reduces satisfaction with family, leisure, and social life, and is associated with lower overall life satisfaction scores. An important component of the intensity of work is the number of hours that people work. Apart from their direct effects on tiredness and nervous strain, long and unpredictable work hours are disruptive of family activities. Data from the Employment in Europe survey show that over a third (37.4 per cent) of those who work 45 hours or more feel that their job prevents them from having the time they want with their partner and family, whereas this is the case for only 11.6 per cent of those working less than 35 hours. Similarly, 36.5 per cent of those working very long hours report that they are too tired after work to do the things they would like to do at home, compared with 17.7 per cent of those working less than 35 hours. This is clearly a potential source of tension within the family. Those who work 45 hours or more are more than twice (18.8 per cent) as likely as those working either less than 35 hours (8.0 per cent) or between 35 and 44 hours (9.0 per cent) to say that their partner always or often gets fed up with the pressure of their job.

Finally, it is clear that job insecurity is closely related to people's broader satisfaction with different life domains. Whether one takes the actual experience of unemployment, the length of the contract, or people's beliefs about the likelihood that they will lose their job involuntarily over the next twelve months, the picture is very much the same. Lack of security is associated with lower satisfaction both with the work situation and with life outside of work.

The destructive effect of unemployment on people's psychological well-being and family lives has been well documented (Warr, 1987; Gallie *et al.*, 1993; Whelan *et al.*, 1991; Gallie and Russell, 1998). But those in temporary jobs are also less satisfied with their job,[5] with their family life, with their leisure life, and with life as a whole (Table 4.6). Moreover, the shorter the term of the contract, the lower the satisfaction. The causal effect of temporary work is confirmed by longitudinal research. European panel data has shown that changes from temporary to permanent status affect job satisfaction (European Commission, 2001*c*), while British longitudinal research has shown that non-standard contracts reduce men's (although not women's) psychological well-being (Bardasi and Francesconi, 2000). A very similar

---

[5] See also the evidence from the European Community Household Survey, reported in European Commission (2001*c*: 68).

pattern emerges for those who thought they were at risk of unemployment, although in this case the adverse effects are also evident for people's social lives.

Such patterns of association cannot in themselves establish causality. However, earlier longitudinal research has shown that the degree of decision latitude that people have at work spills over onto the quality of their non-work lives (Kohn and Schooler, 1983). Moreover, the general negative effect of insecurity on psychological well-being is supported by longitudinal research. Analysis of the European Community Household Panel has shown that people's level of satisfaction with their activity status is driven predominantly by labour market transitions into or out of unemployment (European Commission, 2001c). Earlier research had shown that the psychological pressures associated with unemployment set in from the time that people know that their jobs are at risk (Warr, 1987: 149–51).

Poor quality of work then is detrimental not only for people's capacity for self-development through work, but also for the quality of non-work activities and for people's general psychological well being. It is clear, then, that low quality of work does not provide social integration in the sense that is usually understood but rather a restricted form of social participation. Its negative implications for non-work life are also of great importance in relation to the issues raised in Chapters 2 and 3, with respect to gender relations, family life, and children's cognitive development. It thereby risks undermining the supportive nature of the family for children and to make it more difficult to establish balanced roles between the sexes.

Employment Disadvantage in the Life Course

Poor Jobs: Temporary Transitions to Better Work or Persistent Disadvantage?

The importance of such negative job characteristics for life chances clearly depends on their persistence over time. If there is a great deal of upward job mobility, they will amount principally to short-term inconvenience. But if people remain in such jobs for any length of time, or if the main transitions they experience are to even less favourable labour market situations such as unemployment, they are likely to become sources of entrapment that will curtail their capacity for self-development and social participation.

The view that there is considerable job mobility has been mainly argued in terms of people's experience of low pay. Although there is a great deal of variation between countries, in most countries studied a considerable majority of the low-paid would appear to move out of this situation in a period of five years (Sloane and Theodossiou, 2000). But there are three important reservations about such evidence. First, British data suggest that the low-paid consist of rather different groups. Much of the mobility can be accounted for by people who move out after only a very short period indeed. However, longitudinal analysis shows that the chances of moving out of low-paid employment fall very rapidly with increased duration of time in low-paid jobs (Stewart, 1999). Second, the extent of income mobility is very limited: those who move out of 'low-paid' work while remaining in employment tend to receive only minor increases in earnings. Finally, a considerable proportion of those who move out do not enter higher paid jobs but move into unemployment or economic inactivity. Nearly half of the low-paid (45 per cent) were 'permanent low-paid' over a four-year period if spells out of work were included (Stewart, 1999: 240). Those who leave employment fall into a 'low pay–no pay' cycle, since they have particularly high probabilities of moving back again into low-paid work when they find a new job.

It has been seen that many of the most negative aspects of jobs are associated with broad occupational class position, in particular semi- and non-skilled occupations, and with temporary contracts. Whatever the mobility with respect to low pay, the evidence certainly suggests that people tend to be trapped over time in such broad sectors of the labour market. The data from the European Community Household Panel show that the great majority (85 per cent) of those in non-skilled occupations in 1994 were in the same type of occupation in 1996. Although there was greater mobility out of temporary work, it is notable that only a third of those in temporary work were in permanent jobs after a year, while 20 per cent had become unemployed or economically inactive (European Commission, 2001c).[6] This suggests very limited mobility out of the poor quality job sector.

Sources of Cumulative Employment Disadvantage

Why should this be the case? It is clear that prevailing systems of adult skill formation tend to reinforce rather than to compensate for early disadvantage. As was argued in Chapter 2, those brought up in disadvantaged families

---

[6] Rather similar results were found for mobility out of 'dead-end' jobs more broadly defined in terms of low security and lack of training, with only 24 per cent moving into jobs of 'good' or 'reasonable' quality in the following year, while 26 per cent became either unemployed or economically inactive (European Commission, 2001c: 77). However, transitions into better work varied substantially by country (as was the case for transitions from temporary to permanent work).

have a much higher risk of obtaining poor educational qualifications, thereby heavily restricting their opportunities in the labour market to the less skilled and less secure job sector. However, the cumulative nature of disadvantage does not stop there; it continues through the working career (and indeed spills over from the working career to people's resources and opportunities in retirement). Once people have entered low-skilled jobs they find far fewer opportunities for upgrading their skills than are available to people in more skilled work. As a result, over time, they are likely to suffer an accumulating skill deficit, given the rapid processes of upskilling in the rest of the workforce, which both acts as a source of entrapment in the poor job sector and leaves them highly exposed to job loss in periods of economic restructuring.

Taking the workforce as a whole, there is substantial evidence of a long-term process of skill upgrading in the EU countries. This is evident in changes in the composition of the occupational structure, with the expansion of professional/managerial occupations and the decline of manual work. In the UK, for instance, where there is broadly comparable data over a century, manual workers declined from 75 per cent of the workforce in 1911 to 38 per cent in 1991, while professionals rose from 4 per cent to 19 per cent (Gallie, 2000). It is also clear that at least in recent decades there has been a substantial process of upskilling *within* occupations that has affected a wide sector of the workforce. Overall, the Employment in Europe survey showed that half of EU employees had experienced a significant increase in the level of skill used in their job the last five years (Table 4.7). In contrast, only a very small proportion (6.8 per cent) had experienced deskilling.

This sharp rise in skill demands is likely to have reflected a number of factors. It was a period in which heightened competitiveness led to a stronger emphasis on product quality. Employers were seeking to reduce numbers and increase flexibility, which required an extension of multi-skilling. But perhaps most crucially, this was a decade that saw the rapid spread of information and computer technologies. By the mid-1990s, nearly half (46.8 per cent) of the EU workforce were in jobs that involved some use of computerized or automated equipment and a quarter (24.7 per cent) spent more than half their time at work using such equipment. Among those who did use computerized equipment, 59 per cent had seen an increase in the skills used in their jobs, whereas this was the case for only 42 per cent of other employees. Technological factors would appear to be even more important than industry exposure to international trade in driving up skill levels (Green *et al.*, 1999).

But, with respect to the risk of social exclusion, the crucial point to note is that one occupational class fared much less well in this general context of rapidly rising skills, namely that of semi- and non-skilled workers (Table 4.7). A majority of professional/managerial workers (58 per cent), lower non-manual employees (55 per cent), technicians and associates (54 per cent) and even skilled manual workers (52 per cent) experienced upskilling. But, this was the case for only a minority (41 per cent) of the semi- and non-skilled workforce. It was not that there was widespread deskilling in these categories but rather that there had been little or no change in skills. This points to a polarizing occupational structure in which the great majority of the workforce was experiencing skill upgrading, while the low-skilled were left progressively behind.

The poor opportunities for skill development for people in low-skilled work are reinforced by the pattern of in-career training provided by employers. Taking those who had experienced one week or more training in the previous five years, it is notable that only a small proportion of the European work-force (26 per cent) had received any significant formal training over this

Table 4.7 Occupational class and experiences of skill change and employer training in the last 5 years (EU employees)

	Significant increase in skill requirements	1 week+training from employer
Class		
Professional/managerial	57.6	42.0
Lower non-manual	55.2	21.8
Tech/supervisory	53.7	32.6
Skilled manual	51.6	16.1
Non-skilled	40.5	14.3
All employees	50.3	26.0
Size of Workplace		
Works alone	44.2	16.9
<10 people	48.5	19.0
10–99 people	49.1	25.8
100–499 people	48.4	35.7
500+ people	52.1	39.8

Source: Employment in Europe Survey, 1996.

period.[7] But equally striking is the extent to which this is stratified by skill level (Table 4.7). Nearly half (42 per cent) of those in professional and managerial occupations had received a week or more training, compared to only 16 per cent of skilled manual workers and 14 per cent of semi- and non-skilled workers.

Lack of skill development is accentuated by a number of other factors. There is a marked gradient by age, with older workers less likely than younger to have experienced an increase in their skills or to have received significant periods of training. This may reflect reluctance by employers to invest in the skill development of employees with relatively few years left in the organization before retirement. Alternatively, older workers may lack the self-confidence or motivation to learn new skills. Whichever the case, the pattern implies a growing risk for older workers of falling behind in an economy of rapidly changing skills. While they may be protected temporarily by employment in specific organizational niches, they are likely to be highly vulnerable in periods of economic restructuring, where their skills may no longer be sufficiently up-to-date to switch to jobs in other organizations.

Part-time employees are also less likely to have experienced skill development (44 per cent compared to 52 per cent of full-timers). This is true within each occupational class. Since part-timers are overwhelming female, this implies a significant gender disadvantage. Again differences in skill development experiences are closely related to differences in training opportunities. Whereas 28 per cent of full-time employees had received at least a week's training, this was the case for only 16 per cent of part-timers.

Finally opportunities for employer training are heavily affected by the size of the workplace in which people are employed (Table 4.7). In large workplaces, employers are more likely to have the infrastructural resources (such as personnel departments) to lay on training programmes and where there are larger numbers it is also likely to be easier to provide cover arrangements while people are absent on training. Employees in the largest organizations have roughly twice the chances of training of those in the smallest. In workplaces with less than ten employees, only 19 per cent of employees have received training, while in those with 500 or more employees, the figure rises to 40 per cent.

---

[7] The data from the European Community Household Panel show that, even taking both employer-provided training and private training measures, only 28 per cent of the employed had participated in training measures in the previous year. There was a sharp contrast by skill, with 40 per cent of the high skilled, compared with 17 per cent of the low-skilled participating in training (European Commission, 2001c: 73).

In short, those who enter low-skilled employment find themselves to a significant degree caught in a skills trap. They find it difficult to get access to the types of in-work training and informal skill development that would allow them to escape from the poor job sector. These problems are particularly acute for those who are older workers, part-time employees or employed in small establishments. An effective set of policies for social integration needs then to take into account not simply the quantity of jobs, but also of the importance of providing jobs that give people the opportunity to extend their skills and to move into better quality work.

Where insufficient provision is made to update skills, the lower skilled are likely to find it increasingly difficult to remain in employment. Where the demands of work lead either to physical disability or to sustained psychological stress, then people may be forced to leave employment before the formal retirement age. In systems where pensions vary with time spent in employment, this in turn may lead to inadequate pension provision and the risk of poverty in retirement.

Skill Deficit, Unemployment, and Labour Market Reintegration

There are then strong forces leading to the perpetuation of the disadvantage of people in low-skilled work. Perhaps the most severe of all is their considerably enhanced risk of becoming unemployed. For unemployment then sets in motion another dynamic, which accentuates the problems of skill deficit and leads to yet further decline in people's position in the labour market.

It was seen earlier that the risks of unemployment are very much higher for the low-skilled. This reflects both macro-structural change and the nature of skill formation in work. Sectoral and technological change has led to a marked decline over time in the prevalence of manual jobs and particularly low-skilled manual jobs. Those in lower-skilled jobs have typically had much lower levels of general education and during their careers have received far less training from their employers. They are then poorly placed both to update their skills over time and to adjust to changes in the labour market. This clearly greatly increases their vulnerability to unemployment and their difficulties in re-finding work in an employment structure that is characterized by a continuous process of upskilling of job tasks.

The main response to this problem has been to multiply and generalize special training and work experience programmes for the unemployed. In the past, European countries have differed substantially in terms of the relative emphasis they gave to active and passive labour market policies. Sweden was much earlier involved in active intervention than other countries and indeed even in the mid-1990s still spent considerably more on such measures as a proportion of GDP than most other countries. The variations were and still are very substantial. In the mid-1980s, Sweden spent 2.2 per cent of GDP on active measures, whereas Greece spent a mere 0.2 per cent and Spain 0.3 per cent. In the mid-1990s, the Swedish figure had risen to 3.2 per cent, whereas that for Greece had scarcely changed (0.3 per cent). However, taking the overall picture, there was a rise from the 1980s to the 1990s in expenditure on active measures in the majority of the European countries.

At the same time, there has been a general shift in many countries towards some version of the 'workfare' principle whereby financial assistance to the unemployed has been made conditional upon accepting work. As Loedemel and Hickey (2001) have pointed out the notion of 'workfare' can cover a very wide range of institutional realities (for instance, a much stronger version was applied in Norway than in Denmark, France, the Netherlands, Germany, and the UK). Schemes differ in the relative emphasis placed on longer-term human resource development rather than on immediate job placement. Danish schemes for instance reflected a greater priority to integration and human resource development, while the Norwegian were more concerned with labour market discipline and job placement. Nevertheless generally such programmes have tended to be justified and judged in terms of their success rates in getting people back into jobs in a relatively short space of time. This is likely to impose constraints on the extent to which they can cater for longer-term skill development needs, since the training required is likely to have very slow returns in terms of job acquisition.

One feature of the programmes is that they are usually specifically for the unemployed. This is understandable in terms of the distinctive nature of many of their short term objectives (for instance developing skills in the presentation of CVs and in techniques of job search). It also imposes some limits on the financial commitment that would be involved if they were more widely open say to those who were non-active. But it runs the risk that participation reinforces the stigmatic character of unemployment. They represent in a sense a formal recognition of failure on the labour market.

There has been little rigorous assessment of the most recent wave of 'workfare-style' reintegration programmes. The very comprehensive nature of the new 'workfare' policies, which in principle are supposed to be applied to all people in a given category, make evaluation difficult, since there is no longer a comparison group of non-participants available. But we know from careful analyses of 'partial' schemes that, while they do appear to have some effect, its extent is disappointingly small. For instance, the evaluation of the effects of the British government's major 'Training for Work' programme for the unemployed over the period 1995–7 showed that, compared to equivalent non-participants, those who had taken part in the scheme spent one extra month in seven in work and this advantage was maintained for at least a year and a half after training (Payne *et al.*, 1999). This was not simply a matter of a higher proportion of people being channelled into part-time or temporary work. But, taking the hourly wage people received, it was certainly not evident that people secured a more skilled job than those who had not participated. The rather limited effects in terms of longer-term employment stability and the quality of jobs that people obtained found in this study confirm those from the evaluation of earlier programmes (White, 1998).

Perhaps the most worrying aspect of the results to date on the jobs acquired by the unemployed is their very low level of stability. Across the EU the unemployed have a very high probability of moving into temporary jobs. UK longitudinal research has shown that the typical duration of the jobs taken by the unemployed is substantially lower than that of new jobs taken by people already in employment. The main causes of this shorter job tenure are vulnerability to lay-offs and the prevalence of temporary contracts (Boheim and Taylor, 2000). Of the jobs taken by the unemployed 14 per cent end through quits, 22 per cent with lay-offs and 24 per cent through the termination of a temporary contract. Individuals who enter a job from unemployment are four times more likely to be laid off than those entering from another job and three times more likely to be in temporary employment (ibid.: 13, 15).

Stability of employment is likely to be heavily conditioned by the quality of the jobs people get. The classic evaluation studies tell us relatively little about the nature of the jobs that people obtain. But if these involve routine work, low pay, poor work conditions, limited opportunities for skill development, and job insecurity, people are likely to find themselves trapped in a sector of employment that also heavily constrains their ability to participate in the activities of the community. Such programmes can only be judged to have made a substantial contribution to reintegration if they provide people with the skills that make it possible to escape from the secondary employment sector. The provision of real choices that offer people the prospect of more stable and long-lasting careers is also likely to be important for the motivation of the unemployed to be involved in such programmes. There may be a resistance to the idea of participation in a programme that is perceived as a form of 'cooling out', attempting to make them reduce their aspirations for a job providing interesting work and good employment conditions.

As can be seen from Table 4.8, the jobs occupied by people with previous experience of unemployment are in several respects of even worse quality

Table 4.8 Characteristics of current jobs by experience of unemployment in previous 5 years (EU skilled manual and non-skilled employees only)

	Not unemployed	< 6 months	6 months+
Current contract <3 years	5.6	21.9	27.3
Job very or quite insecure	29.1	51.2	54.7
Risks unemployed in 12 mths	4.9	16.8	14.8
Learns on job (very true)	19.3	19.6	20.1
Received employer training	26.6	19.4	25.7
Completely/very satisfied with job	36.7	26.0	24.7
No variety in work	19.9	23.5	30.1
No say over way job is done	23.9	29.0	27.9
No participation in decisions that affect work	26.9	30.2	36.9

Source: Employment in Europe Survey, 1996.

than those typical of people at the same occupational level (skilled manual and non-skilled occupations). The previously unemployed are at least four times as likely to be in jobs with short-term contracts and at least three times as likely to think that there is a high probability that they will become unemployed within the following twelve months. They are in jobs with lower variety and giving fewer opportunities either for the exercise of initiative in the work or participation in decisions affecting the work. Furthermore, as with jobs more generally at this skill level, they offer very low chances of self-development through either learning on the job or employer training. These are not, then, the types of jobs that could be expected either to reverse long-term skill deficiencies or to provide the motivation and security required to ensure employment stability.[8]

Overall, then, there are good grounds for thinking that there are deeply entrenched skill deficiency barriers to sustained labour market reintegration. Given the trends in the job structure towards higher skills, longer-term employability depends crucially on access to opportunities for skill development. The unemployed typically come from jobs where there were very

---

[8] Very similar results emerge from longitudinal analyses of the European Community Household Panel, which show that of those previously unemployed who take up a job, two-thirds take up a job of relatively poor quality (European Commission, 2001c: 78).

limited opportunities for updating skills or indeed retaining basic learning skills. While considerable effort is put into short-term remedial programmes for people when they become unemployed, they are poorly placed to engage in any intensive retraining. Moreover, they typically return to jobs that are more insecure and poorer in overall quality than those of people in the same occupational classes. These are jobs that are characterized by very poor opportunities for training and thus perpetuate the labour market vulnerability that comes from low skill levels. Sustained reintegration clearly requires much more extended processes of skill development than are likely to be achieved under these conditions.

In the longer term, the foundations for a more highly skilled workforce need to be set by a much greater investment in tackling educational disadvantage in early life (see Chapter 2). But the impact of such changes inevitably will be slow and, given the rate of technical change, they will need to be reinforced by mechanisms that ensure that skills are continuously updated. An effective strategy for tackling skills deficiencies in the current workforce requires a more systematic effort to improve the quality of lower skilled work, so that learning skills are maintained and developed over people's working lives.

Welfare and Work: The Future Agenda

It is clear that, while undoubtedly an important precondition for improving the situation of those who are marginalized, employment does not in itself resolve the problems of social inclusion. Many jobs do not provide people with the opportunities for self-development that are necessary to participate adequately either at work or in the community, there are trends in the developing forms of work organization that increase the vulnerability of low-skilled groups to social exclusion and the provision of a job to those that have experienced unemployment does not ensure longer-term employability. What does this imply in terms of the types of social policies that are needed to provide effective social inclusion?

A central conclusion of this chapter is that the traditional social policy emphasis with respect to labour market problems, which has focused primarily on remedial measures in the context of labour market failure, needs to be accompanied by a much more active preventative policy. In particular, there is a need for a European-level programme for the improvement of the quality of working life. There are two core aspects to this: first an improvement in the quality of work conditions to provide more adequate opportunities for self-development for the low-skilled and effective mechanisms to prevent the escalation of levels of work stress; second, a major expansion of in-career training provision. While such a programme will have initial costs, it must be seen in terms of a social investment that is likely to have very considerable medium and longer-term rewards. It will not eliminate job insecurity, although it will reduce the risks that loss of employment will lead to eventual labour market marginalization. It must then be accompanied by a marked improvement in measures to support those in positions of job insecurity and to ease employment transitions. The objective of creating greater flexibility in employment is more likely to be realised if there is seen to be adequate institutional support for those affected by job insecurity.

Improving the Quality of Work

A substantial proportion of jobs in the EU do not offer the types of opportunities for personal development, intrinsic job interest, adequate income, or reasonable stability that are assumed by those who emphasize the integrative potential of employment. The problem is very widespread in semi- and non-skilled occupations, but it is particularly acute in part-time non-skilled jobs and among older workers in non-skilled jobs. There are also many indications that recent decades have seen a marked intensification of work, as a result of staffing reductions, pressure for higher quality standards, and rapid organizational change. It is likely that this underlies the high levels of reported work stress, a problem that is becoming increasingly recognized at European level (European Commission, 2000f). Work stress is clearly accentuated by excessively long hours of work by many employees and by the problems that people confront in reconciling the demands of their work and family lives. A continuation of current trends is likely to pose substantial problems of premature withdrawal from the workforce and will certainly act as a major barrier to attempts to extend work careers. In the longer run, this can only add to the difficulties faced by welfare systems in providing adequate social protection for those in retirement (see Chapter 5).

The development of effective protection against poor work task quality and potentially hazardous levels of stress poses new challenges for the development of policies of health and safety at work. In the past, these have been primarily designed to reduce physical risks and it is likely that they have been an important factor in the major decline in deaths and serious physical injuries at work. But policy has failed to keep up with the changing nature of work risks, which require quite different methods of assessment and control. Some Northern European countries have been experimenting with ways of improving work organization and task quality and there is some tentative evidence that these may have had a real impact (see, for instance, Gustavsen *et al.*, 1996). New measures need to be developed, which build upon these experiences, and ensure their integration into basic employment norms.

Any effective policy approach to improving the quality of work would require action at several levels. National governments and the EU would need to take responsibility for enhancing the salience of the issue, diffusing information about best practices and establishing a set of social indicators, derived from high quality representative national surveys, that will show trends over time in employees reports of, and satisfaction with, the different aspects of their working conditions. The feasibility of developing sensible indicators of working conditions has now been established. What is lacking is the investment to provide comparative survey samples of the size and quality that are required to provide reliable evidence about trends over time and to allow sufficient disaggregation to inform policy making about key subgroups.

A first important step in this direction has been taken by the Commission with the publication in June 2001 of the Communication, *Employment and Social Policies: A Framework for Investing in Quality* (European Commission 2001*a*). In the wake of the calls in the Lisbon, Nice, and Stockholm Councils for the modernization of the European Social Model and for greater concern with issues of quality, it argues for the need to establish a set of common indicators that would track changes over time in both the characteristics of jobs and the wider work and labour market contexts. It proposes the creation of indicators relating to ten broad domains: intrinsic job quality; skills, life-long learning, and career development; gender equality; health and safety at work; flexibility and security; inclusion and access to the labour market; work organization and work–life balance; social dialogue and worker involvement; diversity and non-discrimination; and finally overall economic performance and productivity. This is clearly a potentially vast programme, covering a much wider field than that dealt with in this chapter. Hard choices will doubtless have to be taken about priorities and careful thought will be needed about the meaning and adequacy of specific indicators. The quality of available indicators is very variable, and the assumption that existing data sources will suffice could lead to the selection of inadequate measures of the underlying issues of interest. But the general approach is clearly in the right direction.

Implementation of changes will necessarily operate at a decentralized level. There are now some widely recognized general principles about the way in which job characteristics affect the experience of work. But the implementation of improvements to the work environment will vary with the specific work situation and will depend for their effectiveness upon the nature of intra-organizational decision-making processes. This underlines the importance of recent developments with respect to participation procedures and the need for them to be adequately resourced. There is now a great deal of research that shows that organizational change is most effective in meeting employee needs and enhancing employee satisfaction when it is introduced through a participative process. Improvement in the quality of work conditions should be an integral and explicit part of the extension of procedures for employee participation. Further, meaningful participation requires not only that employees should be consulted but also that they should have access to up-to-date knowledge. A system will need to be established to ensure that employee representatives have the necessary time and funding to obtain relevant training.

In the longer term, effective action could well require the generalization of a system of periodic 'health audits' in organizations, which will provide for an external evaluation of an organization's strategy in relationship to both physical and psychological health, of the internal system for monitoring working conditions, and of the internal procedures for acting upon issues that are likely to be detrimental to the health of employees (in the broad sense of the term). Such audits would require organizations to develop systematic risk assessments, which would clearly need to take account of employees' reports of their jobs and working conditions, as part of the evidence collected. As well as providing a strong incentive to organizations to improve their practices, such audits would provide a means for the diffusion of best practice information to individual work organizations. Such a system would require the development of specialized health-audit organizations that would be licensed to assess and approve company policies.

With respect to the pressures facing older workers, attention needs to be given to the possibility of encouraging transitions from full-time to part-time work. If governments seriously wish to increase the labour force participation of older workers, they may need to encourage the extension of contractual rights to reduce working time for people of a given age or with specific types of disability. We need to move from a system that largely provides for abrupt transitions between work and retirement to one that allows a smooth and progressive transition that favours both the optimum use of people's skills and a work regime that is adapted to individuals' physical well-being.

Maintaining and Developing Workforce Skills

The rapidly changing nature of skills in advanced economies accentuates the risk of marginalization of those who do not have access to regular training opportunities. Current skill development and training opportunities are heavily stratified and in-career training for both skilled manual and semi- and non-skilled employees is very poor across the European Union. It is also evident that there is a major problem of ensuring adequate training provision in small firms. Failure to provide for regular updating of skills increases the risk of long-term exclusion if people become unemployed, since they may well have lost many of their basic learning skills. An adequate social policy should be one in which ongoing opportunities for skill improvement are seen as an essential aspect of socially responsible employment.

It is clear that adequate training provision does not emerge as a spontaneous outcome of current employment relationships. This is doubtless partly because of the significant short-term costs for both employers and employees. For employers, training involves immediate costs both in terms of organization and personnel, as well as the loss of work time. For the employee, there are substantial financial costs if training is not directly funded by the employer and there is the non-financial cost of an additional burden on already strained time budgets. Employers then are likely only to provide training where it is perceived to be most crucial to the organization, thereby producing the heavy concentration on higher skilled employees. Employees that are excluded from employer provision are unlikely to be in a position to compensate through personal training initiatives. The extension of a more pervasive system of training provision, that will help reduce the longer-term social costs of current arrangements, will require new types of policy and a significant investment of public resources.

The cornerstone of the development of an effective training policy must lie in some system of citizen's training entitlement. This would both greatly enhance the salience of the issue and provide the stimulus for the development of appropriate institutional mechanisms. Individuals should be able to build up training credits across time that will provide a guarantee both of time for training outside the workplace (without risk to employment) and of access to financial resources that will give adequate protection of their living standards for the training period. Such credits would need to be portable between employers. Individuals should be able to have a significant choice in the way that such training credits are used. While courses would need to be certified as vocationally relevant, they would not necessarily be linked to the specific needs of the current employer. Employers could however influence the incentives for particular directions of training, for instance through provision for skills-based pay increments.

While there could be diverse funding formulas for such a programme, it would be unlikely to prove effective without substantial state subsidies for training non-skilled and older workers. This needs to be accompanied by a major programme of development work on the training practices that are best adapted to the needs of such workers. It is clear that there are many problems that are specific to these categories of workers—such as enhancing competences in situations of disability and addressing underlying problems of learning skills—which are not catered for by conventional training provision and require individualized assistance. There are already experiments in this direction in Denmark and the Netherlands that would be worth careful assessment (Guillemard and de Vroom, 2001). More generally, the extension of training provision would need to be supported by a network of specialist advice centres that could provide assessments of individual needs and information about the most suitable opportunities.

Such credit entitlements would be only one aspect of the more general training provision. A great deal of training already occurs in a relatively informal way at work and the issue is how to build upon this in a way that institutionalizes a dynamic training culture in the workplace. Employers in many countries have taken steps to improve the monitoring of individual training needs through systems of individual appraisal. But in the longer term, the salience of training issues and the development of effective organizational policies would be best enhanced by making it a central component of issues that are subject to processes of consultation. This underlines again the importance of the development of participative procedures as a mechanism for improving the quality of working conditions in the broad sense of the term.

One of the most difficult problems that needs to be addressed in improving training provision is that of the relatively low levels of training in small firms. There are clearly major structural obstacles here in terms of the organizational resources available to develop training strategies and deliver adequate training provision. The solution clearly lies in the development of some type of shared training resource, on a geographical or sectoral basis, which would enable small organizations to make economies in terms of the provision and training staff. Many of the skills required, especially in the middle and lower echelons of organizations are of a relatively general type—for instance the development of information technology skills—and could be well catered for on this basis. However, given the co-ordination problems, small organizations are likely to find it difficult to create such structures themselves and hence any such institutional development will require active public intervention.

The Affordability of a Quality of Working Life Strategy

Inevitably proposals for the improvement of the quality of working and employment conditions in low-skilled jobs raise the issue of cost. Can this be achieved without either making such jobs too costly to be attractive to employers or imposing unacceptable burdens on governmental budgets? Is there a necessary trade-off between a greater number of poor quality and a smaller number of better quality jobs?

A first point to note is that, in terms of the costs associated with job design and work conditions, perhaps the most important resource that such a programme requires is not a major investment in the technical infrastructure of firms, but managerial knowledge and skills in the organization of work. This is likely to involve ensuring access to information and stimulating motivation rather than high cost. Second, available evidence suggests that the types of reforms in job design that are emphasized here have major positive implications with respect to both the commitment and health of employees. They tend to be associated with lower absentee and turnover rates, both of which involve high costs in term of discontinuity in production and service provision and new recruitment costs. At the same time, they involve a more effective mobilization of workforce knowledge and are likely to be associated with higher quality work performance. They may well then be associated with improved rather than diminished competitiveness. Certainly, countries (such as Sweden and Denmark) that have moved ahead most strongly in this direction do not seem to have suffered in terms of relative economic performance.

The improvement of mechanisms to provide safeguards for employee health (psychological as well as physical) through a system of health audits may certainly increase costs of management time and may potentially reduce the short-term financial advantages that can be obtained through very intensive exploitation of the workforce in terms of hours and work pressure. However, there is a long tradition of research in industrial psychology that has shown that exceptionally long and intense patterns of working have high costs in terms of diminished quality of performance, leaving it doubtful whether they do provide economic gains over time compared to systems of work organization better geared to employee health needs. Further, any sensible system of overall cost calculation would need to take into account the very high costs that poor work conditions impose on society more generally in terms of the need to provide care for the victims of industrial injury.

Finally, a major extension of in-career training is certainly likely to involve substantial *initial* costs, both in terms of the provision of training and work days forgone, even though the burden of these will depend upon the ways in which such reforms are phased in. But this is a clear case where budgeting has to be seen in the context of a more extended time frame. Training is a form of social investment that will lead to major economic benefits in the longer-term. The economies of the European Union are moving remorse-lessly to a higher skill base and to ever more rapid change in techniques and working practices. The failure to provide the workforce with the capacities to meet these new challenges will result in severe skill bottlenecks and low levels of workforce flexibility in times of change, thus leading to heavy costs in terms of sub-optimal economic performance. At the same time, the provision of adequate training in the course of people's careers is likely to save very substantial costs with respect to programmes to financially maintain and reintegrate those experiencing labour market marginalization. With such a crucial form of social investment, the issue is perhaps better formulated as one of whether advanced societies can afford *not* to take such steps, given their importance for human capital development and for long-term economic flexibility and performance.

Overall, whether one takes job design, improved health and safety, or more extensive training, the view that better quality jobs are markedly more costly than poorer quality jobs is highly questionable if the full range of costs is taken into account. Good work organization and well-designed job tasks are primarily a matter of good management rather than heavy financial investment. Even in the short term there is little evidence that improvements in labour standards undermine competitiveness. Indeed it can be argued that, in certain respects, they may be beneficial for performance. It must be remembered that there are major costs to efficiency arising from extensive labour turnover, ill-health in the workforce, work systems that are poorly adapted to employees needs and low employee motivation. There are also major costs to welfare systems that have to pick up those who suffer ill-health as a result of poor work practices. In the longer run, in a steadily more technologically sophisticated and high skill environment, it is clear the performance of the EU economy will depend crucially on its willingness to invest in the skills and motivation of people, and this in turn will be heavily conditioned by the importance attached to improving the quality of working life.

Regulating Insecurity and the Reintegration of the Unemployed

A central argument of this book is that effective action against prolonged unemployment needs to begin well before an individual becomes unemployed. We need to move from a curative to a preventative concept of social policy with respect to work risks. It is the failure to update skills and to maintain learning skills that makes an individual exceptionally vulnerable at a time of employment restructuring. Improving the quality of work life, particularly with respect to opportunities for regular updating of skills, is one of the major policy measures that can be taken to ensure a more rapid and sustained reintegration of people when they become unemployed. Significant numbers of the unemployed, who in the majority of EU countries are drawn heavily from lower-skilled workers, are caught in a 'skills trap'. They come from jobs in which there is little provision for updating skills and they return to jobs that are as poor, if not poorer, than those typical of their occupational group. The current reliance on short-term remedial training and work experience programmes is not adequate to reverse years of skill fossilization and cannot compensate for the lack of on-going skill development when people return to work. It leads to a pattern where a substantial proportion of the unemployed return not to sustained employment but to precarious and poor quality jobs, where they are at risk of entering a cycle of recurrent unemployment.

But apart from underlining the necessity of much better resourced policies for maintaining skills across the career trajectory, a preventative policy also points to the need to consider carefully the regulations which condition the way in which organizations lay off their personnel. Given the stigmatic effect associated with unemployment and its negative effects on later job acquisition, the objective should be to reduce as far as possible the risks of a person becoming unemployed in the first place. There are two factors that are crucial in this: the length of advanced notice that employees get of the fact that their current job is at risk and the degree of support that they receive before the termination of their existing contracts with respect to guidance about other job opportunities and the provision of additional training to enhance their labour market position. The traditional image of redundancy is one of organizations reacting to situations of largely unanticipated crisis. But the reduction of personnel has now become a widespread policy even of highly successful and profitable firms that are engaged in strategic modifications of their operations in terms of localization or subcontracting policies. At least in this latter case, there should be very strong presumptions about the social responsibility of employers to provide a high level of support for the staff affected. This is likely to require a significant recasting of existing redundancy regulations.

A good deal of discussion about ways of limiting insecurity has focused around the issue of temporary work and a common suggestion is that it could be limited by extending controls over the use of temporary contracts. At the extreme, it is sometimes advocated that the use of such contracts should be strongly discouraged through reducing the grounds on which employers can resort to the use of temporary workers and through tight constraints on the length and renewability of such contracts. It has been seen that some of the claims about the likely trends in the growth in temporary work appear unduly alarmist and that the nature of temporary work is considerably more diverse than is often recognized. But, taking the longer-term perspective, it also has to be recognized that the objective of improved training rights (as well as improving maternity and paternity leave rights) implies that organizations will be confronted with increasing discontinuity in their staffing of specific posts. While the extension of flexible teamworking within organizations can help to offset this, it is still likely that there will be a persisting and possibly rising requirement for temporary personnel to cover organizational gaps.

Given that the need for temporary work will be driven by social as well as economic objectives, it is likely to be a persisting feature of the employment structure and the policy focus should be primarily on what can be done to improve the conditions associated with temporary work. The principal requirement is not ever-stronger restrictions on the use of temporary work, but rather better regulation of temporary work as an industry. There is no reason why temporary work agencies should not provide conditions of employment, with respect to training, holidays, consultation, and even security broadly comparable with those in other industrial sectors. Given that the demand for temporary workers is likely to move in the direction of skilled staff, with the motivation needed to provide high quality work, both user and provider employers have a long-term interest in the skill development of temporary workers. The greater the investment of employers in their personnel, the more likely they are to wish to retain their staff on a longer-term basis and the lower the insecurity of employees in this sector. The proper organization of temporary work then could do much to offset the tension between the need for greater labour flexibility and the concern to provide adequate job security.

Finally, it has to be recognized that whatever the improvements in long-term workforce training, in the management of redundancy processes, and in the employment conditions of temporary workers, the problem of recurrent crises of unemployment is unlikely to disappear from the agenda. Greater understanding of techniques of macro-economic management of the business cycle may provide greater stability in the medium term, but the advanced economies will remain exposed to relatively unpredictable external shocks in an increasingly integrated international economy. A policy that is premised exclusively on the view that the problem of the unemployed can be resolved through finding more effective ways of getting people into employment and that ignores the need to provide proper resources for those without work can only lead to unacceptable levels of poverty and distress at such times of economic difficulty. Research in the last two decades has established clearly the very high costs of unemployment in most countries in terms of both financial deprivation and psychological distress.

A European policy that is genuinely concerned about social integration will have to maintain the provision of adequate protection of living standards for the unemployed as one of its core objectives. The reluctance of some countries to do this has been rooted in the belief that relatively generous financial assistance for the unemployed inevitably poses major problems of work incentives. But the view that high levels of benefit necessarily undermine work motivation is not supported by the comparative evidence (Gallie and Paugame, 2000). Employment commitment is at least as high in societies with generous benefit systems as those with low benefit levels. Rather poverty constitutes a significant barrier to effective job search and therefore accentuates the problems of reintegration. EU societies currently differ substantially in terms of the principles underlying the provision of unemployment benefits and the level of protection they provide. The models for convergence should be those that provide higher levels of protection.

5

A New Social Contract for the Elderly?

John Myles

Introduction

The democratization of retirement must surely count as one of the great achievements of the affluent democracies in the twentieth century. *Retirement* in its contemporary sense—an extended period of labour force withdrawal driven by the accumulation of sufficient retirement 'wealth' to make work unnecessary—was, until recently, the privilege of the few. In the past, the rank and file of elderly workers were often 'retired' due to lay-offs or disability but not because work was *economically* unnecessary.[1] Even as late as the 1960s, 'old age' was a virtual synonym for poverty in many industrial democracies. All this changed in the past quarter century. Old age incomes have been rising, retirement ages have been falling, and the elimination of old age poverty is now well within the reach of most developed nations.

That today's *elderly* are also *retirees* who, on average, enjoy living standards little different from working age households (OECD, 2001*b*) is the result of two developments. Modern retirement is, in the first instance, a result of the rising affluence associated with the long post-war boom from the 1950s to the 1970s. Today's elderly are able to enjoy a relatively prosperous old age because they enjoyed prosperous working lives compared to their parents who spent their adult years in depression and war.

The *sine qua non* of modern retirement, however, was the widespread reform of public pension schemes during the post-war decades. By itself, rising incomes would have produced a growing share of older employees with sufficient wealth to allow for retirement in advance of physiological decline.

---

[1] US surveys of new retirees conducted by the Social Security Administration in the 1950s found the vast majority—90 per cent—had 'retired' because they were laid off by their last employer or due to poor health. Less than 5 per cent reported retiring voluntarily or to enjoy more leisure. By the 1980s, involuntary lay-off and poor health accounted for only 35 per cent of retirees and the majority claimed to have left work voluntarily (Burtless and Quinn, 2001: 384).

But without the post-war expansion of mandatory, universal pension schemes that essentially 'democratized' access to retirement, voluntary retirement that results from the 'wealth effect' would still be significantly skewed in favour of those with higher lifetime earnings.

In the twenty-first century, the cost of maintaining the status quo will escalate substantially as a result of population ageing brought about by continued gains in life expectancy and by lower fertility. The net effect is that the ratio of retirees to workers will rise dramatically in the decades ahead: fewer working age adults will be supporting more elderly adults. With very few exceptions, fertility rates in the developed countries have fallen below replacement levels so that, when combined with increasing longevity, the phenomenon of population ageing is likely to continue even after the baby boom works its way through the demographic age structure.

Demography is producing a qualitative as well as quantitative change among the elderly. The fraction of the elderly most at risk of disability, the 'oldest old' (80+), has been growing much faster than the elderly population in general. As importantly, the capacity of the traditional pool of informal care givers (elderly wives, daughters, and daughters-in-law) who provide about three-quarters of all care to the frail elderly (OECD, 1996: 63) is declining relative to this increased demand. Social policy has traditionally focused on the needs for income security and mainstream (i.e. acute) health care. Care for the chronically ill, the physically frail, and the mentally confused elderly is a policy challenge that few nations have begun to meet (ibid.).

It is widely recognized that a second factor, independent of demography, has been raising 'retirement' costs in the affluent nations, namely the falling age of retirement. Part of this decline might be expected simply as a result of rising affluence (the 'wealth effect') so that more workers now acquire sufficient retirement wealth to exit from the labour force at earlier ages. But it is equally clear that a significant share of the decline has been 'policy induced' by both firms and governments. As a result, many older workers face a situation where continued employment simply 'doesn't pay.' These institutional factors clearly vary among countries. We think it unlikely that one could account for the enormous variation in employment rates among the affluent democracies (Table 5.1) simply by reference to national differences in living standards, health status, labour demand, or cultural preferences.[2]

---

[2] We hasten to add, however, that institutions profoundly shape cultural preferences. Once established, the expectation that 'normal retirement' occurs at age 55 or 60 may be extremely difficult to change.

Table 5.1 Employment rates by age
group, 1999

	55–59	60–64
Australia	55	31
Canada	58	34
Ireland	51	36
UK	62	36
US	68	45
Denmark	71	34
Finland	55	22
Norway	77	55
Sweden	77	46
Belgium	37	13
France	53	15
Germany	55	19
Italy	37	18
Netherlands	48	16
Portugal	59	43
Spain	45	25
Average	57	30

Source: OECD, *Older Workers: A Statistical
Description* (OECD: Paris, 2001).

The big question for the future is not whether retirement will survive these
challenges. It will. Economic growth will be slower than it would be in the
absence of population ageing but for the (already) rich democracies, the
results will be hardly catastrophic. According to a recent OECD scenario
(Turner *et al.*, 1998: 17), real living standards in Europe, North America, and
Japan could be 80 to 100 per cent higher by 2050 despite population ageing.
While there is good reason to rewrite the retirement contract, there is no
reason to abandon it.

Rather, the key issue is whether the progress made in democratizing retirement during the post-war decades is about to erode, and whether further
democratization (e.g. equalizing retirement opportunities for men and
women) is precluded? Does redesign mean convergence on some hypothetical neo-liberal model for the allocation of retirement wealth, one in which

the rights of citizens contract while the importance of markets expands? Will, in short, the pressures of population ageing on the public budget prove to be an additional source of dualism and polarization in the twenty-first century?

The risk is real. The major impetus for reform since the 1980s has come from rising pressures on the public budget (Schludi, 2001), creating incentives for policy makers to offload the rise in retirement costs to firms and individual workers. In the absence of appropriate regulation, cost-shifting to private sector institutions does raise the risk of an expanded role for markets and diminished democracy in the allocation of retirement opportunities. The risk, however, is diminished by the distinctive character of the politics of pension reform. As the policy record of the past decade has shown (Myles and Pierson, 2001), significant reform is unlikely in the absence of a widespread social consensus among relevant social, political and economic actors. As we highlight later in the chapter, the politics of pension reform typically elicits an unusually intense form of 'democratic' consensus-building. The political constraint on policy makers to reach reform through a 'negotiated settlement' with a broad range of relevant actors makes radical demolition of the post-war retirement contract improbable.

Our optimism about the future is not unqualified however. To produce a modern retirement contract, one adapted to the conditions of the twenty-first century, it is important to recall the conditions that produced the initial contract. Over the post-war decades a rising tide was lifting all boats so that the benefits of economic growth were widely spread.[3] The emergent dualisms and polarization of life chances that began to appear at the end of the 1970s, divisions captured by the new debates over 'social exclusion' (in Europe) or the 'declining middle class' (in North America), were largely absent. Where specific groups, such as the elderly, were apparently 'missing the boat,' support for innovative policy intervention was widespread. The 'risks' associated with old age were perceived as widely shared rather than concentrated among 'les exclus' or divided between an 'A-team and a B-team'. Our optimism concerning the future of old age in an ageing society, then, is bracketed by the proviso of national 'success' at addressing the policy challenges raised in earlier chapters. Our children and grandchildren will *share* a 'successful' old age to the extent that they also *share* in 'successful' childhoods and work careers.

---

[3] A remarkable feature of the post-war expansion was that while income inequality did not generally decline neither did it increase. The rich were getting richer but the poor were getting richer as well.

The main policy challenge posed by population ageing *per se* is neither demographic nor economic but distributional. Our demographic future is more or less destiny. Though unexplained, declining fertility is a worldwide phenomenon, unlikely to be substantially reversed by public policy interventions. Immigration may make a difference at the margin and there (inevitably) will be more immigration as young people move from developing to developed countries. But these young immigrants will quickly adopt the fertility behaviour of their host countries and want to bring their ageing parents when they move.[4]

The distributive challenges, in contrast, are profound. As retirement costs rise, how are they to be allocated within and between generations? We can, and no doubt will, offset some significant share of the additional costs by working longer. But can we ensure that that the social welfare losses (reductions in leisure time) associated with longer work careers do not disproportionately affect the least advantaged, those with shorter life expectancies, and low-income workers (who are often the same people)? We can finance the increase in retirement and health care costs by raising the public debt but this simply transfers the costs to future generations, our children and grandchildren. These are the key issues we aim to address here: how to manage the transition so as to satisfy principles of intergenerational equity and intragenerational justice while also contributing to the further democratization of retirement among men and women.

Managing the Transition: Some Initial Assumptions

As usual, the challenge is one of choices and trade-offs. The ten objectives for pension reform embraced by the European Union (Box 5.1) illustrate *grosso modo* the kinds of dilemmas facing policy makers in all affluent democracies in the first half of the twenty-first century.

We want many things simultaneously: *adequate pensions* for all combined with incentives to ensure high levels of *employment*; a fair balance between the *contributions* of workers and the *benefits* of the retired; *flexibility* in the face of societal change but *predictability* of pension benefits. The aim, in short, is to manage the transition to achieve intergenerational fairness, intragenerational solidarity and gender equality while at the same time creating

---

[4] Though we do not pursue the topic here, we note that to the extent higher levels of immigration form part of a strategy to offset population ageing, policies aimed at successful migrant incorporation are an essential part of the policy discussion on the ageing society.

Box 5.1 The EU's ten principles for pension reform

1. Ensure that all older people enjoy a decent living standard and are able to participate actively in public, social and cultural life.
2. Provide access for all individuals to appropriate pension arrangements.
3. Achieve a high level of employment so that the ratio between the active and the retired remains as favourable as possible.
4. Ensure that effective incentives for the participation of older workers are offered.
5. Ensure that public spending on pensions is maintained at a level in terms of per cent of GDP that is compatible with the Growth and Stability Pact.
6. Strike a fair balance between the working and retired population through appropriate adjustments to the levels of contributions and taxes and of pension benefits.
7. Ensure that private pension schemes will continue to provide the pensions to which scheme members are entitled through appropriate regulatory frameworks and through sound management.
8. Ensure that pension systems are compatible with the requirements of flexibility, security, and mobility on the labour market.
9. Review pension systems with a view to eliminating discrimination based on sex.
10. Make pension systems more transparent, predictable, and adaptable to changing circumstances.

For the exact formulation of these objectives see European Commission, 2001d.

---

conditions for a strong economy and sound public finances. Is it possible to have all of these good things at the same time?

Many of these objectives are mutually reinforcing. For governments everywhere, a major objective is to ensure that increases in retirement costs do not undermine public finances, either by increases in public debt or by 'crowding out' other essential public expenditures. Managing public finances to contain public debt and 'crowding out' effects is a *sine qua non* for achieving intergenerational equity and intergenerational justice since both have inevitable distributive implications in the way the increase in retirement costs is allocated both within and between future generations. Moreover, debt reduction in the short term is necessary to give governments the flexibility to meet rising public costs that will result from population ageing in the long term. However, we see no good reason *a priori* for financing debt reduction disproportionately from the retirement budget and so resist the implicit conclusion that it is desirable or necessary to fix, *a priori*, an upper limit or 'hard budget line' for future retirement expenditures. Setting 'hard' constraints on the retirement budget undermines flexibility and, we will argue, makes it unlikely that the desired distributive objectives can be realized.

Second, we assume that the distributive objectives, along with those of ensuring adequacy, predictability, flexibility, and transparency, refer to the *entire* 'retirement budget,' not simply to the share that appears on the public side of the national ledger.[5] Current efforts to shift rising retirement costs off the public budget by encouraging diversification of the sources of retirement income among the three 'tiers' of old age security make this assumption especially important. On average, it makes little difference for the working age population whether higher retirement costs are paid for out of tax revenues, occupational pensions, or personal retirement savings. 'Privatization' of retirement costs aimed at stabilizing public finances does not provide a solution to the larger issue of allocating the costs of population ageing between or within generations. Measuring the allocation of rising retirement costs that result from demographic change by reference to the public budget alone under such conditions would, justifiably, erode any public trust in the policy process.

Two implications follow from this last assumption. The first is that national benchmarks or measures of the level and distribution of rising retirement costs must be based on both 'public' and 'private' (= *total social*) costs, not merely the former (Adema, 1997).[6] The second is that any commitment to manage the allocation of costs of population ageing involves not only the redesign of public sector benefits but also a corresponding commitment to the regulation of private sector retirement wealth. The favourable tax regimes available to second and third tier retirement savings instruments clearly warrants that they too be charged with social goals.

Our aim here is not to prescribe a 'one size fits all' design for pension systems in the twenty-first century. It is now widely understood that existing institutional designs severely restrict the menu of feasible options available to policy makers. The large sunk costs in existing pension institutions make

---

[5] As a recent EU document points out, a 'common emphasis' in recent reforms is to limit the future retirement transfers that 'governments are responsible for' (see European Commission, 2000e). But in contrast, see the discussion of these issues in European Commission, 2001d.

[6] Such a commitment was made clear in the Commission's communication of 3 July 2001 (Commission of the European Parliament, 2001b: 3) which states: 'The present communication responds to the need for clear and integrated strategies to cope with the challenges of an ageing society for pension systems. Such strategies should not only focus on pension schemes belonging to the first pillar as the two other pillars will have an important role to play in achieving the overall objectives of pension systems.'

'regime jumping' highly unlikely for both economic and political reasons (Myles and Pierson, 2001). Rather, we take the status quo as given and focus our attention on the dynamic problem of allocating the *change* in costs associated with sustaining the retirement contract under conditions of population ageing.[7]

We do not have a crystal ball that tells us what the future will bring. We do know, however, that reforms made in the present may have huge 'lock-in' effects that will constrain future generations. Sometimes 'lock-in' effects are desirable: national constitutions, for example, are typically written with precisely this goal in mind. However, we assume that the sad historical record of the social sciences in forecasting future demographic and economic developments will continue well into the future. Accordingly, we attach considerable importance to the principle that a main requirement of any new pension design is that it provides future generations with sufficient flexibility to adjust to the changing circumstances of both the old and the young.

We begin in the next section with a discussion of four key dilemmas policy makers must face when determining how the 'costs' of an ageing society are to be allocated. From these, we derive four criteria or litmus tests for evaluating policy responses to these dilemmas. In the following sections, we move from principle to practise. Drawing on the wide array of national reform initiatives since the 1980s, we highlight both the benefits and trade-offs of alternative reform strategies.

The Economics of Population Ageing: Four Dilemmas in Search of Solutions

Following Thompson (1998), we can highlight the problems facing societies with ageing populations with a simple accounting identity. The economic cost of supporting the retired population is simply the fraction of each year's economic activity given over to supplying the goods and services the retired consume or:

$$Cost\ of\ Supporting\ the\ Retired = \frac{Consumption\ of\ the\ Retired}{Total\ National\ Production}$$

---

[7] Our focus on *change* rather than *level* essentially bypasses the question of judging the status quo among member states, i.e. whether the current level of retirement costs are too high or too low.

which in turn, following Hicks, can be written as:[8]

Cost of Supporting the Retired =

$$\frac{Number\ of\ retirees}{Number\ of\ employees} \times \frac{Average\ consumption\ of\ retirees}{Average\ production\ per\ employee}$$

Assuming all else remains fixed, population ageing raises total retirement costs. A 10 per cent increase in the ratio of retirees to workers results in a 10 per cent increase in the cost of supporting the retired. Higher retirement costs are not a problem *per se*. In a stable population (with no population ageing), we might expect future generations to behave much like earlier ones and take some of the gains that result from higher productivity (the 'wealth effect') in the form of more retirement. Population ageing, however, acts as a 'multiplier effect,' raising the costs for the same amount of leisure over each person's life course.

Cost shifting to the private sector does not *per se* change this scenario.[9] Public and private pensions are simply alternative ways for working age individuals to register a claim on future production (Barr, 2001). The share of total consumption of the retired rises irrespective of whether it is financed with state pensions or with investment returns from bonds and equities. Indeed, as Thompson (1998: 44) observes, proposals to shift towards group or personal advanced funded accounts are often made on the grounds that retirees will receive higher returns from their contributions. If this turns out to be true, the effect of change will be to *raise* future retirement costs.

The policy challenge, then, is to determine how these additional costs are to be allocated both within and between generations. The problem facing the rich democracies is not an 'equilibrium' (or point-in-time) problem but a dynamic one: how to allocate the *change* in costs as countries move through the transition.

One solution is to leave the problem of cost allocation to markets and families.[10] In a totally privatized system based on advance funding and other personal assets, the business cycle and changes in demand for labour and capital that are uniquely attributable to population ageing would solve the problem of cost allocation by producing lucky and less lucky generations (Thompson, 1998). Some cohorts and individuals would benefit from

[8] Peter Hicks, personal communication, December 2001.

[9] Advocates for privatization typically argue that the result would be higher investment and hence larger gains in productivity under a privatized system but as discussed later this is a result over which there is considerable scepticism.

[10] On this see the exchange between Richard Epstein and David Braybrooke in Laslett and Fishkin (1992).

favourable wage histories and returns to their capital and so be in a position to retire early in relative comfort. Other cohorts and individuals would be less fortunate and be required to work longer to avoid an impoverished retirement. Families would decide about the intergenerational transmission of wealth so that (perversely), *within* generations, children from wealthy families and with few siblings would be the winners.

For most nations, however, relinquishing the problem of cost allocation to markets and families is not a feasible option for both political and economic reasons, hence utopian. Even if one believes such a choice to be desirable, it is simply not on the menu of feasible options available to most countries since they are not starting from a *tabula rasa*.[11] The possible choices available today are, in the jargon of political economy, *path dependent*, constrained by choices made in the past. For example, because of the high transition costs (see below) associated with moving from a mature pay-as-you-go to a private advanced funded design, the public pension systems now in place will endure well into the future so that policy makers have no option but to make choices about cost allocation. Even in the absence of the economic constraint, the past decade has shown that popular support for established retirement income programmes is both broad and deep so that truly 'radical' reform of this sort faces an equally daunting political constraint (Myles and Pierson, 2001).

There are also sound normative reasons for a public role in allocating the transition costs arising from what is essentially a collective risk created by a changing population structure. We rarely expect markets to allocate the costs of wars or natural disasters. And there is no more reason to have markets allocate the transition costs of the 'baby dearth' in the twenty-first century than of the 'baby boom' of the mid-twentieth century.[12]

To throw into relief the core issues facing policy reformers, it is helpful to begin from an imaginary starting point—a 'useful fiction'—in which all of

---

[11] The important distinction between *tabula rasa* choices and transformation choices is developed by Orszag and Stiglitz (1999). As they note (1999: 7), the social effects of *transforming* a mature pension system into a system of individual accounts may be substantially different from the social effects of the initial choice between a public defined benefit system and individual accounts.

[12] As Hernes (1976: 516) observes, aggregative outcomes such as marriage, divorce, and fertility rates 'are partly under human control and partly the result of chance processes; in part they can be affected by conscious action but to a considerable extent they are unintended'. Like prices, they depend on all individuals but not on any (one) individual. The normative implications of this observation are important. If one assumes that only individuals, not collectivities (e.g. cohorts or generations), are moral agents, it is difficult on normative grounds to sustain claims (e.g. Thomson, 1996) for allocating the costs that result from such aggregative outcomes to particular cohorts or generations.

the consumption of the retired (including health care and other service costs) comes from pensions financed from payroll taxes on the wages of the non-retired, assumptions that can be relaxed once the main elements of the story are in place.

Needless to say such a starting point more closely approximates the real world situation in countries with highly developed pay-as-you-go defined benefit plans, countries that also were the most active reformers during the 1990s.

Intergenerational Equity[13]

The challenge facing policy makers in the pay-as-you-go countries is in the first instance an intergenerational dilemma that can be illustrated by contrasting two ideal typical pay-as-you-go designs. In the standard defined benefit model with a fixed replacement rate (FRR) common to the majority of developed countries, retirees are entitled to a given fraction of their earnings in the form of benefits plus an adjustment factor to reflect productivity gains and higher wages in the subsequent generation. When the ratio of retirees to workers changes, workers must adjust their contribution rates accordingly. In effect, benefits drive taxes (so that taxes are the dependent variable) and *all of the costs associated with demographic change fall on contributors and their dependants.*

An alternative to a fixed replacement rate is a pay-as-you-go design based on a fixed contribution rate (FCR).[14] The working population is required to

[13] In the context of the issues addressed in this chapter, the principle of *equity* should be understood as referring to 'fair burden sharing', i.e. to an equitable sharing of the costs (or benefits) of demographic transition between citizens. Still, every parent who has tried to explain to younger children why it is 'fair' that they are put to bed before their older siblings knows that determinations of what is equitable are often highly contested. It is not surprising, then, that the contemporary notion of 'intergenerational equity' and its range of application should also be contested (Laslett and Fishkin, 1992). In some contexts, the concept is used to discuss point-in-time differences between generations currently alive (the old, the young), while in other contexts it pertains more to the legacy that one generation (all those now living) will leave to future generations (those not yet born). Here, we make use of both senses of the term (see text below). The range of outcomes considered also varies. Should policies aimed at effecting equity between generations be applied only to the activities of government or to the entire social, economic, and natural infrastructure left to future generations?

[14] It is important to recall that we are describing a fixed contribution model in a *pay-as-you-go* design, not to be confused with a fixed contribution model in a funded scheme where benefits reflect contributions plus (or minus) realized gains (or losses) on invested contributions. Few readers outside of France will be familiar with the pay-as-you-go FCR model. The French model is discussed briefly in the text.

contribute a fixed fraction of its income for the support of retirees. In this design, taxes drive benefits so that benefits are the dependent variable. As the ratio of retirees to workers rises, benefits must decline and *all of the costs associated with demographic change fall on retirees.*

How might a three-generation household faced with the prospect of demographic ageing but committed to intergenerational risk sharing resolve this dilemma? Assuming they are satisfied with the status quo (current consumption levels of the generations relative to one another are neither too high or too low), the solution would undoubtedly approximate the fixed ratio or fixed relative position (FRP) model advocated by Musgrave (1986, Chapter 7).[15] Contributions and benefits are set so as to hold *constant* the ratio of per capita earnings of those in the working population (net of contributions) to the per capita benefits (net of taxes) of retirees. Once the ratio is fixed, the tax rate is adjusted periodically to reflect both population and productivity changes. Along with the fixed contribution method it obviates the need for projections but, in addition, allows for proportional sharing of risk. As the population ages, the tax rate rises but benefits also fall so that both parties 'lose' at the same rate (i.e. both net earnings and benefits rise more slowly than they would in the absence of population ageing).[16]

French second tier pensions (AGIRC, ARRCO) come closest to approximating the Musgrave solution. In theory, second tier French pensions were designed as fixed contribution schemes.[17] In practice, however, plan administrators have discretion to adjust either benefits or contributions and thus can (and do) mediate regularly between the interests of contributors and beneficiaries (Reynaud, 1995). Though not intended as such, the plan's

---

[15] The FRP principle, however, would not satisfy a concept of fairness defined by the notion that each generation ought to pay the same proportion of salary to get the same level of pension rights during retirement. On a three generational 'family farm,' for example, the *share* or proportion of output required to support ageing parents in retirement under FRP will be larger when there are two producers in the working age generation than when there are four.

[16] This is not the place to engage in an in-depth discussion of the normative merits of reciprocity and equiproportional burden sharing. In line with Musgrave's original approach, stated in terms of the political viability of social security arrangements, we rather note that proportionality indeed often acts as a focal point in negotiation problems (thus lending support to FRP as a benchmark). Political viability, or a policy's sustainability, is not an intrinsic feature of an ideal normative conception of justice. But it is a desideratum, and an important one, when pragmatically implementing a theory of justice. See Vandenbroucke (2001) for a further elaboration of this last point.

[17] In French second tier plans, contributors accumulate credits proportional to their contributions but on retirement the value of these credits is fixed not in relation to their previous earnings but in relation to the total pool of revenue available from contributions made by today's working population.

design would allow it to be run along the lines of a 'fixed relative position' plan.[18] Basic security plans that provide a minimum guaranteed benefit indexed to (net) wages can also be thought of as providing a 'fixed relative position' for less affluent retirees.

The FRP principle says nothing about what the relative position of retirees to workers and their dependants *should* be. It simply provides a rule for allocating the *additional* costs of demographic change between generations once an acceptable ratio is established.[19] From the perspective of multi-generational households facing the prospect of fewer workers and more retirees in the near future, it reflects a joint commitment to maintaining the status quo in relative terms. Just as pension benefits were indexed so that wages and benefits would rise together with increases in productivity, so too FRP in essence 'indexes' *both* contributions and benefits to population ageing.[20]

Our hypothetical three generational household faces a *point-in-time* decision concerning the allocation of costs between generations already alive. Such a situation is very close to the real life political choices facing policy makers both now and in the future: should they raise payroll taxes on younger workers, reduce benefits for retired workers (or those about to retire), or some combination of the two? This perspective is useful since all politics is, in an important sense, 'point-in-time' politics, i.e. in the hands of those currently alive. If payroll taxes rise significantly relative to pension benefits for retirees (the FRR solution), they can anticipate the displeasure of workers and their employers. If, alternatively, real benefits are falling year after year relative to national living standards (the FCR solution) retirees (and those near retirement) will be unhappy.

If we shift our perspective from a 'point-in-time' to a life course framework, however, the case for Musgrave's solution is even more persuasive. What are the implications of the three designs from the point of view of the *entire* life course of cohorts born in the future, the legacy that we will leave to our children and grandchildren?

Under FCR, the living standards of future generations would be preserved during childhood and over their working years but they would experience a sharp decline in living standards in retirement. Under FRR, in contrast,

---

[18] For a review of recent patterns of reform see Moore (2001).

[19] It should be clear that implementation of FRP does not preclude passing judgement on the current distribution (e.g. that it is too high or too low), making adjustments accordingly, and applying FRP thereafter.

[20] Hence, the FRP design can be distinguished from solutions that index benefits but not contributions to the higher retirement costs that result from increased longevity, the latter being essentially an FCR strategy.

successive cohorts would experience declining living standards in childhood and during the working years but a relatively affluent old age. FRP, in contrast, effectively smoothes the change across the entire life course and maintains the status quo with respect to the lifetime distribution of income. In this respect, FRP is a conservative strategy based on the assumption that, on average, the lifetime distribution of income available to current generations should be preserved more or less intact into the future. Future generations may of course disagree with our judgements and conclude they want a different allocation of income over the life course. It would seem presumptuous however, for the current generation to 'lock in' future generations in advance by adopting either the FRC or the FRR design.[21]

The core of Musgrave's life course argument, however, rests on practical, political, grounds. His main rationale for the FRP model is based on the assumption that neither of the alternatives, FRR or FCR, are *politically* sustainable under conditions of population ageing. They are based, in his terms (1986: 109), on an intergenerational contract that cannot be kept or at least generates great uncertainty about its future. As the opinion polls make clear, under the prevailing FRR model, young, working age contributors are now extremely sceptical that future generations will continue to support a system in which the active population bears all of the retirement costs associated with population ageing. The result is a sense of 'injustice' and cynicism rampant among many young adults as a result of being required to contribute to a system that 'won't be there for me.'

Under FRP, taxes/contributions will undoubtedly increase as a result of demographic ageing, though less quickly than under the FRR design. Thus the FRP principle runs counter to the notion that a 'hard budget line' should be established for contribution levels or that there is an upper ('acceptable') limit to tax levels associated with 'sound public finance'. Implicitly, the assumption of an 'upper limit' implies a level of taxation that will automatically trigger a general application of the FCR model ('no new taxes') in response to changes in the retirement dependency ratio. Thus far empirical evidence and historical experience makes us sceptical or at least agnostic concerning

---

[21] As Musgrave (1986: 107–8) observes, at any given point in a cohort's life course, those motivated by their immediate (i.e. myopic) self-interest are likely to make choices that depart from the FRP design. For young workers entering the labour force with foreknowledge that the population is ageing, a 'self-interested' response from a cohort concerned mainly with its immediate living standards (i.e. myopic choice) would lead to a preference for a model base on a fixed contribution rate since their contributions to support the retired would not rise during their working years. These preferences, however, would undoubtedly change as they approach retirement since now they would face an impoverished old age relative to earlier retiree cohorts.

claims that there are 'natural' limits to taxation levels that can be known *a priori*. Consequently, we see no sound reason for 'locking in' specific upper limits as long-term policy targets and should leave such a determination to future generations. As taken up below, however, we do think there is good reason for reconsidering the *mix* of taxes used to finance pay-as-you-go pension schemes.

In a dynamic context of change, 'fixed replacement' (FRR), 'fixed contribution' (FCR), and 'fixed relative position' (FRP) can be thought of as alternative principles for the intergenerational allocation of the *change* in retirement costs attributable to changes in the retiree dependency ratio. Moreover, the choice of which principle is applied is a matter of degree. The choice is a normative one that will be determined via 'politics' and it is conceivable, perhaps even desirable, that the mix of choices might change over time in response to changing circumstances.[22] One reason for expecting future departures from the FRP principle, as Frank Vandenbroucke highlights in his Foreword, is that *proportional* sharing measured in income terms does not guarantee *fair* sharing measured in terms of consumption. To use his example, proportional sharing may be unfair if, for example, there are large changes in the relative prices for essential goods and services (e.g. long-term care vs. education and training) consumed by the old and the young. We will assume, however, the FRP principle is the benchmark or litmus test for intergenerational equity, placing the burden of proof on the would-be reformer who would allocate the costs that result from demographic change in ways that depart from FRP.

A major challenge for policy officials is to provide the appropriate accounting frameworks so that the intergenerational allocation of costs associated with any *specific* reform is transparent to the political process. A full accounting scheme of the allocation of retirement costs among the working and retired populations requires inclusion of both the public and private side of the national ledger, including estimates of likely 'behavioural response' to policy changes. Thus, when policy changes intended to induce greater personal saving for retirement are made, the intended (or likely) effect of such change on the intergenerational allocation of retirement costs (including the possibility that retirement costs could rise) need to be established. As Osberg (1998: 135) concludes, policy models that assume there is no linkage between generations *except through the state* bear little resemblance to empirical reality.

---

[22] The choice of principles might well vary according to the *source* of change in retirement costs. Thus, the FRP principle might be applied to distribute the costs that result from 'demographic change' (i.e. past changes in fertility) while the FCR principle might be adopted to accommodate any decline in retirement ages and some mix of the two to changes that result from greater longevity.

Though we have elaborated our discussion within the context of a national pay-as-you-go design, it is important to highlight that the choice of allocative principles is independent of the financing mechanism in mandatory schemes. Many large corporate sector ('second tier') *funded* schemes have long been run along fixed replacement (defined benefit) as well as defined contribution lines through the use of reserve funds to smooth out temporal fluctuations in returns. A number of countries have been adding partial advance funding to finance existing defined benefit schemes. In a similar way, funded mandatory schemes can be designed to satisfy the FRP principle.

Discussions of *intergenerational* 'equity' must always return to two fundamental points often ignored in such discussions (Osberg, 1998). As highlighted earlier, the aggregate well-being of future generations depends primarily on the quality and quantity of the stock of productive assets (including human capital) they inherit, not on the design of pension systems. Providing an appropriate legacy for a working age population faced with population ageing hinges more critically on the issues taken up in earlier chapters than on pension reform.[23] As importantly, however, the relative size of economic differences *between* generations pales in comparison to those that exist *within* generations. As Wolfson *et al.* (1998) demonstrate, the enormous heterogeneity *within* generations (or cohorts) 'swamps' differences between generations with respect to the distribution of 'winners' and 'losers' that can result from population ageing. It is to this topic that we turn next.

Intragenerational Justice

The *intergenerational* dilemma is compounded by at least three *intragenerational* dilemmas, one among retirees (beneficiaries), a second among the working age population (contributors), and a third by the gender divide within generations.

When pension systems contract: intragenerational justice among the retired

The problem on the benefit side (i.e. among the retired) can be highlighted by comparing a pension system that is expanding with one that is contracting. Expansion/contraction can take two forms: (*a*) an increase or decrease in the number of years of retirement; and (*b*) an increase or decrease in the benefits

---

[23] As Osberg (1998: 132) writes: 'Future generations will have to combine their own labour power with the physical capital, human capital, environmental resources, and social capital left to them by previous generations . . . Hence, in analysing issues of intergenerational equity, it is crucial to measure accurately trends in these stocks.'

received during retirement. When retirement ages are falling, the social welfare 'gains' in additional leisure and free time tend to go disproportionately to the least well off. An additional year of retirement, for example, represents a larger proportional gain for someone with a 7-year life expectancy than for someone with a 12-year life expectancy. But the reverse is also true: an additional year of employment represents a proportionately greater loss for those with shorter life expectancies. Raising the retirement age for public sector benefits has the largest effect on those without sufficient means to finance early retirement on their own and the least impact on those who do. Since health (life expectancy, disability) and wealth tend to be correlated, the equity problem is compounded.

As with changes in the retirement age, the more disadvantaged tend to gain most when public pension benefits are expanding since they are less able or likely to provide income security for themselves. But, conversely, they stand to lose the most when income security systems are contracting. The standard result from studies of savings behaviour is that the savings to permanent income ratio rises with permanent income and does so in a sharply non-linear fashion (Diamond and Hausman, 1984). The implication is that behavioural response to lower mandatory pensions will be a function of income level: low-income families are less likely to compensate with more savings than high-income families. If a proportional share of the costs of population ageing are to be transferred to retirees, how can this be done so that they do not fall disproportionately on the least advantaged among them? We return to this issue later where we highlight two strategies: (*a*) enhanced minimum pension guarantees for all citizens; and (*b*) a larger role for selective interpersonal transfers in contributory schemes.

Financing pensions: intragenerational justice among the working population

On the contribution side, pay-as-you-go pensions are financed with a tax on wage income—the payroll tax—while income from capital and transfers are exempt.[24] The payroll tax is a flat tax, often with a wage ceiling that makes it regressive. Unlike income taxes, there are no exemptions and no allowances for family size. Low-wage workers and especially younger families with children typically bear a disproportionate share of the cost as a result. These effects are compounded to the extent that high payroll taxes discourage

---

[24] For purposes of this discussion, we adopt the standard assumption that payroll taxes, even when borne by the employer, are additions to labour costs which are ultimately born by labour typically in the form of lower wages.

employment, especially at the lower end of the labour market where the social safety net, minimum wages, or industrial relations systems make it difficult for employers to pass such costs on to employees. In effect, charging the costs of the transition to the working age population via a payroll tax creates a huge problem of intragenerational equity among the working age population since the distribution of the additional costs in no way reflects ability to pay. Accordingly, in part two, we propose a larger role for general revenue financing in contributory plans.

Population ageing, gender equality, and the gender contract

A third, if often unrecognized, challenge facing policy makers arises from the fact that generations come in two sexes. Men and women face different life course risks both because they are men and women and because of their relations to one another. These differences greatly complicate the pursuit of normative objectives such as intragenerational justice since any particular policy change may result in a differential assignment of 'costs' between men and women. Since women typically have lower lifetime earnings and longer life expectancies than men, they depend more on public pension income in old age and tend to be disproportionately affected by reforms that reduce or restructure public sector benefits. Thus, current reforms aimed at tightening the link between benefits and individual work histories (see below) will have larger effects on women unless adequately offset, for example, by compensating childcare credits. In the past many countries had lower retirement ages for women, differences that are now being eliminated. While arguably more equitable, this makes it difficult for spouses to harmonize retirement ages with each other since husbands tend to be several years older than their wives. Where couples make that choice, women benefit from a longer period of retirement but pay a price in the form of reduced retirement benefits that must support them over a longer life span.[25]

Enhancing gender equality in retirement primarily involves enhancing gender equality over the working life. The reason is obvious: modern retirement is based on a lifetime of accumulating retirement 'wealth' whether in the form of public benefits or private savings. Consequently, proposals aimed at equalising *retirement* opportunities typically emphasise policies that equalise *labour market* opportunities (e.g. day care provision) for men and women during their working lives as much or more than policies aimed at the design or redesign of pension formulae (Ginn, Street, and Arber, 2001).

---

[25] Differences in life course risks that are the product of the way gender relations are organized make policies to divide retirement wealth (credit-splitting) between spouses at divorce and retirement especially important.

Raising women's labour force participation can be a powerful instrument for offsetting the impact of population ageing. But this may prove difficult where there are large differences in incentives for men and women to engage in paid labour, including gender pay differentials related to retirement benefits.[26] In other words, population ageing introduces more mundane material reasons for gender equalization. As Orloff (2000: 3) observes, issues of gender and care-giving have become central in the contemporary period not only for reasons of gender equality but also because of their broader implications for the economy and the reproduction of the population.

The most difficult challenge, however, arises from constraints on women's labour supply that result from the unequal division of caring work between men and women. Despite the fact that the male breadwinner family model is quickly disappearing into the mists of history, the gendered character of the intergenerational contract remains largely intact (Street and Ginn, 2001). Although dual-earner families are now the norm, women continue to bear most of the burden of reproducing and caring for the next generation and providing care for the older generation.

As highlighted in Chapter 2, issues related to childcare and household reproduction are at the forefront of these debates. Here, we highlight the other side of women's traditional care-giving work, the care of the frail elderly. The rising numbers of frail elderly requiring assistance will generate one of the major 'costs' of population ageing. Working age families but primarily daughters (and daughters-in-law) have been the major providers of elder care, work that generates considerable public savings in long-term care provision and related services (Wolf, 1999). Declining fertility, moreover, creates not only a larger pool of elders requiring care but also concentrates this burden on a diminished pool of potential care providers who are also more likely to be employed than in the past.

Redesigning the Retirement Contract

Pressures for Reform

As the pension systems put in place from the 1950s through the 1970s began to mature in the 1980s and the 1990s, policy makers in all of the large pay-as-you-go countries set about an active agenda of reform that has not come

---

[26] Issues of pension design that are especially salient for women include: (1) full access to earnings-related pensions for low-wage and part-time employees; (2) elimination of minimum contribution periods as a criterion of eligibility and immediate vesting of contribution-based entitlements.

to an end. Paradoxically, as we shall see, the trend in countries that had *not* developed large, earnings-related, pay-as-you-go schemes by 1980 was expansionary, albeit adopting a rather different design.

The model of choice for the large earnings-related programmes that were created or expanded from the 1950s through the 1970s was the now familiar pay-as-you-go defined benefit (FRR) model. Benefits would be calculated on the basis of some combination of the retiring worker's earnings history and employment history. They would be financed from revenues collected from today's workers via a payroll tax.[27]

For the reformers of the period, the pay-as-you-go model provided a number of advantages, both financial and political. The financial viability of the pay-as-you-go design is typically framed by comparing implicit rates of return in a pay-as-you-go scheme to its major alternative, advance funding in a capitalized scheme in which contributions are invested and benefits financed from returns on investments. The return in the advance funded model depends on long term rates of return to capital (real interest rates). The implicit rate of return in schemes financed by payroll taxes is the annual percentage growth in total real wages (returns to labour). Total wages are the product of the average wage multiplied by the number of wage earners. The latter term is a function of population growth and the rate of labour force participation. Quite simply, then, the financial soundness of the pay-as-you-go design depends on high fertility and labour force growth, high rates of labour force participation, and strong real wage growth.

Given the values of these parameters in the 1950s and 1960s—rising wages and a growing workforce—and without a demographic crystal ball, most treasury officials would have (sensibly) advised their ministers to opt for a pay-as-you-go design. Pay-as-you-go also pre-empted objections to state control over large capital pools and sidestepped widespread public distrust of capitalized pension schemes in countries where depression and war had devastated pension funds in the first half of the century. Furthermore, pay-as-you-go systems offered enormous 'front-end' political and social benefits during the initial phase-in period. Since there was no preceding generation of entitled pensioners, politicians could immediately offer a potent combination of modest payroll taxes, generous promises of future pensions and, importantly, address rampant old age poverty immediately rather than waiting for

---

[27] In the start-up phase, a few countries (Canada, Sweden) adopted some measure of advance funding by investing surplus revenues to create future flows of revenue but these investments declined as the plans matured. Others provided for some measure of general revenue financing to meet unexpected shortfalls or to subsidize some forms of interpersonal transfers ('unearned benefits') but in most countries payroll taxes have provided the bulk of the revenue.

Table 5.2 Real growth in total wages and salaries and real
interest rates, Canada, 1960s–1990s

	1960–69	1970–79	1980–89	1990–94
Real growth in Total wages and salaries	5.1	4.8	2.1	0.0
Real interest rates	2.4	3.6	6.3	4.6

Source: Canada (1996). *An Information Paper for Consultations on the Canada Pension Plan*. Ottawa: Department of Finance.

the plan maturation required of an advance funded design. By the 1990s everything had changed. Figures for Canada are illustrative (Table 5.2).[28]

Clearly by the end of the 1980s a 'sensible' treasury official would be advising her minister that the model put in place in the sixties was in difficulty. The conditions that favoured the pay-as-you-go design in the 1960s—strong labour force and real wage growth—had evaporated as a result of declining fertility, relative economic stagnation and high rates of unemployment. To meet future obligations, payroll taxes on current workers would rise inexorably into the future. In the context of relatively slow real wage growth and high levels of unemployment, the downward pressure on take-home pay created an intergenerational dilemma for trade union leaders as well as for employers and treasury officials.

For good or for bad, a wholesale shift from pay-as-you-go to advance funding was not an option for most pay-as-you-go countries by the 1990s. Once mature, a pay-as-you-go scheme acquires a large implicit debt reflecting benefits owed to current retirees and those already earned by current workers. Over some period of time, contributors (or taxpayers) must pay twice: once to fund their own pensions and again to fund the large implicit debt built up by the existing pay-as-you-go design. Analyses of the transition costs for the major industrial countries show that the costs of servicing this debt is likely to be greater than the cost of establishing sustainable contribution rates under their pay-as-you-go pension plans (Thompson, 1998: 128). To solve the public finance problem, these nations set about revising benefit formulas, financing mechanisms, and related reforms aimed at containing the growth in contribution rates that would otherwise occur. Public sector reform was

---

[28] Similar, if less graphic, illustrations for selected European nations can be found in Davis (1995: 37).

often accompanied by reforms aimed at facilitating and encouraging a larger private sector share in future retirement incomes.

The pattern in another set of countries—the 'latecomers'—was rather different. These were countries that had developed no, or only modest, earnings-related pay-as-you-go schemes by 1980 and included Australia, Denmark, Ireland, the Netherlands, New Zealand, and Switzerland. With the exceptions of Ireland and New Zealand, the trend among these countries since 1980 was towards pension *expansion* by means of growing coverage of employer pensions based largely on advance funding rather than pay-as-you-go financing. Switzerland and Australia introduced mandatory, advance funded, defined contribution plans for the whole of the labour market in 1985 and 1992, respectively. Denmark and the Netherlands reached the same outcome—quasi-universal employer plans—at the bargaining table.[29] The UK joined this group in the 1980s when participation in SERPS was made optional and employees were allowed to 'contract out' of the public scheme. The UK was a quasi-latecomer, introducing its earnings-related pay-as-you-go scheme only in 1978 so that by the mid-1980s the implicit debt to be financed was comparatively modest.

In large measure, the latecomer countries, by adopting advance funding and (typically) defined contribution designs have avoided the *public finance* problems induced by population ageing but not the larger economic challenge. As these plans mature, the economic costs of supporting the retired will increasingly occur off budget but will be no less real. Reforms in the large pay-as-you-go countries aimed at reducing public sector costs by encouraging private sector alternatives will have a similar impact. Whether or not private sector advance funded plans also alter the economic cost of supporting the retired depends on their impact on one or other of the ratios in the accounting equation presented earlier.

1. If advance funding raises the level of savings and investment so that productivity gains are larger than under existing arrangements, then total production may rise, and everyone will enjoy higher living standards. The economic literature is generally agnostic about such an outcome, however, since additional pension savings tend to displace other forms of saving.

2. If advance funding, as is often claimed, provides contributors with a higher rate of return than pay-as-you-go alternatives, then the living standards of retirees will rise and total retirement costs also rise as a result. In periods when investments perform poorly, benefits will decline and retirement costs will fall.

---

[29] Danish plans are defined contribution while Dutch plans are typically defined benefit.

3. Depending on fund performance, 'lucky' generations will be able to retire sooner and retirement costs will rise; the reverse situation is likely for cohorts whose funds perform poorly.

The main lesson is that meeting policy objectives such as ensuring intergenerational fairness or maintaining solidarity within generations cannot be achieved without considering the retirement income system as a whole (the public and the private side of the national ledger). The average effect of an increase or decrease in retirement costs on the working age population is the same regardless of which financing mechanism is used.[30] Public sector costs in the United States are low relative to say Sweden but total retirement costs are undoubtedly higher. *Average* relative incomes of US retirees are somewhat higher than in most European nations (Hauser, 1997) and health care costs are also greater.

Shifting retirement costs off the public budget does not imply politics and policy making become irrelevant. In the 'latecomer' countries, for example, future pension politics will focus less on the role of the state in 'taxing and spending' and more on its role as market regulator and to provide remedies for 'market failure.' Similarly, regulatory policy will rise in importance in the traditional pay-as-you-go countries as initiatives to encourage expansion of second and third tier pensions begin to have effect.

For the pay-as-you-go countries, the main target of pension reform in the 1990s was to slow or freeze the rate of growth in payroll contribution rates. This aim is most dramatically represented by reforms aimed at imposing a 'hard' budget line on future benefits so that, post reform, payroll taxes stabilize at a fixed level. Prior to reform, Swedish contribution rates were projected to rise from 17–18 to 24–30 per cent in the next century. The reform aims to stabilize the contribution rate at 18.5 per cent (Palmer, 1998: 30). In Germany contribution rates were projected to rise from 22 to 36 per cent between 2000 and 2030. The cumulative impact of reforms since 1992 stabilizes the rate at approximately 22 per cent (Schmael, 1998).[31]

In our imaginary world where all of the consumption of retirees is financed by payroll contributions, retirement ages remain fixed and the population is ageing, putting a brake on contribution rates, as we have highlighted, places

---

[30] The numerous 'myths' surrounding the supposed advantages of funded individual accounts have been examined (and exploded) by Orszag and Stiglitz (1999) and Thompson (1998) and we do not pursue these issues further here.

[31] In Italy, Germany and Sweden an important strategy in this regard is the introduction of a 'notional accounts' design that transfers the risk of future demographic change from contributors to beneficiaries. These include indexing future benefits to increases in longevity or to future GDP growth.

all of the costs of population ageing on the elderly and, by definition, their relative living standards must decline. The potential result is a world more akin to the situation of the elderly of the 1950s than of the 1990s. Fortunately, the real world is more complex. Redesigning the retirement contract requires consideration of the three major components of the retirement income system: the age of retirement, the benefit structure, and the method of financing retirement incomes. We consider each in turn.

Working Longer

Among public policy makers (see OECD, 1998, 2000a, 2001b), though not necessarily their publics, there is considerable enthusiasm for solutions that keep workers in the labour force longer thereby reducing the retiree dependency ratio. There is good reason for this enthusiasm. The three main reasons why workers exit from the labour market at advanced ages are health, wealth and labour market redundancy. Trends for two of the three suggest considerable optimism that future cohorts could retire later. The 'good news' about growing old in the twenty-first century includes:

- *Increased longevity*: People are living longer which adds to the cost of retirement pensions but also means that somewhat later retirement will not reduce the number of years the average person will have to enjoy retirement.
- *Improved health status*: In general, the health of persons in their sixties has been rising. There is greater reported prevalence of some chronic illnesses (heart disease, hypertension) in older cohorts since these diseases are less likely to lead to early death than in the past but the numbers reporting significant activity limitation has declined substantially (Pransky, 2001).
- *Changing work conditions*: New technologies and post-industrial job structures have reduced the number of jobs requiring strenuous physical effort (Manton and Stollard, 1994).
- *Rising educational and literacy levels* among younger cohorts should reduce one of the major barriers to continued employment among older workers and improve the likelihood of successful retraining at advanced ages.
- *Changes in labour demand*: Perhaps the strongest force working in favour of later retirement ages in the coming decades is the effect of population ageing on labour demand. Slower labour force growth drives up capital–labour ratios so that real wages tend to rise and interest rates to fall. Higher real wages create incentives to remain in employment. Lower interest rates reduce income flows from retirement savings. Under these conditions,

healthier and more skilled workers faced with an age-neutral pension regime may increasingly 'choose' to remain at work longer and employers to adapt employment conditions to be more 'friendly' for older workers.

Given these favourable conditions for an extended working life, the case can also be made that the result of later retirement may be more benign than its alternative, namely reduced living standards for retirees and workers. If the labour market is able to generate sufficient employment to absorb older workers and raise total employment levels, a potential payoff is greater economic growth and higher living standards for all. Recent OECD (2001: 69) estimates show that the effect of small increases in the average retirement age can have an equal or greater impact on retirement costs than large cuts in retirement benefits.[32] Moreover, on average, the potential 'welfare loss' that might otherwise result from a longer working life will be offset by increased longevity. Since people are (and will be) living longer, *more* working years does not mean *fewer* retirement years.

Policy makers face a formidable political obstacle to implementing later retirement ages. Most workers in most countries look forward to retirement and raising the age of eligibility for retirement benefits is among the least popular reform options. The OECD, however, highlights an important contradiction in popular preferences for retirement. Though most people are opposed to legislating later retirement, the majority of actual retirees indicate that their preferred status would be to have part- or even full-time employment. The authors (OECD, 2001b: 82) conclude that the explanation for this apparent contradiction is that the retirees 'were likely thinking of hypothetical, highly desirable jobs that were particularly suitable for them— ones that are in limited supply for most people'. If correct, these results underline the importance of the issues of job quality raised in Chapter 4.

As highlighted at the beginning of this chapter, rising retirement ratios have three distinct sources: past changes in fertility, increased longevity, and falling retirement ages induced by both governments and firms. As explained in the footnote, of these three, the clearest *normative* case for policy intervention can be made with regard to eliminating inducements created by

---

[32] Simulations for a 'stylized' OECD country indicate a 5 per cent reduction in the number of beneficiaries—equivalent to an effective rise in the retirement age of 10 months—is equivalent to a 10 per cent cut in average retirement benefits. The reason for the difference can be understood by referring to the accounting equation introduced above. An increase in the retirement age changes both the numerator and the denominator of the retiree/employee ratio. A reduction in benefits affects only the numerator of the ratio between the average consumption of the retired and average productivity per worker. I am grateful to Peter Hicks both for the equation and for pointing out its implications to me.

firms and governments to encourage future generations to choose more retirement and fewer working years.[33]

Reversing the downward spiral: the culture of early exit

In many countries, labour market conditions in the 1970s led to the view that early labour market exit by older workers was a socially and economically acceptable alternative to high unemployment among younger workers. Pension systems often became used as pseudo unemployment schemes and unemployment and disability schemes as pseudo pension plans. The result, as Guillemard (2001) highlights, was a downward spiral in the expectations and practises of both firms and workers. Both employers and workers began to view age 55 as a 'normal' age for definitive withdrawal and those beyond 55 as essentially redundant and unemployable. The results 'ricocheted' onto workers in their forties and early fifties as they became defined as employees 'on their way out', workers without a future and hence inappropriate targets for retraining.

What is striking about such changes is the speed with which they became institutionalized. Rather than being viewed as a temporary stopgap measure (e.g. to respond to cyclical downturns in the economy), the introduction of early exit options quickly became established as a permanent 'structural' shift by both sides to the labour contract. For many, the phrase popularized by a large Canadian firm to market their retirement financial services— 'Freedom 55'—became the new standard for 'successful' completion of the economic life course. As Guillemard observes, altering such norms takes more than just reducing incentives for early exit but also requires creating positive incentives for employers and workers to extend employment beyond the expected retirement date since both sides tend to develop large sunk

---

[33] To establish a normative benchmark for changing the retirement age, it is helpful to rethink the way we organize the economic life course in light of our earlier discussion of intergenerational equity. From a life course perspective, intergenerational equity suggests that we hand on to our children a potential life course at least as good as our own. A 'fixed relative position' solution to the division between work and retirement given no economic growth but increased longevity implies a one-for-one trade-off: for every one year increase in the average life span, future generations would work one additional year. However, as earlier generations and we have done, the additional working time would be reduced (be 'indexed') to reflect economic growth that results from higher productivity so that the additional working time would be less than a year. What to do with additional costs that result from past changes in fertility? Implicitly, the FRP principle simply indicates that these costs should be 'smoothed' over the entire life course of future generations. However, it says nothing about *what* should be smoothed—consumption or leisure. Efforts by the current generation to decide whether our children will absorb these 'costs' with less leisure (later retirement) or lower life-time income are likely to be frustrated in any event. They will make up their own minds. In contrast, eliminating *incentives* created by the current generation that *bias* the choices our children will make with respect to these issues is entirely consistent with Musgrave's FRP principle and intergenerational equity.

costs, social as well as economic, around expected retirement timetables.[34] If, as anticipated, labour demand rises in the twenty-first century as a result of population ageing, the market may deliver these incentives. Guillemard, however, notes that both the Netherlands and Finland have had success in reversing the trend to early retirement not just by closing off (or narrowing) 'pathways' to early exit but also by opening up new pathways for continued employment.[35]

Regulating access to retirement wealth

The most powerful force driving early exit from the labour market—economic growth—is also benign but works in the opposite direction, that is to encourage retirement. As Burtless and Quinn (2001: 385) conclude, the 'simplest and probably most powerful explanation for earlier retirement is rising wealth'. National GDP in the affluent democracies has grown dramatically in the last half century and some of this increase has been used to purchase more years of retirement. Moreover, while working years and working hours have declined for individual workers, they have risen for families, a result of higher women's participation. The increase in 'family' years and hours worked helps pay for more years of retirement. For future cohorts, the same factors that make work possible to more advanced ages—better health and education—along with productivity gains will help compound the wealth effect: they will earn more and accumulate their wealth sooner. Future gains in female employment will add to this effect.

In nations where most pension 'wealth' is stored up inside public sector retirement schemes, policy makers have considerable discretion over the age at which individuals can gain access to it. Where public sector benefits provide a smaller share of retirement income (e.g. Canada, the US, the UK), the effects of raising the age of entitlement inside *public* plans may be more modest and even perverse for both macroeconomic and distributive reasons. The largest gains to the economy are to be had if the most productive workers (the healthy, well educated, and presumably better paid) remain in employment longer. Reform can have a potentially perverse effect if changes to retirement incentives in public sector plans mainly produce higher retirement ages among low wage, low productivity workers. In the US, for

[34] Workers develop 'life plans' in anticipation of retirement that involve career, financial, and housing decisions that may affect not only them but younger family members as well. Firms develop recruitment, training, personnel, and wage strategies based on assumptions about probable rates of exit.

[35] In the Netherlands, Guillemard (2001: 6) notes, not only have benefits for disability been reduced, access to benefits also now depends on employee rehabilitation.

example, where public sector benefits provide a comparatively small (about 40 per cent) share of retirement income, most studies conclude that even large changes in Social Security rules regarding the retirement age cause only small changes in the actual retirement age (Burtless and Quinn, 2001: 405). Higher income earners with greater pension and private wealth outside Social Security are particularly immune to such changes.

There is considerable variation in this regard. High-income pensioners in Canada, Japan, the Netherlands, and the US receive less than 10 per cent of their income from public sources and, in Britain, just over 10 per cent. In Italy the figure is about 50 per cent and in Germany and Sweden between 60 and 70 per cent (OECD, 2000a: 44). In Canada, where high income groups depend largely on occupational pensions and personal retirement savings, there is a much higher level of early retirement (before age 60) among professional and managerial than among less well paid occupations (Schellenberg, 1994: 22–3). In Germany, by contrast, workers in higher status occupations rely heavily on public pensions and are less likely to retire early than employees in lower status occupations (Kohli, 1995).

The implication is that reforms aimed at raising retirement ages requires identical rules regulating the age of access to pension wealth in all three tiers of the pension system. Where co-ordination does not take place, public sector reform is likely to have perverse distributional and macroeconomic outcomes.

In the more market-oriented pension regimes of the Anglo-Saxon countries and Ireland, future trends in the retirement age, not surprisingly, depend largely on regulating access to second and third tier pensions. Raising employment incentives inside *public* schemes will have modest effects and mainly impact lower wage earners that receive a larger share of their retirement income from the public budget. In these nations, raising the average retirement age for higher income employees depends more on co-ordinating the age of access to employer plans and personal retirement savings with public sector plans. Policy co-ordination among public and private sectors will also grow in importance in Denmark and the Netherlands in the twenty-first century as the quasi-universal employer plans negotiated by the social partners in the 1980s come to maturity.

The *fiscal* (public finance) challenge posed by population ageing is greatest, however, where large 'encompassing' pay-as-you-go defined benefit plans were created to provide the vast majority of retirement income not only to those with modest incomes but to middle and upper-middle earners as well. The upshot, however, is that governments in these countries also have the greatest capacity for regulating retirement ages across the whole of the labour market, for high as well as low income earners.

Protecting the least advantaged

The challenge, of course, is to ensure that the social welfare losses (reductions in leisure time) associated with these reforms do not disproportionately affect the least advantaged, those with shorter life expectancy and low-income workers (who are often the same people). While average health status is rising among older workers, it is still the case that the proportion that is disabled rises as a cohort ages.[36] Retirement pensions are clearly a blunt instrument for dealing with the disabled minority. However, they obviate the need for, and the administrative costs of, a carefully tuned system able to identify the 'truly' impaired. Meeting this challenge requires the bureaucratic and technical capacity to administer early retirement schemes for reasons of disability and labour market redundancy that are fair and perceived to be so by the larger community. The other side of an active labour market strategy aimed at reversing the 'downward spiral' are better and more effective programmes for the truly disabled and those whose 'human capital' cannot be raised above the minimum level necessary for employment.

By definition and design, old age *insurance* is a mechanism that transfers income from those with shorter life expectancy to those with greater life expectancy.[37] The result as noted, earlier, is that falling retirement ages disproportionately benefit those with shorter life expectancies but the converse is true when retirement ages are rising. Since life expectancy is associated with economic status, old age *insurance* by definition creates an implicit transfer from the poor to the rich. Hence, this yields one clear rationale for compensating vertical transfers, a topic we turn to in the following section.

Redesigning Benefits: Intragenerational Justice among the Retired

Until the second half of the twentieth century, public pension benefits reflected traditional assumptions of *social assistance* rather than contemporary notions of *social security*. Benefits were modest and aimed mainly at putting a floor under the declining wages of older workers and a modest income for their widows. Early post-war reforms hardly changed this. Where they existed, replacement rates in earnings-related public sector plans were modest. Beveridge-type reforms that introduced universal flat benefits for all, contained no notion of providing retired workers with an income sufficient to maintain pre-retirement living standards, i.e. *income security*. Germany in

---

[36] US studies of recent Social Security recipients aged 62–64 indicate that approximately 22 per cent have impairments that prevent employment.

[37] In the United States, for example, it has long been noted that Social Security creates a transfer of wealth from blacks to whites.

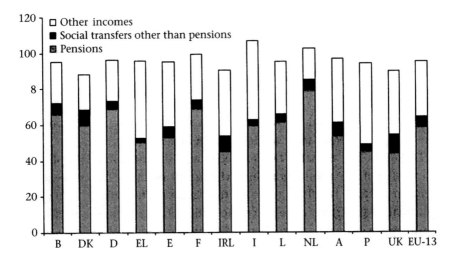

Chart 5.1 Relative equivalized income of persons living in households receiving pensions (100 = all persons in a given country)

Notes: The average (equivalized) income of the whole population in a given country is put at 100. Pensions include retirement and survivor's pensions. For EU-13, persons living in households benefiting form pensions have an average income of around 95%. This means that their average standard of living, as measured by income, is 5% lower than for the total population.

Source: Social Protection Committee on the Sustainability of Pensions, May, 2001.

1957 and Sweden in 1958 took the lead in this respect and, in varying degrees, most countries followed suit in the sixties and seventies. The aim of the new design was to provide retired workers with a retirement wage reflecting past earnings, a form of retirement insurance traditionally available only to civil servants and a minority of private sector workers through their employers. As illustrated in Chart 5.1, *average* living standards of retiree population (pensioners) in Europe now differ little from the rest of the population despite differences in pension design and the OECD (2001*b*: 27) shows identical results for Canada, Japan, and the US. The gap between the old and young would be further reduced if differences in home ownership were taken into account.[38]

The relative economic status of recent cohorts of retirees is not merely the result of better pensions, however. They also reflect cohort history. Today's

[38] There is considerably more cross-national variation in the proportion of older persons who might be considered affluent relative to their nation-specific income distributions. LIS calculations for Italy, France, Spain, and Germany show that between 30 and 34 per cent of elderly households are in the top two population income quintiles. In Sweden and the UK the proportion is 23 per cent and in Denmark and Finland 14 and 17 per cent respectively.

seniors are the workers of the golden age. They have comparatively high incomes today because of relatively affluent work histories compared to earlier cohorts of old people whose adult lives were spent during depression and war. Moreover, current retirees have grown old in a period of slower real wage growth among the working age population. Had real wage growth during the past twenty-five years been like that of the previous twenty-five, the elderly today would look less affluent simply because the incomes of the working age population would be much higher.

The lesson here is that the current economic situation of old people is an uncertain guide to what is good and what is bad about the current design of pension systems. It reflects not only the design of the pension system but also cohort specific life experiences. To anticipate the future we must make assumptions concerning: (a) what the economic history of today's workers will have been like when they reach old age (relatively affluent or not); and (b) what the economic circumstances of the working age population in the future will be like. How does one design a system to allocate the costs of population ageing in the face of such uncertainty. As we noted earlier, the criterion of Fixed Relative Position not only provides a benchmark for inter-generational equity but also has the advantage that it requires no assumptions about the future values of these parameters. The FRP principle essentially allows for intergenerational risk sharing to accommodate the varying fortunes of sequential cohorts.

Unlike the traditional fixed replacement ratio design, however, FRP assumes that a share of these costs will be allocated to future pensioners—benefits will be lower than under the FRR design. This result raises issues of intragenerational justice among the retired: how to allocate these costs so that they are of greatest advantage (or the least disadvantage) to the least well off within the pensioner population?

Clearly, reforms that simply cut all pensioner benefits by a proportional amount (e.g. by reducing all pensions by 5 per cent) do not satisfy this standard. Moreover, behavioural response to such reductions can be expected to increase inequality among the retired. The standard result from studies of savings behaviour is that the savings to permanent income ratio rises with permanent income and does so in a sharply non-linear fashion (Diamond and Hausman, 1984). The implication, then, is that behavioural response to reduced *mandatory* pensions will be a function of income level: lower income families are less likely to compensate with more *voluntary* retirement savings than higher income families.

The notion that the costs of restructuring should be born by those most able to afford it and the weakest members of society should be protected is hardly novel. But how to implement it? Here, we propose two forms of 'targeting' benefits to meet this challenge drawn from the real world experience of Member States and other OECD nations.

Eliminating Old Age Poverty

Declining poverty rates among the elderly have been a distinguishing feature of all OECD countries since the 1960s. Old age poverty rates below 10 per cent are now common and a number of countries have achieved rates of 5 per cent or less (Hauser, 1997; Smeeding and Sullivan, 1998; and Table 5.3).

The most effective anti-poverty systems are not necessarily the most costly. Both high-spending Sweden and low-spending Canada achieve poverty rates of less than 5 per cent (see also Smeeding and Sullivan, 1998) as a result of the fact that both provide guaranteed minimum benefits that raise the vast majority above standard 'poverty lines'. Canada provides a guaranteed annual income to the elderly and Sweden a guaranteed minimum pension. Both make benefits conditional on the presence or absence of other economic resources but in a way that departs significantly from traditional *means-tested* programmes. To distinguish traditional means-testing from these modern variants it is useful to draw some distinctions.

- *Means-testing*: Individuals qualify for benefits on the basis of a test for both *income* and *assets*, requiring individuals to 'spend' their way into poverty to qualify. Tax-back rates (the rate at which benefits are cut as other income rises) are typically high and can be in excess of 100 per cent. Supplemental Security Income (SSI) in the United States is an example. Usually the aim is to restrict benefits to a small fraction of the population (the 'poor'). Because of the intrusiveness of the means test, there is often considerable stigma attached to accepting benefits so that take-up rates tend to be low.

Table 5.3 Poverty rates among the population 65+, 1990s

<5%	5–9%	10–14%	15–19%	>20%
Canada	Finland	Austria		Australia
Sweden	France	Belgium		US
	Germany	Denmark		
	Luxembourg	Italy		
	Netherlands	Norway		
	Switzerland	Spain		
		UK		

Source: LIS Key Figures, Luxembourg Income Study, 2001.

- *Income-testing*: As the term suggests, income-testing is based on a test of income but not of assets so there is no requirement to spend oneself into poverty to qualify. Interest or dividends from investments are included in the test but not the underlying capital that generates the income. Tax-back rates are always *much* less than 100 per cent so that benefits are not 'for the poor alone' but often extend well into middle income groups, albeit at declining rates. The implicit model is closer to Milton Friedman's design for a negative income tax (NIT) or a guaranteed annual income (GAI) than traditional means-tests for the 'poor' (see Myles and Pierson, 1997). Canada's *Guaranteed Income Supplement* for seniors is the exemplar.[39]
- *Pension-testing*, as practised in Sweden and Finland, is a yet more restricted type of test, including only income that comes from *public* pension pro-grammes in those countries. Unlike a Guaranteed Annual Income scheme, it functions to provide a Guaranteed Annual Pension. Individuals with earnings histories and contributions below the minimum, are provided with pension supplements on a sliding scale. Where all or most of the income of retirees comes from the public pension system, of course, the distinction between income and pension testing is merely a formal one.

Providing all citizens with a minimum guarantee above a poverty line indexed to national living standards is well within the reach of most member states since the poverty gap—the difference between family income and the poverty line—of the poor elderly is typically modest compared to that of working age families (see Table 5.4).

Providing retirees with a high guaranteed annual income or minimum pension is less problematic than providing such benefits to working age fam-ilies since the issue of work incentives does not arise.[40] Over some range of the earnings distribution, a high guarantee level may have an impact on

---

[39] Every NIT model is defined by three parameters: the *guarantee level* (the level of benefit pro-vided to people with no other income; the *tax-back rate* (the rate at which benefits are reduced as the recipient gains income); and the *break-even point* (the income level at which benefits disap-pear). A high guarantee level is desirable to provide people with adequate incomes and a low tax back rate is desirable to encourage people to work. But such a combination means that the break-even point is very high and so are the costs. In practice, virtually all NIT proposals are broken into two tiers in order to contain costs and to maintain work incentives. One tier is intended for people who are not expected to work (such as the elderly) with a high guarantee level, a high tax-back rate, and a low break-even level. The second tier, for those expected to work, typically has a lower tax-back rate, and a higher relative break-even point but a lower guarantee level.

[40] For working age families the level at which social benefits affect work incentives is a function of the wage distribution. When wage inequality in the lower tail of the distribution (e.g. when low-paid workers earn about 40 per cent of the median wage) a high guarantee level will have more disincentive effects than when wage inequality is more modest (e.g. where low-paid workers earn about 70 per cent of the median).

Table 5.4 The cost of eliminating old age poverty, National Accounts estimate, 1990s

Country (year)	Number of poor HH's with old people (thousands)	Poverty gap (local currency)	Extra cost as per cent of GDP
Canada (1994)	118	1591	0.025
US (1997)	5565.9	2931	0.201
Finland (1995)	21.7	3708	0.015
Norway (1995)	60.6	6612	0.043
Sweden (1995)	27.2	10524	0.017
Netherlands (1991)	36.9	5312	0.036
Germany (1989)	633.8	3617	0.080
France (1994)	664.1	8083	0.073

Notes: Extra cost as % of GDP = #poor households × poverty gap)/GDP. Estimates are based on the objective of bringing families containing persons 65+ above 50 per cent of the median adjusted disposable income line. This exercise ignores the fact that this, in itself, will alter the overall distribution and, thus, also the median.

Source: LIS Databases and OECD National Accounts.

savings behaviour but this is likely to occur over a short time period, relatively late in the work career, when the impact of more or less savings on retirement income is known.

Building or enhancing generous basic security schemes with a minimum guarantee above the poverty line goes a long way towards addressing the multiple dilemmas facing pension reform outlined earlier. It establishes a floor beyond which the most disadvantaged pensioners bear *none* of the additional costs of population ageing and so meets at least a minimal requirement of intragenerational justice. Since a guaranteed annual income or minimum pension involves interpersonal redistribution, there is a strong case for general revenue (from income, consumption and other taxes) rather than payroll taxes as the source of financing. Payroll taxes impose all of the cost on the working age population with perverse distributional effects within that population. A large or rising share of general revenue financing provides a powerful tool for reallocating the costs of population ageing based on ability to pay among the retired as well as the working age population since, like the young, the old are also subject to income and consumption taxes.

The cost of eliminating poverty among the elderly will be higher in nations with higher earnings inequality over the working life since there will be more retirees who are eligible for such benefits. One might think of these additional costs as an 'inequality tax.' the cost of which must be calculated on the basis of one's prior assumptions concerning the effects of wage inequality during the working life on employment and labour market flexibility.

The modern institution of retirement, however, rests on much more than a promise that retirees will not fall into 'poverty'. Post-war retirement patterns reflect the development of institutions that promised much more, namely that the majority would be able to maintain living standards not unlike those reached during their working years.

All of this suggests that the main challenge raised by reduced public or mandatory benefits, in the presence of an adequate basic security scheme, is the probable impact on workers with average and below average earnings who under current provisions would have retirement incomes well above the guaranteed minimum. The challenge, moreover, is not gender neutral. The distribution of income security 'losses' that can result from lower public pensions will have a greater impact on women since they typically have lower lifetime earnings and longer life expectancies than men.

Rationalizing redistribution in earnings-related schemes

Although earnings-related pension schemes ostensibly reflect individual work histories and contributions, all systems have traditionally incorporated design features that produce significant interpersonal transfers and cross-subsidies. During the nineties, eliminating transfers and cross-subsidies that could be identified as 'inequitable,' 'perverse' or 'out-dated,' (such as special privileges for public employees) provided many countries with an effective means of cost reduction. At the same time, however, it was also common to use some share of the savings to create new interpersonal transfers for risk groups now considered to have legitimate claims. This 'rationalization' of redistributive design features to achieve equity or to more clearly realize socially desirable distributive outcomes offers policy makers a potent tool for solving the Rawlsian problem among the non-poor.

For example, Italian and Swedish reforms of the 1990s eliminated transfers that result from the use of final (or best) earnings formulas. As the OECD (1988: 68) points out, final earnings formulas tend to be biased in favour of higher income groups who have steeper age–wage profiles whereas the age–wage profile of lower-income groups tends to be hump shaped or at least to flatten out sooner in the work career. Swedish pensions were traditionally calculated on the best fifteen years. In Italy, the earnings record was based on the last five years for private sector workers and the *last year* for public sector workers. Both nations modified their formulas so that, in future, benefits will

Table 5.5 Change in assessed earnings
in final/highest earnings plans

Country	1986	1997
Austria	10	15
France	10	25
Italy	5	Career
Norway	20	20
Spain	8	8
Sweden	15	Career

Sources: OECD, *Reforming Public Pensions*, Paris,
1988; Social Security Administration, *Social
Security Around the World, 1986/1997*, Washington:
Office of Research and Evaluation, 1986/1997.

reflect average earnings over the entire working life. Other countries with
final or best earnings models are also moving in this direction (Table 5.5).

The implications of other changes are more ambiguous since they involve
greater *targeting* of interpersonal transfers rather than their elimination.
Adjusting the contribution period to compensate workers for irregular work
histories is one method many countries have used in the past, provisions that
typically benefit women. Rather than basing benefits on a work history of say
forty years, Swedish workers were eligible for maximum pensions after only
thirty years of contributions. Italian workers were able to claim a pension
based purely on years of service (thirty-five years for private sector workers
and twenty years for public sector workers) allowing many to retire on a full
pension in their early fifties (the so-called 'baby pensioners'). This created
markedly different 'rates of return' (and implicit transfers) based on age of
labour market entry and employment sector. In both countries, the reforms
reduced these transfers by basing benefits on total lifetime contributions.

The reforms, however, did not *eliminate* protection against irregular work
histories; rather, social protection against irregular work careers was *targeted*
on specific forms of labour market exit typically associated with child and
elder care or spells of unemployment (insurable risks). In the new design
women (and men) will be compensated for shorter work histories that result
from child or elder care but not for providing housekeeping services to a
spouse. Men (and women) will receive credit for periods of unemployment or
disability (insurable risks) but not for periods of non-employment that are
not insured.

The 1995 Swiss reform is especially striking since the reform was about introducing gender equality and subject to a national referendum (Bonoli, 1997). As in the US, a married man with a dependent spouse was eligible for a 'couple pension' corresponding to 150 per cent of his own pension entitlement, a practice that disproportionately benefits higher income families (Meyer, 1996). Women's organizations successfully took the lead in demanding the end of the couple pension. In the new design all contributions paid by the two spouses while married are added together, divided by two, and counted half each. Strikingly, however, couples with children below the age of 16 now receive additional credit equal to the amount of contributions payable on a salary three times the minimum pension (56 per cent of the average wage). Compensation is provided for child rearing but, unlike the previous formula, not for providing housekeeping services to a spouse. The result is a cross-subsidy to families with children from those who remain childless.

These examples of the rationalization of redistribution among retirees illustrate a more general strategy for restructuring traditional earnings-related pension schemes in ways that simultaneously enhance intragenerational equity and intragenerational equality. Redesigning contributory plans to eliminate horizontal cross-subsidies that now seem outdated or that benefit the most advantaged has proven to be a potent source of cost reduction. At the same time, the addition of interpersonal transfers that are more adapted to meeting contemporary needs such as child and elder care credits has also been a potent tool for *modernizing* traditional earnings-related schemes to meet the needs of contemporary families. If pursued aggressively, the enlargement of well-targeted interpersonal transfers *inside* contributory earnings-related schemes provides policy makers with a way of offsetting many of the negative distributional consequences that may otherwise arise from pension reform. As importantly, the result is to create a new framework for managing the distributions of costs of population ageing among both the working and retired population by refinancing the welfare state.

Refinancing Retirement Costs: Intragenerational Justice for the Young

On the financing side, application of the fixed relative position principle also implies that a proportional share of the increased retirement costs that result from population ageing will fall on the working age population, i.e. that contributions will rise. Clearly, however, allocating these costs based on a flat-rate tax without deductions for children or other circumstances (i.e. flat-rate payroll taxes) is inconsistent with the notion that these costs should be of greatest advantage (or the least disadvantage) to the least well off within the working age population.

As Reynaud (1997) points out, however, a major goal of reforms aimed at rationalizing redistribution within earnings-related schemes during the nineties was to make the division between the contributory and 'solidaristic' (redistributive) elements of payroll-based schemes transparent. Drawing a clear separation between the two creates the opportunity to shift financing of the solidaristic elements from payroll taxes to general revenue, relieving pressure on the former and spreading the transition costs of an ageing society to a larger revenue base.

Bonoli's (1997) interviews with party officials and labour leaders in France and Germany provide striking evidence for the self-conscious character of this strategy. In the words of a French trade unionist: 'the financing of contributory benefits . . . must be done through contributions based on salaries. In contrast, non-contributory benefits must be financed by the public purse.' Tuchszirer and Vincent (1997) highlight a similar logic underlying the 1995 Toledo pact, an all-party agreement on the framework for reforming the Spanish social security system.

A rising share of general revenue financing in the retirement budget provides a powerful tool for reallocating the costs of population ageing based on ability to pay not only among the working age population but among the retired as well. While retirees are not subject to payroll taxes they do pay income and consumption taxes.[41] Assuming the more affluent in both populations also pay higher taxes, their share of the additional costs associated with demographic change rises proportionately with increases in the share of retirement costs financed from general revenue.

At the same time, increased transparency creates a *political* framework within which redistributive issues can be addressed. In the age of expansion, many of the redistributive features of the income security system, some of them perverse, were often concealed in complex technical provisions. This strategy was often deliberate, guided by the assumption that concealment made redistribution politically easier (Derthick, 1978). Increased transparency, in essence, repoliticizes issues of how much redistribution and for whom. We should not assume from all this that the effects of reform will all be benign. Whether, for example, working women will be winners or losers as

---

[41] We do not preclude the possibility that there may be significant advantages to a system of 'earmarked' social security contributions so long as such contributions are based on total income and provide for some degree of progressivity, especially in the lower tail of the distribution, and provide adjustments for family size.

a result of raising the contribution period on the one hand while improving child- and eldercare credits on the other depends on both the relative value of the new credits and future patterns of labour force participation. The point, rather, is that this new architecture creates the possibility for political actors to address systematically the redistributive dilemmas created by redesigning traditional pay-as-you-go defined benefit schemes. The outcomes are clearly indeterminate but the indeterminacy reflects the balance of political forces and institutions of political representation rather than the impersonal forces of the market and/or demography.

If pursued aggressively, if only incrementally, the pattern of reform outlined above implies a strategy that potentially alters the traditional social insurance model of old age security dramatically, at least in the long term. On the benefit side, any reductions implied by the FRP principle are partially offset by new or expanded interpersonal transfers for less advantaged retirees. On the contribution side, these additional costs are met not through higher payroll taxes but with general revenue financing raised among both the retired and the non-retired based on ability to pay. The implication on the benefit side is that with time the earnings replacement function of public sector insurance schemes diminishes somewhat for higher income families (which may be taken up by second and third tier savings).[42] And, with time, the share of general revenue financing for the income security system as a whole rises. The exact mix at the 'end' of the process will vary from country to country since we assume a wide variety of initial starting points and that the strategy is applied incrementally only to the allocation of the *change* in retirement costs that results from population ageing.

Pension reform, the gender contract, and caring work

The issues related to gender equality and gender equity go well beyond those related to the allocation of increased retirement costs due to population ageing that have concerned us here. They are primarily issues of enhancing gender equality over the working life and providing compensating differentials for the uneven distribution of caring work between the sexes, issues that arise even in the absence of population ageing. As we emphasize above, however, they are issues whose broader economic and social importance rise dramatically as a result of population ageing. We have already alluded to the importance of achieving high levels of female employment in an ageing society. The challenges this poses for childcare have been addressed in

---

[42] We hasten to add, however, that there is no intrinsic reason why second tier employer pensions cannot incorporate interpersonal transfers to achieve desirable social objectives.

Chapters 2 and 3. In this concluding section, we turn to the related issue of eldercare, a task that is rising exponentially in ageing societies, and one that has long been the preserve of daughters, daughters-in-law and ageing wives.

Population ageing has brought this issue to the forefront for two reasons. First, the fraction of the elderly most at risk, the 'oldest old' (80+) has been growing much faster than the elderly population in general. Second, the capacity of the traditional pool of informal care givers (elderly wives, daughters, and daughters-in-law) who provide about three-quarters of all care to the frail elderly (OECD, 1996: 63) is declining relative to this increased demand. Increased longevity means that the care provided by spouses to one another (typically by the wife) occurs at an age when care giving capacity is diminished. Declining fertility has meant fewer non-elderly, typically female, relatives to provide support and they are more likely now to be employed. Our aim here is not to provide a systematic overview of the policy issues related to the provision of home services and long term care for the frail and disabled elderly but rather to highlight important parallels with our discussion of family and pension policy.

Like longevity, the onset and duration of frailty in old age is unpredictable and hence an insurable risk for which at this point in time there is little or no market. The emergent market for long-term care insurance in the US is beset with a variety of problems and still modest in scope (OECD, 1996: 39–40) reminiscent of the world before the spread of mandatory public pensions.

As recent historiography (Haber and Gratton, 1994) has shown, in the world before mandatory pensions, intense poverty in old age was still the exception, mainly associated with those elderly persons without working adult children able or willing to supplement the declining incomes of their ageing parents. Mandatory public pensions, in this sense, were a form of risk sharing not only against the risk of one's own longevity (i.e. for the elderly) but also against the risk of one's parent's longevity (i.e. for their working age children) and the imperative of supporting parents financially through an extended old age. Similarly, the expansion of publicly financed long-term care and home help services in the contemporary period represents a welfare gain not only for the frail elderly who receive these services but also for their adult children and other family members who otherwise must provide such services directly.

As with childcare, eldercare still remains largely women's work and much of our discussion of the former can be applied to the latter with little modification, a fact implicitly recognized by countries that now provide elder- as well as childcare credits in their pension formulas. Achieving gender equality requires attention to the caring work women provide to those at both ends of the life course.

Conclusion

Population ageing is not new. Western societies have been growing 'older' for well over a century. Those of us now living grew up in a world with many more elderly parents and grandparents than any previous generation and our children and grandchildren will grow up with even more older persons. There has been enormous variation in the quality of life over the twentieth century but these variations have had little to do with changes in population age structure.

In contrast, modern 'retirement', an extended period of labour force exit driven by wealth, not disability, is new for most people. This change was the result of rising affluence, on the one hand, and, on the other, the post-war pension 'revolution' that expanded access to this new wealth, however unevenly, to the majority of older households. The question then is not whether we will survive 'population ageing' (we will). Rather, in face of an impending acceleration in the rate of population ageing, the big questions concern whether and in what form modern retirement will survive, at what cost, and to whom? Of particular concern is whether the fiscal pressures (i.e. on the public budget) that result from population ageing will erode the democratic gains in equalizing access to retirement achieved during the post-war era of pension reform.

We have little doubt that an extended period of retirement will continue to be the normal conclusion to the economic life course for the affluent, especially for affluent two-earner couples. Because the less affluent depend much more on public pension and other services (such as health care), the political risk associated with population ageing is that public sector reforms could lead to greater inequality in access to retirement and preclude the possibility of a still fuller democratization (e.g. between men and women) of retirement opportunities.

How, then, to respond? The combination of a strong basic security programme and appropriately designed cross-subsidies in earnings-related programmes provide potent tools for addressing issues of intragenerational justice among the elderly and for democratizing pension entitlements among men and women. Both strategies produce a changing mix of revenue sources and benefits that makes it possible to allocate costs based on the ability to pay among both retirees and workers.

The traditional pay-as-you-go model is useful for illustrating the intergenerational dilemma posed by population ageing. The usual defined benefit formula tends to impose all the costs of population ageing on the working age population, a solution that is inconsistent with the principle of intergenerational equity. But shifting to a model based on fixed contribution rates is equally unacceptable. As an alternative, we have advocated Musgrave's 'fixed relative position' solution in which the ratio of per capita earnings (net of contributions) and (net) benefits are set so as to hold constant the ratio of the two. The advantages are several. It provides for a fair sharing of risks with regard to both population and productivity change and obviates the need for planning now based on uncertain and risky projections of the future. Since actual outcomes are unpredictable, the main requirement of any new pension design is that it provides future generations with sufficient flexibility to adjust to the changing circumstances of both the old and the young.

Implementation of such a strategy in the real world where the consumption of the retired is financed from a variety of sources is, of course, decidedly more complex. Paradoxically, however, nations where the public sector share of retirement costs is larger probably have had an historical advantage with respect to facing up to these issues. The maturation of public pension schemes since the 1970s combined with adverse economic conditions compelled these nations to address the fundamental issues of retirement costs well in advance of the demographic shift all nations will experience in the next quarter century. Many of the lessons to be learned from efforts to reform the large public pay-as-you-go systems have already been acquired. The trade-offs and dilemmas are known and there is some experience in addressing these problems. For countries where there is greater reliance on advance funded employer schemes and tax-subsidized personal retirement accounts, the challenges of achieving social objectives related to intergenerational justice and intragenerational fairness will require a sea change in the policy tools and accounting methods used to measure the distributional consequences of alternative strategies. A larger private sector does not imply that markets are in charge, only that the strategies differ: a fair and just cost allocation of retirement costs depends more on regulation and taxation policies when the private sector role is greater.

Maximizing employment among the working age population and raising actual retirement ages among older workers, particularly in countries where employment levels (Table 5.1 above) are very low, provides one of the most potent tools for containing the growth in retirement costs but potentially one of the more difficult to implement. Healthier and better educated older workers are capable of working longer but are unlikely to do so in the absence of healthier and better workplaces.

If we have focused on the distributive challenges generated by population ageing, we have not exhausted the subject. Perhaps the single greatest 'silence' in all recent discussions of these issues concerns the potentially huge impacts of the underlying demographics on the intergenerational transmission wealth both through inheritance and through transfers between older parents and their adult children prior to death.[43] Changes in fertility combined with rising female labour force participation are undoubtedly creating an enormous intergenerational funnel for transmitting wealth across the generations about which we know little and understand less. Although working out the implications is difficult, the arithmetic for the intuition is easy. The demographic shift from three- or four-child families to one- and two-child families *combined* with the dual-earner household is creating it's own set of winners and losers *within* the next generation and those that follow. *Within* generations, children from wealthy families and few siblings stand to be the winners in the intergenerational lottery. The 'lottery' has of course always been present but population ageing and new family forms have raised the stakes. For the 'lucky' few, or perhaps many, the 'retirement' decision in the future—when to work and how much—will possibly depend less on their own work careers and more on the work careers (and longevity) of their parents. If so, the problem of 'class' and intergenerational inheritance will be magnified at the end of the life course as well as at the beginning.

---

[43] In particular, the usual discussions of 'intergenerational accounting' that focus only taxes and transfers has nothing to say on this topic.

6

The Self-Transformation of the European Social Model(s)

Anton Hemerijck

The European Social Model

European welfare states are in varying need of reform. Intensified international competition, ageing populations, de-industrialization, changing gender roles in labour markets and households, and the introduction of new technologies, all pose severe strains to welfare state programmes designed for a previous era. Identifying new social objectives with no regard to their practical political relevance and implementation within diverse European welfare models, would remain a sterile academic exercise. For this reason the analytical focus in this final chapter shifts from the 'problem-oriented' question: 'What sort of new welfare architecture is required in the face of the strains of transformation?', to the 'political-institutional' question: 'What kinds of policies are feasible and fair, given the tremendous differences in welfare state design and in decision making structures across Europe?'

All European welfare states share three distinctive characteristics. Normatively, there is a common commitment to social justice. The vocabulary of reform in most Member States is couched in terms of a solidaristic commitment that society will not abandon those who fail. The preference for minimum guaranteed resources is widely accepted by European publics and deeply entrenched in policy programmes and institutions. The stigmatizing discourse of the 'deserving' versus 'undeserving' poor never really gained currency in the European Union, apart from the Thatcher era in the United Kingdom in the 1980s (Schmidt, 2000).

At the cognitive level, the European social model is based on the recognition that social justice can contribute to economic efficiency and progress. As a 'beneficial constraint', a term coined by Wolfgang Streeck, social policy can reduce uncertainty, enhance the capacity to adjust and the readiness to accept change, bear more risks, acquire more specialized skills, and pursue investment opportunities. Social policy also serves to create and stabilize collective goods, channel and mitigate industrial conflict in periods of structural adjustment, and, in turn, foster political stability and social cohesion (Streeck, 1992; 1997). Last but not least, it should not be forgotten that with social protection outlays averaging 28 per cent of GDP in the EU, social policy acts as an effective anti-cyclical stabilizer (Begg *et al.*, 2001). Against the neo-liberal assumption of a big 'trade-off' between economic efficiency and social justice, European policy elites agree that social policy is an essential factor in promoting economic adjustment, that there is no contradiction between economic competitiveness and social cohesion.

The European social model is marked by high degrees of interest organization and comprehensive negotiations between the government and the social partners over conflicts of interests in matters of economic and social policy. Compared to North America, industrial relations are stable; the majority of workers are covered by collective agreements determining working conditions, employment protection, and living standards. Social partnership, with 'trust' as a constitutive element, moreover, encourages a problem-solving style of policy making, rendering collective actors the necessary social capital to overcome sectionalist interests (Swank, 2001).

Bounded Policy Innovation

Since the late 1970s, all the developed welfare states of the European Union have been recasting the basic policy mix upon which their national systems of social protection were built after 1945 (Scharpf and Schmidt, 2000; Ferrera and Rhodes, 2000; Kuhnle, 2000; Pierson, 2001). In the 1970s, in addressing the threat of stagflation, policy adjustment primarily revolved around macro-economic management and wage bargaining to counter spiralling cost-push inflation and demand-gap increases in unemployment. After the mid-1980s, policy attention moved towards issues of economic competitiveness. In employment policy there was a decisive shift towards supply-side measures. Next to initiatives of labour market deregulation, many welfare states tried to contain open unemployment by reducing labour supply, mainly via early retirement and disability pensions (Ebbinghaus, 2000). The destabilizing consequences of large-scale early retirement and other forms of paid inactivity were only perceived as major policy problems when the European Monetary Union (EMU) set limits to deficit and debt financing. In the wake of the Maastricht Treaty, politicians adopted measures of cost containment, often in conjunction with the introduction of more proactive labour market policies. The institutional make-up of social security arrangements also became a target for reform in the 1990s (Hemerijck and Schludi, 2000).

In retrospect, it is perhaps surprising that policy reforms in the core 'distributive' areas of the welfare state arrived so late in the process of adjustment. The answer is largely political: the more that reform embraces core 'distributive' areas of social protection, the more political conflict is likely to flare up. A change in macroeconomic policy is less likely to ignite conflicts than are cuts in social security benefits. And as social rights are usually attached to strong interest groups, political opposition is likely to render the reform process unpredictable (Pierson, 1994). If wages are sticky, as economists argue, then policies of social protection, enshrined in law, are probably even stickier. This is perhaps most true for pension benefits, which are regarded by large majorities as 'sacrosanct rights' of the elderly (Myles and Pierson, 2001).

We live in a world of path-dependent solutions, and radical change in Europe's welfare states is institutionally ruled out. The challenge is not so much to design, in the abstract, a completely new welfare architecture, but to *recast* prevailing social and economic policies to make them more responsive to the new demands of post-industrial economies. Throughout the neo-liberal 1980s it proved difficult to launch a successful attack on the mature welfare states, especially in Western Europe. Growing citizen disenchantment with neo-liberal recipes subsequently led to political reversal in the 1990s. Voter reaction against the social costs of widening wage disparity and rising poverty revealed a deep popular commitment to their welfare states. This helped return social democratic parties to office in the majority of West European polities, including the four largest countries.

Welfare state popularity does not preclude change. Welfare states are not 'immovable objects' as many observers assert (Pierson, 1998). Even groundbreaking policy changes were implemented in many countries over the past two decades. Moreover, welfare state futures are not foreordained. Path-dependency is about historical contingency: no more, no less. It is indeed striking how many reforms have been enacted in the past decade and how little they followed the textbook neo-liberal recipes (Ross and Martin, 2002). The impact of EMU on social and employment policy is a case in point. Many of the architects of EMU believed that the new macroeconomic environment would, by erecting massive constraints, trigger 'structural reforms' in labour markets, collective bargaining systems, social protection programmes, and in welfare financing. To be sure, the shift to a single currency engendered important direct and indirect repercussions on wage bargaining and social policy. Centre-left parties, back in office during the run-up towards EMU, could definitely not achieve their aspirations of social justice and full employment through traditional expansionary 'demand-side' policies. This was not tolerated by the Maastricht Treaty (1992) or, later, the Stability and Growth Pact (1997). As a consequence, social democratic governments were forced to adopt more painful policy prescriptions. Many embarked upon novel agreements with the social partners, reminiscent of corporatist exchanges between the trade unions and employers' organizations in the 1970s.

Common post-industrial challenges impose quite divergent problem loads from one welfare state to the next. This reflects heterogeneous economic development and social structure, but, more crucially, different social policy legacies, distinct systems of interest organizations and democratic institutions. We identify three welfare regimes, each with a rather unique welfare design and institutional attributes: a Nordic, an Anglo-Saxon, and a Continental European model. The three vary significantly in their relative vulnerability to the new challenges of post-industrial change. The Scandinavian welfare state faces a 'flexibility' problem of creating the appropriate conditions for an expansion of private services. This is closely related to fiscal pressures. The Anglo-Saxon countries face increasing social exclusion of both the 'working' and 'non-working' poor, even in a booming labour market. The Continental countries suffer from low employment rates, especially among women and elderly males, and are especially pressed to transform their inclusive pay-as-you-go pension systems. The Mediterranean welfare states are additionally faced with the difficult task of weakening their traditional 'familialism'. Although the principal site of reform and policy innovation is the nation-state, the process of reform is no longer exclusively a national affair. Today social and employment policies are, under conditions of growing international economic and political interdependence, severely constrained by the Economic and Monetary Union and increasingly shaped by initiatives like the European Employment Strategy (EES). The impact of European integration on domestic employment and social policy reform in the fifteen Member States therefore features prominently in this final chapter.

The character of the reforms pursued under centre-left governments in the 1990s is best captured in terms of institutionally bounded policy change. Most of the policy changes in wage bargaining, employment policy, social services, and pensions have evolved through experimentation. As prevailing employment and social policy ran into severe problems of sustainability, because they were built on political, economic, demographic, and household conditions that no longer prevailed, this triggered a dynamic of *renovation* and *recasting* of current policy so as to achieve a better 'fit' with new societal challenges and pressing economic constraints. The precise policy mixes that have ensued have not only been critically shaped by past policy legacies and institutional structures of decision making, but also by policy makers' capacity for *innovation*, intelligently using the policy resources at their disposal (Crouch, 2001).

Many reform efforts across Europe during the 'social democratic moment' of the 1990s were couched in terms of the idea of 'social protection as a productive factor'. The challenges of post-industrialism should be met by novel synergies between social policy and economic policy (Kaufmann, 2001). As noted, essentially all European governments agree that comprehensive welfare policy is a 'productive factor' in the competitive knowledge-based society (European Council, 2001). This is captured in the normative commitment, formulated at the Lisbon Summit (2000), 'to become the most competitive and dynamic knowledge-based economy in the world, capable of sustainable economic growth with more and better jobs and greater social cohesion'. Institutionally, moreover, it is again generally accepted that a productive balance between economic and social policy is best achieved through a dialogue with the social partners, also at the level of the European Union.

In this chapter I first highlight the main characteristics and vulnerabilities of the three welfare regimes. They all represent a different manifestation of the so-called 'service sector trilemma' (Iversen and Wren, 1998). This trilemma suggests that welfare states today confront a tough choice between full employment, income equality, and fiscal restraint. Next, I present the notion of *bounded policy innovation* and turn to examine available policy responses and concrete experiences of policy innovation in four key policy areas. These concern, respectively, adaptations in wage bargaining in the shadow of EMU, different approaches to activation at the interface of labour market policy and social insurance, policies enabling parents to combine career and family life, and, last but not least, efforts at making pensions both sustainable and fair in the face of ageing. Finally I examine the potential contribution of the EU in employment and social policy reform to the ongoing process of *self-transformation of the European social model(s)*.

Welfare Regimes and the 'Service Sector Trilemma'

Each welfare state displays unique features in policy design, based on deeply held national aspirations of equality, social justice, and solidarity. Since World War II, the expansion of social security, social services, pension rights, minimum wages, collective bargaining procedures, and dismissal protection was a fairly autonomous domestic political affair. In terms of policy design, European welfare states vary significantly along several dimensions (Esping-Andersen, 1990; Scharpf and Schmidt, 2000; Ferrera *et al.*, 2000).

- *Eligibility and risk coverage.* Access to provisions of social protection can be based on citizenship, need, work-related contributions or private contracts.
- *Benefit structure and generosity.* Benefits can be generous or minimal, means-tested, flat-rate, earnings-related, or contribution-related. Benefit structure is also related to country-specific objectives of social protection: income maintenance, poverty alleviation, or equality.
- *Methods of financing.* Financing can range from general taxation, payroll contributions, and user charges, or some combination thereof.
- *Service intensity.* Social services can be provided for through professional (public) services, through the market, or, informally, by the (extended) family.
- *Family policy.* Family policy can be passive, with a strong emphasis on cash transfers in support of traditional single breadwinner family patterns, or very active in its support for gender equality within and outside households with a strong emphasis on servicing through public day-care and generous parental leave provisions.
- *Employment regulation.* Under the heading of employment policy and regulation we group together highly diverse sets of 'industrial rights', such as employment protection (e.g. in the case of dismissals), (minimum) wage regulation, collective bargaining rights and procedures, work councils, and active labour market policies.
- *Logic of governance.* Management of welfare and employment policy does not necessarily fall within the jurisdiction of national public administration. Of special importance is local administration and the degree of extra-parliamentary institutional integration of the social partners (representatives of employers and employees) and private or 'third sector' sector parties in the management and delivery of welfare policy.
- *Industrial relations.* Closely related to the employment regulation and logic of governance in social and employment policy, is the degree of co-ordination in national systems of industrial relations, ranging from fragmented un-coordinated systems to sectoral pattern bargaining and centralized co-ordination. Co-ordination in industrial relations is crucial to employment, primary income distribution, and the extent to which externalities like inflation and unemployment can be mitigated through co-operation (Crouch, 1993; Traxler *et al.*, 2001; Scharpf, 2000*a*).

The rich literature on welfare 'models' has shown how these variables are systematically related to one another, producing distinctive, but not exclusive, nation clusters. Basically we can distinguish between three different 'social Europes' (Esping-Andersen, 1990; 1999). The comprehensive Scandinavian welfare states are characterized by (1) citizenship-based universal entitlements; (2) generous replacement rates in transfer programmes; (3) general revenue financing; (4) a broad supply of social services beyond health and education; (5) active family policy encouraging gender egalitarianism and women's integration in the labour market; (6) low (Denmark) to high (Sweden) levels of employment protection, with a strong emphasis on active policies and training programmes linked to general education; and (7) corporatist industrial relations with peak level bargaining, strong unions, and high levels of collective bargaining coverage. Historically, Scandinavian welfare states featured a strong commitment to full employment macroeconomic policy.

The Anglo-Saxon model, more guided by utilitarian market principles, is characterized by (1) a bias towards targeted, needs-based entitlements; (2) low replacement rates in transfer programmes; (3) general revenue financing; (4) underdeveloped public social services beyond health and education; (5) poor family services; (6) low levels of employment protection, largely confined to ensuring fair contracts, and no legacy of active labour market policy, nor vocational training and education; (7) un-coordinated industrial relations with moderately strong unions, decentralized wage bargaining, and low levels of collective bargaining coverage.

The Continental European model, historically influenced by a mix of statist, corporativist, and familialist traditions (Kersbergen, 1995), is characterized by (1) occupationally distinct, employment-related social insurance; (2) very unequal levels of generosity in transfer programmes, combining generally very high pension replacement rates with occasionally very modest income support (such as unemployment benefits in Italy); (3) a contribution-biased revenue dependency; (4) very modest levels of public social services beyond health and education and often a considerable reliance on 'third sector' and private delivery; (5) passive family policies premised on the conventional male breadwinner family; (6) generally strict levels of employment protection, that is meant to protect, once again, the male breadwinner combined with passive labour market policies, but comprehensive systems of vocational education and training, especially in Germany, Austria, and the Netherlands; (7) strong social partnership that extends into the administration of social insurance; and (8) co-ordinated industrial relations, with a predominance of sectoral wage bargaining, with high levels of bargaining coverage and moderately strong unions.

Differences in policy design are closely related to variations in employment performance, service intensity, levels of income inequality, and also to

Table 6.1 Employment performance in the European Union (2000)

	Employment rate[a]	Unemployment rate[b]	Long-term unemployment[c]	Female employment rate	Youth unemployment rate[e]	Public employment ratios[d]
Denmark	76.3	4.7	1.0	71.6	5.3	22.7
Finland	67.5	9.8	2.8	64.4	11.2	14.6
Sweden	73.0	5.9	1.3	71.0	5.5	21.9
Austria	68.3	3.7	1.0	59.4	2.9	10.0
Belgium	60.5	7.0	3.8	51.5	6.5	10.3
France	62.2[f]	9.5	3.8	55.3[f]	7.1	14.5
Germany	65.4[f]	7.9	4.0	57.9[f]	4.6	9.3
Greece	55.6[f]	11.1	—	40.9[f]	—	6.9
Italy	53.5	10.5	6.4	39.6	11.8	8.9
Luxembourg	62.9[f]	2.4	0.6	50.3[f]	2.5	—
Netherlands	73.2[f]	2.7	0.8	63.7[f]	3.6	6.8
Portugal	68.3	4.2	1.7	60.3	4.2	12.0
Spain	55.0	14.1	5.9	40.3	11.4	7.5
Ireland	65.1	4.2	1.7	54.0	3.3	9.3
UK	71.2	5.5	1.5	64.6	8.3	9.5
EU 15	63.3	8.2	3.6	54.0[f]	7.8	11.7

[a] Total employment/population 15–64 years. [b] Standardized Ratio. [c] Long-term unemployed (12 months and over) as per cent of labour force.
[d] Per cent of population 15–24, 1998. [e] Unemployed as per cent of population aged 15–24. [f] Eurostat estimation.

Source: *Employment in Europe 2000*, European Commission, *2000a*; OECD (*1999a*) (Public employment figures).

structures of taxation. On the employment side, the Nordic countries out-perform both the Anglo-Saxon and Continental models (see Table 6.1). Ireland and the United Kingdom display favourable levels of employment with relatively low rates of public employment (but in Ireland, female employment is very low). The Continental European countries present a mixed picture, with above average employment performance in the North-Western part of the European continent (including Austria, Belgium, France, Germany, the Netherlands, and Luxembourg), and very low employment rates (especially among women and older workers) in the Mediterranean countries (Portugal being an exception).

With respect to social expenditures, the Nordic countries, as shown in Table 6.2, are by far the most generous, followed by Continental Europe with the Anglo-Saxon countries occupying the low end. The spending bias differs, however. The Mediterranean countries are very pension biased, most notably in Italy where pensions absorb 16.13 per cent of GDP. In contrast, the Nordic welfare states are unusually biased in favour of social services to families and children.

What follows, quite surprisingly, from these figures is that the relation between distributive results, employment performance, and tax-spending levels is very weak. The most redistributive welfare states (Denmark and Sweden), have the highest tax burdens, and do better in terms of employment than the low tax Anglo-Saxon countries. The medium–high tax Continental welfare states and the moderate–low tax Southern welfare states perform worst in terms of employment, and also in terms of redistribution. Indeed, the low rates of employment in Continental Europe have less to do with the overall level of taxation and more to do with the heavy reliance on social security contributions.

Persistent unemployment remains the Achilles heel in most European economies. Although it has declined from its peak of 11.1 per cent in 1994 to less than 8 per cent in 2001, long-term unemployment remains at 4 per cent of the labour force. More than 40 per cent of European unemployed people have been out of work for more than a year. Youth unemployment, at 8.4 per cent in 2000, is only two percentage points lower than in 1994.

Employment growth, like everywhere, is skill-biased, service intensive, and gender-specific. The highly educated workers are the winners, both in terms of job security and pay (Lawrence and Slaughter, 1993; Freeman, 1995). The low skilled and less experienced workers are the losers; they either face declining wages, as in the US, or rising difficulties in finding employment.

High-skill jobs account for two-thirds of net employment creation since the mid-1990s. Between 1994 and 1999, over 60 per cent of the 6.8 million new

Table 6.2 Levels of social security, active labour market policy, and collective bargaining coverage in the European Union

	Social expenditures as per cent of GDP 1998[a]	Total taxation as per cent of GDP 1997[a]	Old age and survivors as per cent of GDP 1998[a]	Family/children as per cent of GDP 1998[a]	Social exclusion 1995[c]	Active labour market policy as per cent of GDP 1995[d]	Labour market training 1995[e]	Coverage collective wage bargain as per cent of workers 1995[d]
Denmark	30.0	52.2	11.49	3.90	1.1	2.01	0.48	0.52
Finland	27.2	47.3	9.38	3.48	0.4	1.66	0.21	0.67
Sweden	33.3	53.3	13.12	3.60	0.1	0.87	0.28	0.72
Austria	28.4	44.4	13.69	2.84	1.5	1.89	1.07	0.97
Belgium	27.5	46.5	11.77	2.34	0.7	1.23	0.41	0.82
France	30.5	46.1	13.42	2.99	0.3	0.42	0.09	0.75
Germany	29.3	37.5[c]	12.69	3.03	0.3	0.44	0.15	0.80
Greece	24.5	40.6	12.89	1.98	0.7	1.29	0.29	—
Italy	25.2	45.0	16.13	0.91	0.6	1.27	0.34	—
Luxembourg	24.1	—	10.65	3.40	0.4	0.30	0.01	0.79
Netherlands	28.5	43.3	11.71	1.28	0.7	1.76	0.22	0.80
Portugal	23.4	34.5	9.99	1.24	—	0.35	0.06	0.80
Spain	21.6	35.3	9.96	0.45	0.0	1.08	0.01	0.67
Ireland	16.1	34.8	4.01	2.04	0.5	1.37	0.35	—
United Kingdom	26.8	35.3	11.77	2.30	0.1	0.72	0.21	0.35
Average	27.7	42.6	12.66	2.30	0.5	1.1	0.27	

Sources: [a] 'Statistics in Focus: Social Protection in Europe,' Theme 3–15/2000, Eurostat (2000); [b] OECD (1999c): *Benefit systems and work incentive*, own calculations; [c] Social Protection Expenditures and Receipts, European Commission/Eurostat (1999) (there may be some overlap with other categories of expenditure); [d] OECD Online Social Expenditures Database, workers covered, figures not including Greece, Italy, Luxembourg, and Ireland; [e] OECD Online Social Expenditures Database, 1995 data, or latest year available.

jobs in the European economies went to women (European Commission, 2000a). The majority of newly employed women in the 1990s have taken up service related jobs. Employment levels of workers over 55 continue to decline in the larger economies of Germany, France, and Italy, while in the Netherlands the employment rate of men over 55 rose by 5.5 percentage points over the past decade.

The problems which beset different welfare regimes are inevitably connected to the nature of de-industrialization, and the rise of the service sector. In particular, countries differ substantially in terms of the longer run dynamics of exposed and sheltered sectors (Scharpf, 1997a). Since the mid-1970s, European economies, with the notable exception of the Netherlands and Ireland, have experienced substantial employment decline in the exposed sectors, especially in agriculture, mining, manufacturing, and transport. Sweden and Finland stand out in terms of suffering a continuous loss in industrial employment. In other Member States, employment in the exposed sector has stabilized at a rate of about a third of the working population.

The decline of jobs in the exposed sectors is probably less related to competition from Third World markets (considering that the rest of the world accounts for only a small proportion of European trade) than to the removal of regional barriers to the free movement of capital, firms, goods, and services by the completion of the European internal market. This has required the economies of Sweden, Germany, and the Netherlands, for instance, where wage costs are high, to exploit all opportunities of increasing the efficiency of production and the quality of innovation. To the extent that employment in the exposed sectors has remained stable since 1985, the decline in low-skilled jobs has been offset by significant increases in highly skilled jobs (Scharpf, 1997a).

Within the sheltered sectors, employment depends mainly on the expansion of domestic services, like wholesale and retail trade, restaurants and hotels, community-, social-, and personal-services. These, in theory, should be dynamic given the new demand structure that comes from population ageing (health, care services, and recreation), from household transformation (dual career households are more inclined to buy personal services), and from increased female employment which generates demand for 'reproductive' social services, such as childcare.

The combination of de-industrialization, the rise of the service sector, and the fiscal constraints that derive from the EMU, pose a thorny trilemma. Iversen and Wren (1998) argue that the goals of high levels of employment, income equality, and fiscal restraint can no longer be achieved simultaneously. The ability to maximize service employment today depends on a number of constraints, all of which are linked to the nature of national welfare systems (Scharpf, 2000):

- International competition is driving up productivity and skill requirements in the exposed sector, and this means that most employment growth will be biased in favour of medium and high skilled jobs, while the low skilled will continue to shrink (Wood, 1994).
- The loss of jobs in exposed sectors can be offset by employment gains in the sheltered service sectors, which can be either private or public. However, public employment is stagnant, in large part because of the fiscal constraints associated with the EMU and, subsequently, the Stability and Growth Pact. Job opportunities in private social services are on the rise, but their growth potential is constrained by welfare state regulation of private provision (Scharpf, 2000).
- For the less skilled, employment opportunities are doubly constrained. On one hand, well-paid public sector jobs are stagnant. On the other hand, the growth of private services, such as retail trade, restaurants, and personal services, are constrained by prevailing levels of social protection, the size of the minimum wage, and by the high tax wedge that derives from heavy payroll contributions or from general taxation.

The service sector trilemma generates quite distinctive policy problems for different welfare systems. It is worth summarizing these regime-specific problems before we go on to assess policy responses in the areas of wage bargaining, labour market policy, social services, and pensions.

The Scandinavian Problem

The Scandinavian welfare states are undoubtedly expensive in terms of revenue requirements. Nonetheless, they are demonstrably better adapted to the exigencies of post-industrial change—in large part due to their service intensive, women and child 'friendly' public policy profiles.[1] Social exclusion due to poverty and long-term unemployment is largely avoided. Denmark and Sweden embarked on the road to high public employment already in the 1960s, and what emerged was a self-reinforcing mechanism whereby the expansion of 'welfare state jobs' encouraged women and lone parents to enter the labour market. As the welfare state 'de-familialized' many caring functions it also fostered demand for more social services. The net result was near-maximum employment among men and women alike, less

---

[1] For details, see Chapters 2 and 3 in this book.

early retirement, and relatively high birth rates, all helping to reduce the long-term financial strains on pension systems.

The main difficulty confronting the Scandinavian model is that financing the welfare state is made more difficult due to high capital mobility, the fiscal and budgetary constraints that ageing and European monetary integration impose, and increased political tax resistance (Hemerijck and Schludi, 2000; Scharpf, 2001). Since the 1980s, tax revenues as a share of GDP have been stagnant and, consequently, so has public employment. Indeed, with falling tax revenues during the 1990s, public employment fell markedly in Sweden. There is a clear need to expand private sector jobs to compensate for losses in public sector employment. This is where the trilemma raises its head: the Nordic countries face the hard choice between liberalizing private services, which entails more wage inequality, or a continued adherence to wage equality which, under conditions of budget constraint, implies more unemployment.

The Anglo-Saxon Problem

The Anglo-Saxon experience represents a response to the trilemma that has sacrificed egalitarian goals for the sake of jobs and budgetary restraint. New Labour in effect rejects the pursuit of greater equality via redistribution on moral grounds. The central feature of New Labour's egalitarianism is to promote more earnings income via employment.

The Anglo-Saxon welfare states are comparatively far less threatened by long-term problems of financial sustainability. The conservative adjustment strategy adopted in the UK encouraged wage inequalities and an expansion of low-paid jobs. The result has been a significant polarization of incomes, coupled to an ever-more unequal access to social insurance. Those who can afford private insurance are well covered, while those who cannot are at risk of poverty.

The rise of female employment is, however, not accompanied by active attempts to diminish gender inequities. In the UK, the absence of quality day care provision means that women are frequently compelled to accept low-quality part-time work (Stewart, 1999). And as we have seen in Chapter 2, there has been a marked increase in child poverty and inequality over the past twenty years. Wage subsidies have been introduced to supplement the incomes of low-paid workers and their families (Clasen, 2001). Moreover, radical labour market deregulation has rendered the British system of industrial relations incapable of engaging in co-operative relations between management and trade unions, and it has not helped remedy Britain's long-standing inability to produce a well-trained labour force (Finegold and Soskice, 1988). Skill shortages, low wages, and poverty have produced cumulative cycles of social disadvantage and exclusion of vulnerable groups (Glyn and Wood, 2001).

The Continental European Problem

The Continental European welfare states represent yet another version of the service sector trilemma. Here, a main obstacle to private job growth lies in high wage floors—largely created by very high fixed labour costs. At the same time, public employment is constrained by the fiscal burden of supporting a very large inactive population.

The vulnerability of most Continental welfare states lies less in the Anglo-Saxon ills of widespread poverty and problems of skill-formation, and more in their chronic inability to stimulate employment growth. Job stagnation is directly related to the particular method of payroll-based social insurance financing (Esping-Andersen, 1996; Scharpf, 1997a). This breeds a complicated, mutual interaction between investments, productivity, labour supply, and wage costs. The key to this interaction lies in the strategy of boosting international competitiveness via a combination of early retirement and raising productivity levels of workers through high-quality vocational training and education. The strategy may have put a premium on high productivity, but the indirect effect has been a substantial increase in the 'tax' on labour, as ever fewer workers must shoulder ever more inactive citizens. Put differently, maximizing worker productivity may have resulted in a general 'inactivity trap', whereby a virtuous cycle of productivity growth coincides with a vicious cycle of rising wage costs and exit of less productive workers, all requiring further productivity increases and eliciting another round of reductions in the work force through subsidized early retirement exit. The inactivity trap of the Continental welfare states reinforces existing 'insider–outsider' cleavages and social exclusion, especially where labour markets are heavily regulated, as in Southern Europe (Ferrera, 2000; Guillen et al., 2001).

The primary victims of this self-reinforcing negative spiral have been the young and women (women with children, especially). This goes a long way to help explain fertility and labour supply patterns. As we have seen in Chapters 2 and 3, birth rates are low because of (a) difficulties among youth in gaining a firm foothold in labour (and housing) markets, and (b) the absence of affordable childcare. Hence, women especially are faced with a naked choice between participating or forming families. Hence also the protracted dependency of youth on their parents, in Southern Europe especially (Trifiletti, 1999). As elsewhere, with rising education women's preferences have changed dramatically. But unlike elsewhere, the institutional environment has remained 'frozen' in the traditional male breadwinner mould. In brief, overall job stagnation is worsened by the severe incompatibilities that women face when they opt for a career.

Yet, far higher female employment rates are needed not only to counteract population ageing, but also to reduce household poverty risks. Of course, the low levels of employment imply also that the Continental welfare states have a vast unused labour force potential which, if mobilized, may help sustain future welfare state finances.

Countries all face the service sector trilemma in one form or another. Still, we should avoid exaggerating its actual ramifications. More concretely, it may act as a general constraint but it is not necessarily insuperable. Over the past decade, some countries, among them Denmark and the Netherlands, have managed to increase service jobs while essentially returning to full employment *without* abandoning their commitment to either wage equality or fiscal restraint. Indeed, both countries have in recent years built up substantial budget surpluses. This also applies to Sweden and Finland which, considering the depth of the economic crisis of the 1990s, confronted intense budgetary strains *and* a rise in unemployment.

Bounded Innovation in the Welfare State

Welfare reform is difficult, but it happens. Feasible policy reforms are conditioned by at least three distinct sets of causal factors. These are: (1) the relevant policy challenges; (2) differences in structures of political decision making; and (3) variation in welfare state design (Scharpf and Schmidt, 2000).

As we have shown in the first five chapters of this book, European welfare states face similar challenges and, yet, these do not seem to lead to convergent policy responses. The neo-institutionalist approach to comparative social policy assumes a relatively tight connection between path-dependency and policy inertia: there is a 'lock in' effect, whereby policy choices made in the past become difficult to reverse, even in the face of serious external pressures. Institutional arrangements become resistant to reform because of high sunk costs, reduced co-ordination and transaction costs, and ingrained popular expectations. Still, domestic reform is guided by far more than path-dependency. Innovation occurs when the incentives for change are strong. In the face of accumulated anomalies and policy failures, policy makers are likely to become convinced that they need to innovate.

If we really wish to understand the dynamics of welfare reform, we need to identify the cognitive and normative orientations of policy actors

(Scharpf, 1997*b*). Policy making is the outcome of *puzzling*—diagnosing the nature and magnitude of the problems at hand, setting priorities and identifying potentially effective solutions—and of *powering*—organizing the political and societal support for the selection of particular solutions (Heclo, 1974). Policy reform is not merely 'a contest for power' but depends also on 'playing with ideas', the extent to which policy actors agree over the cognitive definition of policy problems, and the normative benchmarks for effective policy solutions. Governments may be capable of welfare adjustment through policy learning, which is the 'deliberate attempt to adjust the goals or techniques of policy' in the light of the consequences of past policy and new information so as to better attain effective and legitimate policy solutions (Hall, 1993).

Crises often trigger policy learning. They force policy makers to evaluate existing policy and to consider alternatives. At such critical junctures, the authoritative nature of politics—also in multi-actor political systems—offers strategic opportunities for policy changes (Wood, 2001).

The recessions of the mid-1970s served as triggering devices, discrediting many left-of-centre coalitions and paving the way for conservative governments, restrictive policies of fiscal consolidation, privatization, and welfare retrenchment (Pierson, 2001). Policy mistakes can energize the policy process by allowing political decision makers to overcome institutional rigidities. The cathartic experience of the 'Dutch disease' in the early 1980s is a good example of how policy mistakes generate positive learning effects: after a lengthy and painful period of immobility, a process of self-correction in the Netherlands spurred a remarkable economic recovery without sacrificing core welfare goals. In 1986, the Irish government and social partners prepared their first central agreement for economic recovery, when the Irish economy was said to have reached its nadir. Italy's political and economic crisis in the early 1990s, which led to a comprehensive redesign of the Italian pension system, was to a large degree fostered by the challenge of EMU. Typically, reforms are preceded by deep political crises, major hikes in unemployment, government deficits, exchange rate pressures, and irresistible economic and political imperatives like EMU participation. Policy failures, however, are not a sufficient condition for policy change. The capacity to translate a crisis into bounded policy innovation depends on political forces and institutional factors.

Besides the political orientations of governments, domestic institutions exert a tremendous influence over the pace of electoral rhythms, the scope, character, and style of policy change. They make up the political incentive structure of policy making, determining the degree of influence and power that relevant policy actors can bring to bear on the policy process (Scharpf,

2000*a*). They shape the structure of political debate, mediate preferences, and alter policy choices. At one end of the scale, majoritarian political systems, as in the United Kingdom, give single-party governments the mandate to adopt radical and comprehensive reform. At the other end of the scale, the consensual German and Dutch democracies, based on proportional representation with multi-member constituencies and coalition governments, are more biased towards slow, incremental, disjointed, and negotiated patterns of policy change because of the many veto players that need to be accommodated (Bonoli, 2001). German federal governments are, however, subject to more constitutional limitations than the Dutch. With respect to administrative capacities of policy implementation and delivery, there is also huge variation, ranging from the highly centralized French state to the Italian.

Institutional structures also affect individual policy areas. In some countries industrial relations are fully autonomous from state intervention, as in Germany with its constitutional requirement of *Tarifautonomie*. In others, there is a long tradition of state intervention, as in Belgium and France. In corporatist political economies political authority over industrial relations is 'shared' by the state and the social partners. In Bismarckian social protection systems, there is a strong heritage of associational self-regulation by the social partners. Germany and France share strong elements of union involvement in the management of occupational insurance schemes. This implies that adjustment and reform will require agreement from all parties involved. No matter how weak they might become in terms of union membership strength, unions with this kind of institutional role cannot be easily marginalized, and this will constrain state action (Hemerijck and Schludi, 2000).

Political institutions may limit the repertoire of feasible policy options, but they may also act as a resource, encouraging particular styles of decision making (Scharpf, 1997*b*; 2000). Consociational democracies and corporatist systems of industrial relations encourage consensual or problem-solving styles of decision making, characteristic of Scandinavian and Austrian systems of industrial relations (Swank, 2001). This contrasts the self-interested bargaining style in more fragmented systems, or the confrontational style in statist systems of industrial relations, like the French, with its deeply divided trade union movement and weak employers' organizations (Crouch, 1993).

In theory, three directions of policy innovation are possible. One is to preserve the prevailing logic, principles, and institutional format of previous policy. This implies essentially instrumental and incremental change. More daring reforms include changes in the institutional rules of the game and/or changes in the goals and principles of policy. These are best understood, respectively, as institutional adjustment and paradigmatic change (Visser and Hemerijck, 1997). They include new administrative and policy delivery arrangements, new modes of financing, and new roles assigned to public and private actors. When change fails to establish a workable equilibrium, this often prompts domestic political actors to adopt 'best practices' from elsewhere. In the early 1980s, the Irish followed the British strategy of radical labour market deregulation. After government officials, trade unionists, and employers discovered that this strategy was ineffective in countering industrial decline, Irish policy makers shifted to comprehensive social pacts (Hardiman, 2000).

The next three sections highlight recent experiences of bounded policy innovation in different welfare states, in the area of wage bargaining, activation, social services, and, finally, pension reform.

EMU and the Wage Bargain

The introduction of the Economic and Monetary Union (EMU), incorporated in the Maastricht Treaty (1991), is a major watershed in the process of European integration. EMU, with its independent European Central Bank (ECB), statutorily dedicated to price stability as its primary objective, and the single currency, marks a paradigm shift in macroeconomic policy (Dyson and Featherstone, 1999). It is part and parcel of a more general shift to a hard currency policy across the European economies going back to the EMS (European Monetary System) of 1979. In important respects, this paradigm shift was triggered by the failure of Keynesian demand policy in response to the recession-prone 1970s, and to the severe macroeconomic instability in the 1980s and early 1990s.

Monetary integration has consequences for macroeconomic performance and distribution at the level of individual economies, but also for labour markets, social protection, and welfare financing. Both the indirect effects on labour market institutions (Franszese and Hall, 2000) and the direct effects of domestic budgetary and fiscal policy have major implications for welfare state finances. The EMU implies that (Keynesian) macroeconomic policy measures can no longer shield other areas of social policy and economic regulation from the need to adjust to international competition. As nominal exchange rate adjustments are ruled out, adjustment must be sought elsewhere.

Many advocates of EMU argue that its monetary and fiscal rules will spur growth and employment, essentially via two mechanisms. In the first place, a stable macroeconomic framework will result in lower and less variable interest rates, with beneficial effects on investment and consumption. Second, it will also affect the behaviour of the labour market parties by nurturing employment-friendly, decentralized, wage bargaining. In contrast, high debt and deficits would threaten the stability of the Euro and put pressure on the ECB to bail out countries in financial distress.

The EMU will also foster low and stable inflationary expectations which, indirectly, will affect wage behaviour, and deficit reduction will create more room for manoeuvre to cope with adverse economic shocks. With the passing of time, as the Euro gains weight in the world economy, this should result also in lower interest rates worldwide. Many proponents of the EMU, however, argue that its fruits do not come cheap. It will only prove truly advantageous if it is bolstered by structural reforms in the core areas of European welfare states, i.e. in wage bargaining, labour market regulation, social protection, and public services.

A more sceptical note is struck by egalitarians who worry that EMU acts as a 'Trojan horse' for a neo-liberal policy shift, undermining the European Social Model (McNamara, 1998). They believe that EMU, given its restrictive mandate, will reinforce low growth and high unemployment, and thus increase pressures on welfare financing. Their remedy lies primarily in more expansionary 'demand-side' policies. Moreover, a unified interest rate is likely to affect countries differently, with the consequence of divergent inflationary and deflationary pressures. Since the ECB can only respond to average conditions, its actual policy may turn out to be either too tight or too loose for particular Member States (Scharpf, 2000b). By the same token, there is little scope for macroeconomic adjustment to deal with country-specific or 'asymmetric shocks'. Some even argue that the EMU could undermine Europe's growth potential by triggering a vicious cycle of deflationary 'beggar-thy-neighbour' strategies of internal devaluation through competitive wage moderation. They also fear, finally, that the Stability and Growth Pact is wholly inappropriate to the long-term shifts in public finances related especially to population ageing (Begg et al., 2001).

With the completion of full monetary integration, it is also feared that tax competition will intensify, leading to an under-provision of public goods (Genschel, 2001; Ganghoff, 2000). In order to attract and preserve capital, countries will feel pressed to provide advantageous taxation and/or regulation for internationally mobile firms (Cacheaux, 2000; Steinmo, 1996). Other countries will follow suit, which in the end will cause a lower level of taxation and regulation than was previously found appropriate. Such developments would jeopardize current systems of social protection (Tanzi, 1998).

Following the logic of tax competition, economic integration would result in two significant adjustments in national tax systems (Genschel, 2001):

- a decline in the level of total taxation because the exit-threat of mobile tax bases makes high taxes unsustainable;
- a change in the composition of tax revenues because governments are forced to shift taxation from mobile to immobile bases, such as labour, consumption, and real estate.

The empirical evidence, however, suggests that tax competition has so far been limited. First, there has been no decrease in total taxation levels across Europe; to the contrary. Second, there is no clear indication of a shift from taxing mobile to immobile factors. Empirical data show that while property and consumption taxes have declined, corporate taxes have gone up.

Some conclude, then, that there is no significant pressure on taxation (Garrett, 1998; Swank, 2001). But this may be misguided. For one, when we consider increasing unemployment, rising poverty, expanding pensions, and health care costs, we would have expected that taxation should have risen. Instead, during the 1980s most welfare states turned to deficit spending. If countries were not affected by tax competition, they would not have been forced to seek recourse to deficit financing rather than more taxation in order to finance higher spending requirements. Empirical evidence shows that total tax revenues as well as tax ratios appear to be more or less 'frozen' since the mid-1970s. This suggests that some downward pressure on taxation has indeed been operative. However, there is no evidence that governments have been pushed into a 'race to the bottom'.

The assumption that immobile tax bases are not subject to tax base erosion should also be challenged. Higher taxes on labour increase the labour costs for employers and thus decrease labour demand, especially in an open, competitive economy. What is more, high taxes on labour generate incentives to engage in the black economy. A similar argument can be applied to consumption taxes: consumers will want to buy products without paying taxes and producers will want to sell products without having to remit consumer taxes (Genschel, 2001).

Looking back over the 1990s, we can only conclude that the introduction of EMU has been an immense success. It forced Member States to commit to budgetary discipline within the constraints of 3 per cent for the deficit and 60 per cent for the debt (as a percentage of GDP). Following the liberalization of capital mobility in the early 1990s, the creation of the European Monetary Institute (EMI) to monitor convergence in 1994, and membership qualification in 1998, the Euro was adopted by twelve member countries in

January 2002. The UK, Denmark, and Sweden remained outside. Throughout the process, we observe a clear convergence in performance across Europe with respect to inflation, public deficits, and government debt ratios. The EMU has inaugurated a more stable economic environment, and moved the EU towards a more closely synchronized business cycle. Today, deficit spending is no longer a viable option. In an environment of internationally mobile capital, welfare state reform is high on the agenda so as to lower the burden on the public budget and to dampen the growth of wage costs, irrespective of participation in EMU. Indirectly, the Maastricht criteria, negotiated in 1991 and ratified in 1993, put considerable pressure for budgetary consolidation even on those countries that did not join EMU (Scharpf, 2000a).

Politically, the need to qualify strengthened the relative position of finance ministers and central bankers, at the cost of other actors in the polity. The Maastricht criteria clearly operated as triggering devices, helping to overcome political resistance to unpopular reform. Italy in this respect is exemplar. The Italian welfare state was in effect 'saved by Europe' (Ferrera and Gualmini, 2000).

The Resurgence of Social Pacts

Remarkably, these new constraints have not provided policy makers with a 'window of opportunity' to launch bold strategies of labour market deregulation. To the contrary, EMU seems to have spurred a resurgence of national social pacts aimed at ensuring welfare state sustainability. It is true that in the 1980s there was strong pressure to decentralize collective wage bargaining (Calmfors and Driffil, 1988). The shift to a hard currency has brought the social partners closer together, leading to a remarkable resurgence of social pacts (Fajertag and Pochet, 2000). This process began in the Netherlands with the 1982 'Wassenaar' accord, followed by the 1992 'New Course' agreement and the 'Flexicurity' accord of 1996. Denmark established more informal norms of wage moderation under the D-mark zone in 1987. Finland followed suit with the 'Stability Pact' of 1991, and later with the 'Social Pacts I' and 'II' in the second half of the 1990s. Similar attempts were made in Belgium in the first half of the 1990s, but these failed until the 1998 'Central Agreement'. Similarly, the German 'Alliance for Jobs' of 1995–6 under Kohl and the 'Alliance for Jobs, Training and Competitiveness' of 1999 under Schroeder, turned out to be fragile agreements. Ireland embarked on a series of tripartite accords in the late 1980s, beginning with the 'National Recovery' accord, which ran between 1987 and 1991, succeeded by the 'Economic and Social Progress' agreement between 1991 and 1994, the 'Competitiveness and Work' accord of 1994, and finally, the 'Partnership 2000' agreement between 1997 and 2000. In Italy, the first pact was the 'National Agreement' on the *scala mobile* in 1992, followed by pension reform in 1995, labour market reform in 1997, and the 'Social Pact for Growth and Employment' of 1998. In Portugal a number of agreements were reached throughout the 1990s (without consent from the largest union), running from the 'Economic and Social Agreement' of 1990, to the 'Short Term Social Concertation Agreement' of 1996, and the 'Strategic Concertation Agreement' of 1997. In Spain important agreements include the 'Toledo Pact' of 1996, and the 'Stability of Employment and Bargaining Pact' of 1997 (Moreno, 2000). Similarly, in Greece a 'Pact of Confidence' was reached in 1997. Especially for hard currency latecomers, like Italy, Portugal, and Greece, EMU helped to rekindle co-operative, positive-sum solutions (Cameron, 2000; Ferrera and Gualmini, 2000; Rhodes, 2000). Even in Sweden attempts were made to establish a 'Euro' wage norm in 1995, followed by the bipartite agreements in 1997 and the 1998 Pact for Growth. Also Jospin promoted a national social dialogue in 1997 with, however, little success. Except for the United Kingdom, all these social pacts affected wage bargaining systems, strengthening rather than weakening trade unions (Martin and Ross, 2002).

Denmark and the Netherlands have emerged as something of an alternative to neo-liberal deregulation and to traditional 'social democracy' as well, both in terms of institutional and policy change (Benner and Vad, 2000; Visser and Hemerijck, 1997). The Dutch strategy of wage restraint has undoubtedly spurred a substantial growth of (mainly part-time) service jobs. This may have had a moderately negative effect on productivity growth due to the large share of low skilled employment involved. Regardless, the Dutch experience suggests a way for other countries, like Germany and France, to boost service employment. To the extent that wage developments in the private and public sector are coupled, wage moderation can lower the public sector wage bill, ease the costs of social security, and broaden the revenue basis (Ebbinghaus and Hassel, 1999). Finally, there is some empirical evidence from Denmark, Ireland, and the Netherlands that policy co-operation establishes a smoother interplay between income, monetary, and fiscal policy, thus stimulating economic growth with low inflation.

In short, caught between fiscal strain and the need to address new social risks, significant adjustments are required in order to sustain European welfare states. The resurgence of social pacts and tax reforms in the wake of the EMU indicates the presence of a distinctly European search for a new, economically viable, politically feasible, and socially acceptable option. Some authors maintain that the social pacts will decline in coherence and

stability once the goal of EMU participation is reached, especially considering falling union membership. To counteract this, efforts must be made to
initiate bargaining co-ordination at the EU level (Boeri *et al.*, 2001).

Realigning Work and Welfare

Contemporary policy fashion emphasizes gainful employment as the axial
principle of effective citizenship (Clasen, 2000). The new vocabulary of
'employability', 'lifelong learning', 'activation', 'insertion', 'make-work-pay',
and 'welfare to work', signals a shift in favour of microeconomic supply management (Fay, 1997; Esping-Andersen and Regini, 2000). The new objective is
to maximize employment rather than induce labour force exit, and this
implies new links between employment policy and social security (Schmidt
et al., 1996; Vandenbroucke, 1999).

A main priority everywhere is to upskill workers through either vocational
training or education. If social and employment policies are increasingly
aimed at developing the quality of human resources for a high-skill equilibrium, they can assume the role of a 'productive factor'.

The consensus over lifelong learning begins to weaken at the moment one
must decide on responsibilities (Crouch *et al.*, 1999). Leaving skill formation
to the market may result in under-investment since private firms fear the
danger of 'poaching' from competitors. Hence, the inclusion of the social
partners may be essential. The key problem, as discussed in Chapter 4, is how
to ensure training opportunities for those workers who are most likely to
become marginalized, such as those in low-skilled jobs, part-time or older
workers, and immigrants.

In the 1990s, some countries promoted voucher schemes, tax incentives,
and Individual Learning Accounts (ILAs) to promote more training. ILAs, like
vouchers and co-payments, are based on the principle that: (*a*) individuals
are best placed to choose what they need to learn and how they want to
improve their skills; and (*b*) costs should be shared by all the actors involved,
employers, workers, and government.

Activation

Improvements in vocational training and education are unlikely, by themselves, to solve the problem of skill deficits, particularly for those who have
already entered the workforce. Hence, in the 1990s, several governments
experimented with various forms of 'activation' programmes (Eardley *et al.*,
1996; Lødemel and Trickey, 2000). The underlying philosophy is one of

reciprocal obligations: welfare recipients must be obliged to accept employment or training in order to receive benefits, while the state has the obligation to enhance the employability of benefit claimants (Clasen, 2000).

The Danish activation policies combine successful employment strategies with an extremely generous benefit system. They have been singled out by the European Commission as a 'best practice' for others to follow (Kvist, 2000). While the level of unemployment benefits remained unchanged, restrictions were introduced with respect to duration and eligibility.[2] In the United Kingdom, by contrast, the emphasis on training and skill enhancement remains limited and is accompanied by less generous income support than is the case in Denmark (Clasen, 2001). The direct involvement of the social partners in activation is part and parcel of the Danish success story.

Employment subsidies

Demand for low skilled workers can also be raised by subsidies. The US, Ireland, and the United Kingdom have followed this approach by extending work-conditional benefits, while other countries have favoured a reduction in social security contributions (France, Belgium, Germany, the Netherlands, Spain, and Portugal) (Cantillon and De Lathouwer, 2001). As a result, the number of subsidized jobs has grown dramatically.

Different wage subsidy strategies are appropriate to different welfare states. In the United Kingdom, where income guarantees and unemployment benefits are modest, individual tax credits to support low-wage workers and their families are very popular. In Continental Europe, the main problem is that heavy social contributions price less productive workers out of the market. Hence, reducing fixed labour costs is one way to stimulate jobs. Targeted wage subsidies are seen as a means to spur job growth without, at the same time, accepting American style inequalities. Wage subsidies are far less important in countries such as Denmark, in part because public employment is massive; in part because basic income support is generous.

Employment subsidies are not without problems. The British experience reveals that poverty risks for those outside employment have been aggravated by tax credits (Clasen, 2001). Moreover, subsidies may simply permit employers to lower wage rates without necessarily creating new jobs. Since many Continental programmes are targeted to the long-term unemployed, they may spur employers to substitute long-term unemployed for short-term unemployed, or to delay hiring until the subsidy can be collected. Also, a policy of reducing social security contributions could jeopardize employers'

---

[2] See Chapter 2, and Kvist (2000) for details.

incentives to upgrade skills. The danger is that employment subsidies may lock low-skilled workers into persistent low-wage employment: the erstwhile 'inactivity trap' may, in other words, become a 'low-skill trap'.

Labour market de-segmentation

In the 1980s, it was widely believed that full employment could only be achieved by a redistribution of existing jobs. The most popular strategy was compulsory working time reduction. In the 1990s, the policy consensus has moved in favour of voluntary work sharing through the expansion of part-time work.

The new policy environment requires more labour market flexibility in terms of work patterns, wages, and working time. This may promote a better use of human resources within firms, but also welfare improvements for workers and their families. An effective employment policy must reconcile flexibility with minimal precariousness. There is no inherent contradiction between these objectives. To the contrary, acceptance of flexible labour markets is enhanced if matched by strong social guarantees.

Labour market de-segmentation implies a relaxation of employment protection for the core workforce combined with increased protection for the peripheral and more precarious labour force. The Netherlands are an example of how labour market de-segmentation prevents marginalization (Barrell and Genre, 1999). With the 1995 flexi-security agreements, the legal position of part-time and temporary workers was strengthened in exchange for a slight liberalization of dismissals among regular, full-time employees.

Even in the very 'insider biased' Southern European labour markets, labour de-segmentation is possible. The Treu reforms in Italy sought to favour part-time and temporary work, and in Spain improved conditions for short-term contract workers were accompanied by reduced dismissal costs for those with permanent contracts. In the UK, the introduction of a statutory minimum wage may also imply labour market de-segmentation.

The reforms discussed above have also triggered a change in governance in the promotion of welfare and employment. This is obvious in the case of Danish activation with its individualized guidance and service provision, because it necessitates new institutional connections between social security and employment policy and between the public and private sector. Three trends are clear: (1) the liberalization of public employment service systems; (2) the widening scope of co-ordination between social protection and employment provision; and (3) emerging sub-national employment pacts in response to problems associated with regional economic conditions (Regalia, 2001).

The new approach to labour market policy has been accompanied by a major restructuring of public employment services. In a number of countries we witness a liberalization of the regulations governing private employment agencies and of market mechanisms, such as contracting out arrangements. In some countries, this has gone hand in hand with a regionalization and, sometimes, tripartization of institutional responsibilities, so as to include organized interests, especially employers, in job placement organizations (Ferrera, Hemerijck, and Rhodes, 2000).

Another example of institutional change is found in welfare state financing. In France, for example, the bulk of health care and basic income support (the RMI) financing has been shifted from social insurance contributions to general taxation (Palier, 2000). This would serve the double goal of reducing payroll taxes and of increasing the leverage of the state over social policy.

Reconciling Work and Family Life

Strategies of labour market de-segmentation are related to the feminization of the labour market. As examined in Chapter 3, women now account for the majority of job growth in the European Union but, still, substantial differences in participation rates and also in the nature of female employment remain (Daly, 2000). Low birth rates indicate severe compatibility problems for women across much of Europe, and in Southern Europe especially. Hence the urgent need for policy change.

As argued in Chapter 3, a first policy priority has to do with childcare, leave arrangements, professional care for the elderly, and the tax treatment of spouses' earnings. More social services like childcare, could provide additional employment opportunities, especially for women (Behning and Serrano Pascual, 2001). Yet, it is also clear that the nature and quality of jobs play a key role for working mothers.

In Scandinavia, followed by Belgium and France, the expansion of services to families began in the 1970s in tandem with the rise in female labour supply. It was in large part this policy of 'de-familialization' of caring responsibilities which catalysed the dual-earner norm. In most other European countries, female employment growth has come somewhat later (Sainsbury, 1999). In Southern Europe it is only during the past decade that we see a sharp rise (Saraceno, 1994). The big question is whether such a strategy of 'de-familialization' is feasible under current economic and social conditions?

Recent policy, especially in the Netherlands, seeks to expand childcare through the organizations where parents are employed. The Netherlands now has the highest rate of firm-provided and privately subsidized day care. While this shows that childcare does not necessarily need to be provided by the government, the problem is that private provision is generally limited to high-skilled and full-time workers. The ambition of the so-called National Childcare Strategy in the UK, on the other hand, is to establish childcare facilities in every neighbourhood. Workers receiving Working Family Tax Credits (usually low skilled and low paid workers), are credited 70 per cent of their childcare costs. Furthermore, opening hours play a significant role in the accessibility of childcare facilities. In many Continental European countries, day care institutions generally open only during mornings, which severely constrains the possibilities of full-time or even part-time employment.

Parental leave arrangements are of critical importance so as to avoid career interruptions. The duration and generosity of entitlements is obviously key. The Nordic countries combine very generous provision and also provide incentives for fathers to participate. In the UK, parental leave is underdeveloped. Indeed, the Thatcher government sought to remove parental leave for fathers from the scope of the EU Parental Leave Directive of 1984. Progress has, however, been made under New Labour. The National Action Plan of 1999 contains an extension of Maternity Allowance to those under the lower earnings limit. In the majority of Continental welfare states there are provisions for either fully or partly paid maternal leave, but additional parental leave schemes are not all that generous, leading to low take-up rates.

Job security is of crucial importance to the continuity of female employment. The cumulative wage penalty, caused by interrupted working careers, may discourage continuity in female careers, but may also make it prohibitive to have children for career-oriented women. Several countries guarantee the right to return to work, after having cared for young children.

Flexible working hours are often a requirement for family-friendly employment, and there is a clear relation between the ratio of part-time jobs and female employment growth. But the ability of part-time employment to harmonize careers with family depends very much on regulation, whether it is recognized as a regular job with basic social insurance participation, and whether it offers possibilities for career mobility.

In Scandinavia, part-time employment has been stagnant and even in decline in recent years. This can be seen as testimony of the highly developed policies for reconciling work and family life; part-time employment is increasingly not *necessary* for working mothers. However, especially in the UK and the Netherlands, part-time jobs have grown steadily over the past decade and account for a large share of female employment growth. Nonetheless, the regulatory framework remains decisive for whether part-time jobs expand. Their growth in Ireland and the UK is in large part the product of labour market deregulation in the 1980s. Here part-time work is mainly a coping strategy among low-skilled and low-paid female workers. The Netherlands exemplifies a more 'women-friendly' approach to part-time employment. The Working Hours Act (2000) gives part-timers an explicit right to equal treatment in all areas negotiated by the social partners, such as wages, basic social security, training and education, subsidized care provision, holiday pay, and second tier pensions. As a result, hourly earnings differences between full-time and part-time jobs have narrowed to 7 per cent. Dutch employers essentially recruit part-time workers to obtain organizational flexibility, not as a low-price competition strategy, as is the case in the United Kingdom. Indeed, 69 per cent of all employed Dutch women work part-time, which means that further increase in female employment is most likely to follow the Nordic lead of full-time contracts. In the Mediterranean countries, the pervasive absence of part-time jobs means that fewer women are employed, and if employed they are mainly on full-time contracts.

Since women are more likely to compromise their careers for family reasons, they risk accumulating fewer pension entitlements than their partners. A policy of labour market de-segmentation requires that pension entitlements be universalized, and also that taxation be gender-neutral. To achieve more universal pension coverage, one step would be to introduce a basic, non-contributory pension. Again following the Scandinavian tradition, some countries have begun to make access to a basic pension easier for part-time and temporary employees.

Pressures for more women-friendly policy are no doubt intensifying now that the EU has adopted the 60 per cent female employment target by the year 2010. The pressures are obviously stronger in the Continental European and Anglo-Saxon welfare states with undeveloped leave and care provision. For these countries, Scandinavia might exemplify a 'best practice'. It should, however, be remembered that the conditions that obtained when, in the 1970s and 1980s, the Nordic countries embarked upon their servicing strategy were quite different. This was a period of full employment, and governments then enjoyed considerably greater financial leeway. With the EMU and with fears of tax competition, major public expenditure increases become far more difficult.

In light of this, Dutch policy may provide an alternative model for others to emulate. In its first phase, Dutch part-time job expansion was based on rather short hours contracts. Soon it became evident that further female employment growth would necessitate not only improved access to childcare but also an upgrading of part-time contracts. From this followed the strategy of encourageing firms (often via subsidies) to provide day care for their employees (OECD, 2001a).

The Quest for Fair and Sustainable Pensions

Demographic ageing constitutes one of the most pressing policy problems throughout the advanced welfare states. As examined in Chapter 5, the real challenge lies in how to allocate the *additional* expenditures that inevitably accompany population ageing. Clearly, the demographics vary substantially between countries. With very low birth rates and, simultaneously, high rates of early retirement, the Continental European countries face far greater pressures.

Demographic pressures are compounded by design characteristics in public pension systems. Except for the Netherlands, all Continental welfare states have mandatory PAYGO systems, financed through social contributions. These systems imply high non-wage labour costs that can have seriously negative consequences for employment at the lower end of the earnings scale (Scharpf, 1997a; Schludi, 2001). It is also argued that PAYGO systems yield lower rates of return than do fully funded systems (Hinrichs, 2001). Funded pension systems face far less fiscal strain as a result of population ageing. Whereas PAYGO is based on an intergenerational contract according to which the 'young' finance the pensions of retirees, in funded systems each cohort is in principle responsible for its own welfare in old age. As Myles argues in Chapter 5, relying on funded schemes means that the entire burden of additional future pension spending is allocated to the aged themselves; relying fully on PAYGO schemes means that the entire burden is placed on the 'young'.

A few countries, including Denmark, Sweden, and the Netherlands, combine a general revenue financed, basic pension guarantee with funded pensions. Such a combination would in principle produce a better risk diversification combined with higher rates of return (Manow and Seils, 2000).

Ongoing efforts at pension reform offer, once again, an example of path-dependent policy. As is well known, no reform project can assume a *tabula rasa*. There are huge sunk costs in whatever system obtains in any country. Hence, an overnight shift from PAYGO to a fully funded system would impose a double financial burden on at least one generation. The upshot is that radical change is unlikely, but not that reform is impossible as long as it remains loyal to prevailing principles and starting conditions.

Policy makers must simultaneously secure sustainability and distributional fairness. In terms of sustainability, reforms in Europe will have to adhere to the fiscal constraint of EMU and the Stability and Growth Pact. In terms of fairness, as argued in Chapter 5, intergenerational equity can be assured with the adoption of a fixed relative position (FRP) benchmark, holding constant the income ratios between the working population and retirees. But if we also aim to ensure intragenerational justice, that is, more equality among retirees, this would be best assured by adding a basic, general revenue financed retirement guarantee to the system—more or less in line with current Nordic and Dutch practice.

There is almost unanimous agreement that pension system reform must be coupled to employment policy. Sustainable pensions will be difficult to achieve unless we raise employment rates among women and older workers. For some countries this involves a double-bind: high non-wage labour costs depress job growth and, yet, they serve to finance pension schemes. It is additionally clear that a reduction of public debt by the time that huge cohorts enter into retirement, around year 2030 in most cases, is vital in order to create greater financial leeway for anticipated spending increases. And, finally, there is a broadly recognized need to match old-age security with more flexibility and 'active ageing'.

If governments were able to bring down the national debt over the next twenty years, so interest payments would fall, and this would, at once, enhance financial sustainability and release funds to meet the needs of an ageing population. In the 1990s, a number of countries, notably the Netherlands, France, Portugal, Ireland, and Belgium, have started to build up pension reserve funds in order to maintain adequate pension provision when the 'baby-boom' generation retires.

A variety of measures have been adopted in order to strengthen the actuarial link between contributions and benefits. These include incremental adjustments in the retirement age, replacement rates, and indexation systems. A dominant feature in current reform is to raise contribution rates, which has been done in Denmark, Finland, Greece, Germany, and the Netherlands. These measures, when simply applied 'across the board', like in Denmark, usually disadvantage lower income earners. At the same time some countries, like Germany and the Netherlands, have established ceilings to contribution rates that are linked to commitments not to reduce replacement rates.

Raising the retirement age means increasing contributions and reducing benefit payments over a citizen's life span. Under pressure from EU equality legislation, most countries are in the process of equalizing the legal retirement age of men and women. Increasing the number of years used to define the reference earnings usually leads to reductions in benefit levels. In

Finland, for example, pension benefits are now calculated on the basis of the last ten (instead of 4) years; in Italy, the reference period has been extended to the entire career.

Changes in indexation rules for pensions are now common, and these also help reduce pension liabilities. In Sweden, for example, a new proviso states that if pension liabilities exceed assets, then pension indexation will automatically fall behind the income index until the balance between assets and liabilities has been restored. Austria and Germany have moved from gross to net wage indexation, while France and Italy have shifted from wage to price indexing. By and large, these reforms are justified by the argument that the primary purpose of pensions is to preserve the purchasing power of retirees and not to compensate them for productivity improvements.

In Southern Europe, such restrictions have gone hand-in-hand with attempts to upgrade minimum pension benefits. This, of course, ensures greater intragenerational equality and helps create trade union consensus, as evidenced in the Spanish 'Toledo Pact' (Moreno, 2000). Italy provides another example. Here, high income earners were subject to indexation adjustments and also an extension of the reference period for full pension earnings, while the minimum pension was raised.

Groundbreaking pension reforms cannot be ruled out. Here Britain offers an example. The Conservative governments of the 1980s succeeded in privatizing old age social security by giving employers and the middle classes the incentive to 'opt out' of the public SERPS system and contract private occupational pension insurance. One consequence was a marked decline in public pension liabilities, but this has been accompanied by substantial increases in poverty and inequality among the aged. To diminish such inequalities, the Blair government has, in 1999, introduced a 'Stakeholder Pension', aimed at providing pensions for people with insecure employment. In the long run, this basic income guarantee should increase in line with earnings to allow pensioners to benefit from rising prosperity of the country as a whole.

Both Italy's and Sweden's reforms move in the direction of a defined-contribution pension scheme. This means that the costs associated with demographic change will fall more on future retirees than on current contributors. These are far-reaching reforms, but their implementation is very incremental, allowing for a long transition period which enables younger cohorts to anticipate a decline in prospective pension benefits by building up supplementary private pension entitlements. Radical, though incremental, changes like these are more viable if accompanied by incentives to take up supplementary (private) pension schemes.

In Italy the transition towards a defined-contribution pension system was enacted and implemented in two steps. In the 1992, the Amato government extended the number of contributory years, raised the retirement age, and lengthened the period determining the reference salary for pension calculations. In 1995, the Dini government went still further, introducing a form of capitalization through the creation of individual retirement accounts. This reform was made possible by support from the unions. In this case too the reform is based on a long transition period.

With respect to increased pre-funding, there has been little progress in most Continental welfare states. Germany has gone furthest with reforms to encourage private occupational pensions, and in many countries private plans now enjoy favourable tax status. Since tax deductions favour higher incomes, German policy makers plan to support low-income earner plans with state subsidies.

Interrupted careers cause a disproportional gap in acquired pension rights. Countries like Austria, Belgium, France, and Germany now add contribution years to the insurance records of parents who raise children. In the Netherlands, part-time and temporary workers are granted access to basic pension and health care entitlements.

Policy makers now advocate 'active ageing' as an alternative to early retirement. The idea is to keep older people in the work force by measures that make it possible to combine work and retirement. In Finland, part-time retirement was already introduced in the late 1980s. Tax allowances for older workers who remain employed and for those working part-time, as introduced in Denmark, can also enhance the choice-menu among older workers. In Belgium older employees can reduce working hours progressively until they reach retirement age in exchange for a partial pension. And in the Netherlands a supplementary tax credit will be introduced to keep older workers employed. Still, most welfare states have abstained from more proactive policies to raise the employability of older workers and to counter widespread age discrimination by employers.

The degree of success of reform efforts varies considerably, even among countries with similar pension systems (Hinrichs, 2001). The political feasibility of reform depends to large degree on the institutional capacities to orchestrate a consensus among major political parties and/or between the government and the social partners, especially the trade unions (Schludi, 2001). Groundbreaking reforms (except in the a-typical Westminster model), are almost impossible to achieve without broad partisan support. In Sweden, reform began with a broad political consensus between the social democrats and the bourgeois parties and was subsequently extended to the social partners. In Italy, support from the trade unions was a *sine qua non* for the shift to a defined-contribution system. More recently, in Germany, the Schroeder government sought in vain to gain support from the Christian Democrats. The government did finally gain the approval of the Bundesrat, as not only the SPD-led Laender, but also Berlin and Brandenburg, supported the reform. The other CDU Laender still refused (Schludi, 2001). *Ex negativo,* the absence of co-operation among mainstream French parties and the social partners is an important cause for the lack of progress in pension reform (Palier, 2000; Levy, 2000).

In Southern Europe reform initiatives were part and parcel of encompassing 'package-deals' in the run-up to the EMU, covering wider areas of social protection over which the trade unions have an important say. This was the case in the Spanish Toledo Pact, and also in Italy, where on the basis of trade union consent cuts in pension benefits for the 'better off' were 'traded' for improvements among the lower income earners. Through such issue-linkages, governments in Italy, Spain, and also Portugal managed to obtain union support to make substantial changes in their pension systems. The social partners, especially the trade unions, were apparently able to internalize the trade-off between increasing pension demands and the fact that those pensions need to be financed out of contributions from the working age population (Myles and Pierson, 2001). Using such methods of 'positive co-ordination' on the basis of a common agreement on overarching policy goals, the scope for effective policy reform increases dramatically (Hemerijck and Schludi, 2000).

All told, with the exception of Scandinavia, there has in reality been little progress to encourage employment among older workers. Guillemard's (1999) appraisal of the lack of substantial reforms in France applies basically to all Continental welfare states: the ageing debate tends to focus on pensions. Proposals for delaying the retirement age by simply increasing the number of contribution years required for a full pension provide insufficient incentives to continue working. Extending working life longer calls for an active employment policy.

Deepening Social Europe through Open Co-ordination

In the European Union we observe some convergence of employment and social policy objectives over the past decade. All Member States are explicitly dedicated to raise employment, promote social inclusion, invest in the productivity and skills of future workers, and enhance innovation in the pursuit of a competitive knowledge-based economy. The Treaty of the European Union (Title XI, article 136) already lists a number of common social policy ambitions, ranging from 'the promotion of high levels of employment, the raising of the standard of living and working conditions, adequate social protection, the social dialogue, the development of human capital and the fight against social exclusion'. This convergence in objectives and ambitions not only reflects shared aspirations, but perhaps more precipitously a common concern with the new risks of social polarization.

If Europe's social concerns are not merely symbolic, then we face the question of a possible common European welfare strategy. Economic integration has made it easier for citizens and corporations to opt out of national social insurance schemes. By the same token, European citizens increasingly fear a race-to-the-bottom, involving tax competition and/or social dumping between rival economies. Accelerated economic integration without any meaningful social progress could confront the European Union with severe legitimacy problems.

For three reasons a fully-fledged European welfare system in the near future is rather unlikely to emerge: (1) the room for a European Union employment and social policy is already occupied by strongly entrenched national policy (Leibfried and Pierson, 1996; 2000); (2) national policy makers are generally unwilling to transfer social and labour market policy competencies to EU institutions; (3) it may very well be that Member States face broadly similar challenges, but 'the devil lies in the detail'. In this case, the detail encompasses not only policy legacies but also substantial institutional diversity.

The principal site for welfare reform remains the nation-state and, yet, domestic reforms are severely constrained by the EMU and increasingly shaped by supranational regulation and policy initiatives. While domestic policy makers are wary of surrendering any authority, there is nonetheless a case to be made for greater co-ordination at the EU level. In a period of growing international interdependence, the performance of one national economy will hinge ever more on the performance of other Member States. As governments search for solutions to pressing policy problems, they may first turn to their own past experience. However, in the face of increased uncertainty, policy makers can hardly be expected to effectively build on their own past policy experience to come up with new answers.

From Rome to Laken

The formative period of the European Union, culminating with the Treaty of Rome in 1957, included only six countries and there was an implicit assumption that social policy harmonization would evolve naturally. With each wave of enlargement the barriers to harmonization obviously rose. Indeed, the harmonization of employment and social policy eventually became an important impediment to economic and monetary integration. In the 1980s, European integration was biased in favour of 'market-building', of eliminating trade restrictions and competitive distortions. The Single European Act (1986) strengthened the legal basis of the Commission by extending qualified majority voting on issues of the internal market. Countervailing initiatives of 'market correction' in the area of common employment and social policy remained subject to unanimous consent. This clearly inhibited ambitious European-wide employment and social policy initiatives (Scharpf, 1997a; 1999; Streeck, 1992). Notwithstanding the dominance of 'negative integration', the Delors commission managed to become more active in the area of social policy once the Single European Act was ratified in 1987. In 1989 several directives and recommendations were put together under the 'Charter of Fundamental Rights', to be incorporated into the Maastricht Treaty. However, due to the veto of the Thatcher government, a 'social chapter' in the Treaty of the European Union was ruled out (Lange, 1993). As a result, EU-wide employment and social policy initiatives were largely absent from the completion of the Single Market and the introduction of EMU. But this began to change with the Dutch Presidency in 1997.

A first real breakthrough was the insertion of an Employment Chapter in the Amsterdam Treaty (1997). At the European Council of Essen in December 1994, European leaders adopted a medium-term strategy for the fight against unemployment (Goetschy, 1999). Five priority objectives were identified: investment in vocational training and lifelong learning, increasing the employment intensity of economic growth through flexible employment and wage restraint, reduction in non-wage labour costs, improvement in active labour market policies and targeted measures to help the long-term unemployed. In terms of institutional procedures, the Essen Council proposed annual evaluation procedures in order to monitor progress. The European Summit in Dublin (1996) sought to add an employment chapter to the revised treaty, and a High-Level Employment and Labour Market Committee was established with this aim in mind. This was the precursor to the Amsterdam Treaty which officially raised employment to the status of a common European concern (Larsson, 1998).

The employment chapter stipulates that Member States participate in policy co-ordination around a common strategy defined by the Council. The chapter does not confer competencies to the EU to interfere in domestic labour markets. Institutionally, the employment chapter formally assigns a public status to the social partners in the process, both at the level of the EU in formulating guidelines and at the level of individual nation-states with respect to the drafting of national action plans (NAPs).

Agreement over the employment title was helped along by the rise to power of centre-left governments in the EU, in particular in large countries, like France, Italy, the UK, and Germany, which triggered a search for a new European approach to employment and social policy. After the victory of New Labour in the British general election of May 1997, Blair instantly put his support behind the European employment strategy. Shortly after, France also endorsed the employment strategy. Meanwhile, social unrest in Belgium, Germany, Italy, and France in 1995–7 added to the fear of competitive social dumping.

In 1998, the European Employment Strategy (EES) was formalized and Member States, with the involvement of employer organizations and trade unions, were required to report on its implementation. On the basis of the annual evaluation, the Council was allowed to issue recommendations to individual Member States to revise their policies. Such advice, however, does not carry the penalty of sanctions (Porte, Pochet, and Room, 2001). Its sanctioning power lies entirely in 'peer pressure'.

Contrary to what sceptics might have feared, first results reveal progress. Institutionally, the EES has helped extend social partnership involvement in the guidelines. Also, the Joint Employment Reports signal a reorientation of national policies from passive to active measures. Moreover, the new 1999 guidelines on gender mainstreaming, including policies on career breaks, parental leave, and part-time work, reveal new priorities in favour of reconciling work and family life (Bercusson, 2000). Another groundbreaking change is the requirement to introduce policies to keep older workers in the workforce. In 2001, numerical targets for increasing participation rates were established.

Following the second evaluation exercise of the NAPs, the Council identified eight areas where national implementation remained insufficient: youth unemployment; preventing long-term unemployment; tax and unemployment benefit reforms; job creation in services; modernization of work organization; making taxes more employment friendly; the fight against gender inequalities; and improving statistical indicators.

Progress in terms of European social protection also emerged in the second half of the 1990s (Falkner, 1998). Here, too, development flowed from the notion of a 'convergence of objectives' rather than 'harmonization'. The Commission presented in 1999 its proposal for 'A Concerted Strategy for Modernizing Social Protection', a framework for closer co-operation in social protection, again based on annual reporting with a view to identifying best practices (European Commission, 1993; 1997; 2000*d*).

The Lisbon Summit marked a watershed in the Europeanization of employment and social policy. It produced concrete commitments to increase the rate of total employment in the European Union to 70 per cent (60 per cent for women) by 2010, the promotion of lifelong learning, and increased employment in services. With respect to social protection, it launched the open method of co-ordination to new policy initiatives for fighting poverty, combating social exclusion, and modernizing systems of social protection. The Portuguese presidency agreed to draw up European guidelines for social protection, which would be implemented in the same manner as the Employment Guidelines; setting common objectives that are ambitious and realistic, using clear indicators whenever possible, ensuring necessary flexibility for Member States to implement policy, and fostering co-operation among Member States (European Commission, 2000*b*). More recently, the Swedish Presidency proposed to apply the method of open co-ordination to health, elderly care, and pensions (European Commission, 2000*e*; European Council, 2001). It also included targets to raise employment among workers aged 55 to 64 to 50 per cent by 2010. The Belgian Presidency in 2001 forged a political agreement on quantitative indicators for monitoring progress with respect to social inclusion across Member States. It also sponsored, at the Laken Council in December 2001, common objectives for pension reform. The fight against unemployment and social exclusion has thus become part of the EU constitution.

Strengths and Weaknesses of the Open Method of Co-ordination

With fifteen different welfare states, not to forget a possible enlargement with ten candidate countries, there obviously does not exist any single 'European social model' towards which Member States of the European Union could possibly converge in the next decades (Ferrera, Hemerijck, and Rhodes, 2000). Clearly, the issue is not one of subordinating domestic policy to EU directives but rather one of joint policy learning and co-operation.

The European Employment Strategy inaugurated a new model of cross-national policy making through monitoring and benchmarking, and the Open Method of Co-ordination (OMC) launched a new mode of European governance. The latter promotes a 'learning-friendly' environment for policy innovation and experimentation while recognizing that national welfare states are profoundly different. This is a major breakthrough in an environment which, for long, remained paralysed by resistance to supranational harmonization and fears of a race to the bottom.

OMC is a procedure whereby domestic policy actors respect national differences while accepting commonly agreed guidelines and taking inspiration from 'best practices' abroad. The objective is not to achieve common policies, but rather to share policy experiences and practices. The conclusions of the Lisbon Summit list a number of key elements of OMC:

- setting short-, medium-, and long-term guidelines for the EU with specific timetables for their achievement;
- establishing performance indicators and benchmarks tailored to each Member State to allow comparison of best practice;
- translating targets from European guidelines to national policy responses;
- periodic monitoring, evaluation, and peer review and evaluation with an emphasis placed on mutual learning processes.

Open co-ordination should be located somewhere between the modes of 'intergovernmental negotiations' and ' mutual adjustment' (Scharpf, 2000b). Government competencies remain entirely national but are no longer pursued in isolation.

As an iterative process, OMC provides ample opportunities to tackle employment and social problems in a medium-term perspective. It helps de-politicize the issues at stake, and it encourages a problem-solving style of policy making. Moreover, it facilitates policy in areas where EU competencies are relatively weak, where regulation is infeasible and impracticable. The experience with EES reveals that Member States seem to be more willing to accept initiatives of Community action when the EU does not have legally binding powers.

Contextualized Benchmarking

Benchmarking and monitoring are central to OMC. Benchmarking requires (a) collection of data on policies and their outcomes; (b) assessment of the outcomes and of how policies affect such; and (c) some determination about whether the institutional environment surrounding the policy is comparable (Romanelli, 1999).

OMC exemplifies a 'contextualized' method of benchmarking, allowing consultation over guidelines and national action plans, with ongoing feedback on implementation (Hemerijck and Visser, 2001). Most often, a 'decontextualized' benchmarking prevails, leading to the promotion of one exemplary case for others to follow. A quote from the Joint Employment

Report 1999 is instructive in this respect: 'The essence of this method is an examination of the transferability of a policy presented by a 'host country' by several interested 'peer countries'. The core activity in each peer review is a seminar complemented with a site visit. It is a structured activity based on a number of expert papers prepared in advance specifically for this exercise' (European Commission, 2000b).

Benchmarking and monitoring offers the possibility of acquiring information through standardized evaluations. Relying on elaborate guidelines, targets, deadlines, and evaluations, the strategy is pragmatic in dealing with national contingencies and vulnerabilities. The exposure to others through peer review is a useful motivator because no government wants to be seen to perform badly. More important is the experience gained through peer review. OMC stimulates an understanding of national contexts, whereby policy makers are able to assess why some solutions can or cannot be transposed to their own national context.

Taking learning seriously highlights the importance of ascertaining what is possible *and* of a willingness to experiment. Open co-ordination combines two types of policy learning: *learning from others*, with a large element of 'lesson drawing' and mimicking based on the experience in other countries; and *learning with others*, or 'interactive learning', based on joint processing and exchange of information and experience. OMC can potentially stimulate *'learning ahead of failure'* (Hemerijck and Visser, 2001). It may expand the repertoire of policy responses, and learning from success elsewhere, policy makers may reduce the costs of pure trial and error. In this sense, the open method of co-ordination marks a step towards a *preventive* labour market policy.

Shortfalls of OMC

Some fear that 'soft' policy co-ordination, with its lack of real sanctions, will crowd out 'hard' legislation. Domestic policy innovation can easily be masked by repackaging existing policies. Moreover, rushing towards social benchmarking with reference to vague objectives runs the risk of discrediting the entire process. In the absence of sanctions or rewards, the attempt to co-ordinate social objectives may prove futile.

In short, OMC is no panacea and will possibly need to be accompanied with legislation. To be sure, health and safety at work and regulation of second pillar pensions requires legislation. OMC is especially useful in policy areas where EU competencies are constrained and where policy objectives are ambitious. One of the most sensitive issues, especially in the area of social protection, is the quality and quantity of available statistics on performance.

Additionally, a key political question is how and to what extent feedback from learning processes contributes to the improvement of guidelines. The Europeanization of employment and social policy cannot affect the balance of political power in individual Member States. A change in national governments may, for example, alter nations' policy priorities. A final concern is how much diversity in welfare design, institutional structure, and problem loads that OMC can tolerate. This issue may become acute with the impending accession of many Central and Eastern European countries.

Open co-ordination has the potential to develop into a valuable addition to the modes of governing now available in the European polity. It is imminently more flexible than 'joint decision procedures' or 'intergovernmental negotiations'. Moreover, in contrast to 'mutual adjustment, it can provide useful safeguards against an unintended 'race to the bottom' (Scharpf, 2000b). Policies may even converge in a voluntary process of multi-level diffusion as the experience with new policies accumulates. The OMC does, however, remain fragile, in the sense that it is highly contingent on the extent to which national policy makers see themselves as pursuing convergent or parallel goals. Nevertheless, successes achieved through OMC are likely to enhance the legitimacy of the EU as a social union.

Conclusion

Domestic welfare reforms throughout the 1990s mark distinctive, and sometimes successful, responses to the massive policy challenges ahead, and we would expect the momentum to continue. In contrast to the view of Europe as 'sclerotic', this chapter has highlighted a dynamic and distinctly 'European' type of reform process. It is a process that continues to adhere to deep-seated commitments to equity and solidarity, to the belief that social protection enhances efficiency, and to institutional preferences for negotiated rather than imposed change.

The self-transformation of the European social model has never been guided by some grand master plan, from which policy then ensued. The European reform model is replete with contingencies, policy failures, co-ordination and implementation problems and, obviously, shifts in the balance of political and economic power.

The 'trial and error' nature of European social reform means that attempts to solve problems in one particular policy area may, through a dynamic of spill-over effects, create problems in neighbouring policy areas. New problems trigger yet another search for new solutions, both horizontally (across policy areas) and vertically (between different layers of governance). Since the mid-1970s, macroeconomic instability stimulated a learning process through which the hard currency EMU was established. The imperatives of monetary integration put pressure on systems of industrial relations, leading to new adaptations in wage bargaining. New bargaining procedures, in turn, encouraged a search for more active labour market policies, as well as 'activating' social security provisions. And with the rise of services and female employment occurred a reorientation of policy. Last but not least, steps are being taken to make pension systems fair and sustainable in the face of population ageing. Politically, most of these sequential stages of bounded policy innovation were outcomes of lengthy processes of (re)negotiation between political parties, governments, and often also the social partners.

Policy innovation at the national level has shaped the employment and social policy agenda of the European Union. Persistently high unemployment in the run-up to the EMU raised the urgency of a common European strategy. In the second half of the 1990s, aided by the presence of centre-left governments, we see a deepening of Social Europe. The success of the European Employment Strategy provided a window of opportunity for European employment and social policy which, in turn, catapulted the open method of co-ordination. OMC may very well unleash a process of 'hybridization' in welfare and labour market policy. This could lead to new policy mixes, something which is already apparent in small countries like Denmark, Ireland, the Netherlands, and Portugal. Welfare reform in the first decade of the twenty-first century will increasingly involve a combination of *domestic learning, learning from and with others,* and hopefully also a learning *ahead of failure.*

References

Adema, W. (1997). 'What do Countries Really Spend on Social Policies? A Comparative Note.' *Economic Studies* 28: 153–67.

Alber, J. (1982). *Von Armenhaus zum Wohlfartsstaat*. Frankfurt: Campus Verlag.

Allmendinger, J., and Hinz, T. (1996). 'Mobilitat und Lebensverlauf.' Unpublished paper, University of Munich (January).

Andersen, D., and Hestbaek, A. (1999). *Ansvar og Vaerdier. En Undersoegelse i Boernefamilier*. Copenhagen: SFI.

Atkinson, A., Cantillon, B., Marlier, E., and Nolan, B. (2002). *Indicators for Social Inclusion in the European Union*. Oxford: Oxford University Press.

Atkinson, A. B., and Micklewright, J. (1986). *Unemployment Benefits and Unemployment Duration*. London: Suntory-Toyota International Centre for Economics and Related Disciplines, London School of Economics.

Bardasi, E., and Francesconi, M. (2000). 'The Effect of Non-Standard Employment on Mental Health in Britain.' *ISER Working Papers*, no. 2000–37. Colchester: University of Essex.

Barr, N. (2001). *The Welfare State as a Piggy-Bank: Information, Risk, Uncertainty and the Role of the State*. Oxford: Oxford University Press.

Barrell, R., and Genre, V. (1999). 'Employment Strategies for Europe: Lessons from Denmark and the Netherlands.' *National Institute Economic Review*, April: 82–95.

Bazen, S., Gregory, M., and Salverda, W. (1998). 'Low-Paid Employment in France, Great Britain and the Netherlands.' In S. Bazen, M. Gregory, and W. Salverda (eds.), *Low-Wage Employment in Europe*. Cheltenham: Edward Elgar, 7–24.

Becker, G. (1991). *A Treatise on the Family*. Cambridge, Mass: Harvard University Press.

Begg, I., Berghman, J., Chassard, Y., Kosonen, P., Madsen, P., Matsaganis, M., Muffels, R., Salais, R., and Tsakloglou, P. (2001). 'Social Exclusion and Social Protection in the European Union: Policy Issues and Proposals for the Future Role of the EU.' Policy Report, EXPRO.

Behning, U., and Serrano Pascual, A. (2001). *Gender Mainstreaming in the European Employment Strategy*. Brussels: ETUI.

Bell, D. (1976). *The Coming of Postindustrial Society*. New York: Basic Books.

Bell, I., Houston, N., and Heyes, R. (1997). 'Workless Households, Unemployment and Economic Activity.' *Labour Market Trends*. London: Office of National Statistics.

Benner, M., and Bundgaard Vad, Y. (2000). 'Sweden and Denmark: Defending the Welfare State.' In F. W. Scharpf and V. A. Schmidt (eds.), *Welfare and Work in the Open Economy*, ii: *Diverse Responses to Common Challenges*. Oxford: Oxford University Press, 399–466.

Beramendi Alvarez, P. (Forthcoming). 'The Distributive Consequences of Decentralization.' Ph.D. Thesis (Juan March Institute, Madrid).

Bercusson, B. (2000). 'The European Employment Strategy and the EC Institutional Structure of Social and Labour Law.' Paper presented at the workshop 'Legal Dimensions of the European Employment Strategy', Brussels, 9–10 October.

Berger, S., and Piore, M. (1980). *Dualism and Discontinuity in Industrialised Societies.* Cambridge: Cambridge University Press.

Bernardi, F. (1999). *Donne fra Famiglia e Carriera.* Milan: FrancoAngeli.

—— (2001). 'The Employment Behaviour of Married Women in Italy.' In H. P. Blossfeld and S. Drobnic (eds.), *Careers of Couples in Contemporary Society.* Oxford: Oxford University Press, 121–45.

Bernhardt, E. (2000). 'Female Careers between Employment and Children.' Paper prepared for European Observatory on Family Matters, Seville, 15–16 September.

Bertola, G., Boeri, T., and Nicoletti, G. (2001). *Welfare and Employment in a United Europe.* Cambridge, Mass.: MIT Press.

Bielby, W., and Baron, J. (1984). 'A Woman's Place is with Other Women.' In B. Reskin (ed.), *Sex Segregation in the Workplace.* Washington, DC: National Academy Press, 27–55.

Bien, W. (2000). 'Changing Values among the Future Parents of Europe.' Paper presented at European Observatory on Family Matters, Seville, 15–16 September.

Bison, I., and Esping-Andersen, G. (2000a). 'Unemployment, Welfare Regime and Income Packaging.' In D. Gallie and S. Paugam (eds.), *Welfare Regimes and the Experience of Unemployment.* Oxford: Oxford University Press, 69–86.

—— —— (2000b). 'The Transformation of Life Course Dynamics in Italy.' Unpublished paper, Facolta di Sociologica, Universita di Trento (October).

Blau, F., and Ehrenberg, R. (1997). *Gender and Family Issues in the Workplace.* New York: Russell Sage.

—— Ferber, M., and Winkler, A. (1998). *The Economics of Women, Men, and Work.* Englewood Cliffs, NJ: Prentice Hall.

—— and Kahn, L. (2000). 'Gender Differences in Pay.' *NBER Working Papers*, no. 7732.

Block, F. (1990). *Postindustrial Possibilities.* Berkeley, Calif.: University of California Press.

Blossfeld, H. P. (1995). *The New Role of Women.* Boulder, Colo.: Westview Press.

—— and Hakim, C. (1997). *Between Equalization and Marginalization.* Oxford: Oxford University Press.

—— and Drobnic, S. (2001). *Careers of Couples in Contemporary Society.* Oxford: Oxford University Press.

Boeri, T., Borsch-Supan, A., and Tabellini, G. (2001). 'Would you Like to Shrink the Welfare State? A Survey of European Citizens.' *Economic Policy*, 32: 9–50.

—— Brugivini, A., and Calmfors, L. (2001). *The Role of Trade Unions in the Twenty-First Century.* Oxford: Oxford University Press.

Boheim, R., and Taylor, M. P. (2000). 'The Search for Success: Do the Unemployed Find Stable Employment?' *ISER Working Papers*, no. 2000–5. Colchester: University of Essex.

Bonke, J. (1995). *Faktotum. Husholdningernes Produktion.* Copenhagen: SFI.

Bonoli, G. (1997). 'Switzerland: Institutions, Reforms and the Politics of Consensual Retrenchment.' In J. Clasen (ed.), *Social Insurance in Europe.* Bristol: The Policy Press, 109–29.

—— (2001). 'Political Institutions, Veto Points and the Process of Welfare State Adaptation.' In P. Pierson (ed.), *The New Politics of the Welfare State.* Oxford: Oxford University Press, 238–64.

—— and Palier, B. (1997). 'Reclaiming Welfare: The Politics of French Social Protection Reform.' In Martin Rhodes (ed.), *Southern European Welfare States*. London: Cass, 240–59.

Bradbury, B., Jenkins, S., and Micklewright, J. (2000). 'Child Poverty Dynamics in Seven Nations.' Paper prepared for Conference on Families, Labour Markets, and the Well-being of Children. University of Vancouver, June.

—— —— —— (2001). *The Dynamics of Child Poverty in Industrialised Countries*. Cambridge: Cambridge University Press.

—— and Jantti, M. (2001). 'Child Poverty across the Industrialised World.' In K. Vleminckx and T. Smeeding (eds.), *Child Well-Being, Child Poverty and Child Policy in Modern Nations*. Bristol: The Policy Press, 11–32.

Bradshaw, J. (2000). 'How Effective Are Minimum Income Schemes in Reducing Child Poverty?' Paper presented at the Coloque Comparer les Systèmes de Protection Social en Europe (June). Paris: Ministry of Social Affairs.

—— et al. (1996). *The Employment of Lone Parents: A Comparison of Policy in 20 Countries*. London: Family Policy Centre.

Brewster, K., and Rindfuss, R. (2000). 'Fertility and Women's Employment in Industrialised Nations.' *Annual Review of Sociology*, 271–96.

Bruyn-Hundt, M. (1996). *The Economics of Unpaid Work*. Amsterdam: Thesis Publishers.

Buchel, F., Frick, J., Krause, P., and Wagner, G. (2001). 'The Impact of Poverty on Children's School Attendance. Evidence from West Germany.' In K. Vleminckx and T. Smeeding (eds.), *Child Well-being in Modern Nations*. Bristol: The Policy Press, 151–74.

Burtless, Gary, and Quinn, Joseph (2001). 'Retirement Trends and Policies to Encourage Work among Older Americans.' In P. Budetti, R. Burkhauser, J. Gregory, and H. A. Hunt (eds.), *Ensuring Health and Income Security for an Aging Workforce*. Kalamazoo, Mich.: Upjohn Institute.

Cacheaux, J. le (2000). 'Labor Markets, Social Protection, Tax and Social Competition in the European Monetary Union.' Preliminary paper prepared for the conference on 'Europe: One Labour Market, Challenge for Workers and Employers'. Brussels: SALTSA.

Calmfors, L., and Driffil, J. (1988). 'Centralization of Wage Bargaining.' *Economic Policy*, 6: 14–61.

Cameron, D. R. (2000). 'Unemployment, Job Creation and EMU.' In N. Bermeo (ed.), *Unemployment in the New Europe*. Cambridge: Cambridge University Press, 7–55.

Cantillon, B., Ghysels, J., van Dam, R., and Mussche, N. (2000). 'Skills, Gender Equality and the Distributional Impact of Female Labour Force Participation in the Three Worlds of Welfare Capitalism.' Unpublished paper, Centre for Social Policy, University of Antwerp (June).

—— and Van den Bosch, K. (2001). 'Back to Basics: Safeguarding an Adequate Minimum Income in the Active Welfare State.' Unpublished paper, Centre for Social Policy, University of Antwerp.

—— and Lathouwer, L. de (2001). 'Report on Belgium.' Paper presented at the conference on 'Welfare Systems and the Management of the Economic Risk of Unemployment'. Florence: European University Institute, 10–11 December.

Castells, M. (1996–8). *The Information Age: Economy, Society, and Culture*. 3 vols., Oxford: Blackwell.

Christoffersen, M. (1996). *Opvaekst med Arbejdsloeshed*. Copenhagen: SFI.

—— (1997). *Spaedboernsfamilien*. Rapport nr. 1. Copenhagen: SFI.

Clark, T., and Lipset, S.M. (1991). 'Are Social Classes Dying?' *International Sociology*, 4: 397–410.

Clasen, J. (2000). 'Motives, Means and Opportunities: Reforming Unemployment Compensation in the 1990s.' In M. Ferrera and M. Rhodes (eds.), *Recasting European Welfare States*. London: Frank Cass, 89–112.

—— (2001). 'Managing the Economic Risk of Unemployment in the UK.' Paper presented at Conference 'Welfare Systems and the Management of the Economic Risk of Unemployment'. Florence: European University Institute, 10–11 December.

Clement, W., and Myles, J. (1994). *Relations of Ruling*. Montreal: McGill-Queens University Press.

Cornia, A., and Danziger, S. (1997). *Child Poverty and Deprivation in the Industrialized Countries*. Oxford: Oxford University Press.

Crouch, C. (1993). *Industrial Relations and European State Traditions*. Oxford: Clarendon Press.

—— (2001). 'Welfare State Regimes and Industrial Relations Systems: the Questionable Role of Path-dependency Theory.' In Ebbinghaus and Manow (2001), 105–24.

Daly, M. (2000). 'A Fine Balance: Women's Labor Market Participation in International Comparison.' In F. W. Scharpf and V. A. Schmidt (eds.), *Welfare and Work in the Open Economy*, ii: *Diverse Responses to Common Challenges*. Oxford: Oxford University Press, 511–53.

Danziger, S., and Waldvogel, J. (2000). *Securing the Future. Investing in Children from Birth to College*. New York: Russell Sage.

Davies, H., and Joshi, H. (2001). 'Who has Borne the Cost of Britain's Children in the 1990s?' In K. Vleminckx and T. Smeeding (eds.), *Child Well-Being, Child Poverty and Child Policy in Modern Nations*. Bristol: The Policy Press, 299–320.

Davies, R. B., Elias, P., and Penn, R. (1993). 'The Relationship between a Husband's Unemployment and his Wife's Participation in the Labour Force.' In D. Gallie, C. Marsh, and C. Vogler (eds.), *Social Change and the Experience of Unemployment*. Oxford: Oxford University Press, 154–87.

Davis, E. P. (1995). *Pension Funds, Retirement Income Security and Capital Markets*. Oxford: Oxford University Press.

De Graaf, P., and Ultee, W. (2000). 'United in Employment, United in Unemployment? Employment and Unemployment of Couples in the European Union in 1994.' In D. Gallie and S. Paugam (eds.), *Welfare Regimes and the Experience of Unemployment in Europe*. Oxford: Oxford University Press, 265–85.

Dejours, C. (1998) *Souffrance en France. La banalisation de l'injustice sociale*. Paris: Seuil.

Derthick, M. (1978). *Public Policy for Social Security*. Washington, DC: Brookings.

Dex, S., Gustaffson, S., Smith, N., and Callan, C. (1995). 'Cross-National Comparisons of the Labour Force Participation of Women Married to Unemployed Men.' *Oxford Economic Papers*, 47: 611–35.

Diamond, P., and Hausman, J. (1984). 'Individual Retirement and Savings Behaviour.' *Journal of Public Economics*, 23: 81–114.

Ditch, J., Barnes, H., and Bradshaw, J. (1998). *A Synthesis of National Family Policies in 1996*. European Commission: European Observatory on National Family Policies, vol. i.

Drèze, J. H., and Sneesseens, H. (1997). 'Technological Development, Competition from Low Wage Economies and Low-Skilled Unemployment.' In D. J. Snower and G. de la Dehesa (eds.), *Unemployment Policy: Government Options for the Labour Market*. Cambridge: Cambridge University Press, 250–82.

Duncan, G., Gustafsson, B., Hauser, R., Schamauss, G., Jenkins, S., Messinger, H., Muffels, R., Nolan, B., and Ray, J. (1993). 'Poverty Dynamics in Eight Countries.' *Population Economics*, August: 215–34.

—— and Brooks-Gunn, J. (1997). *Consequences of Growing up Poor*. New York: Russell Sage.

—— Yeung, J., Brooks-Gunn, J., and Smith, J. (1998). 'How Much does Childhood Poverty Affect the Life Chances of Children?' *American Sociological Review*, 63: 406–23.

Dyson, K., and Featherstone, K. (1999). *The Road to Maastricht. Negotiating Economic and Monetary Union*. Oxford: Oxford University Press.

Eardley, T., Bradshaw, J., Ditch, J., Gough, I., and Whiteford, P. (1996). *Social Assistance in OECD Countries*, i: *Synthesis Report*, ii: *Country Reports*. London: HMSO (Department of Social Security Research Report No. 46).

Easterlin, R. (1987). *Birth and Fortune. The Impact of Numbers on Personal Welfare*. Chicago: University of Chicago Press.

Ebbinghaus, B. (2000). 'Any Way Out of "Exit from Work"? Reversing the Entrenched Pathways of Early Retirement.' In F. W. Scharpf and V. A. Schmidt (eds.), *Welfare and Work in the Open Economy*, ii: *Diverse Responses to Common Challenges*. Oxford: Oxford University Press, 511–53.

—— and Hassel, A. (1999). 'Striking Deals: Concertation in the Reform of Continental European Welfare States.' MPIfG Discussion Paper 99/3. Cologne: Max Planck Institute for the Study of Societies (MPIfG).

—— and Visser, J. (2000). *Trade Unions in Western Europe since 1945*. London: Macmillan.

—— and Manow, P. (eds.) (2001). *Comparing Welfare Capitalism: Social Policy and Political Economy in Europe, Japan, and the USA*. London: Routledge.

Erikson, R., and Goldthorpe, J. H. (1992). *The Constant Flux. A Study of Class Mobility in Industrial Societies*. Oxford: Oxford University Press.

Esping-Andersen, G. (1990). *The Three Worlds of Welfare Capitalism*. Cambridge: Polity Press.

—— (ed.) (1996). *Welfare States in Transition*. London, Sage.

—— (1999). *Social Foundations of Post-industrial Economies*. Oxford: Oxford University Press.

—— (2000). *A Welfare State for the 21st Century*. Report to the Portuguese Presidency of the European Union, Lisbon.

—— and Regini, M. (2000). *Why Deregulate Labour Markets?* Oxford: Oxford University Press.

European Commission. (1993). *Social Protection in Europe*. Luxembourg: Office for Official Publications of the European Communities.

—— (1997). *Social Protection in Europe 1997*. Luxembourg: Office for Official Publications of the European Communities.

European Commission (1999a). *Employment in Europe 1998*. Luxembourg: Office for Official Publications of the European Communities.

—— (1999b). *Social Protection Report*. Brussels: DGV.

—— (2000a). *Employment in Europe 2000*. Brussels.

—— (2000b). *Building an Inclusive Europe*. Communication from the Commission, Brussels, DGV, Employment and Social Affairs.

—— (2000c). *Acting Locally for Employment. A Local Dimension for the European Employment Strategy*. Communication from the Commission, Brussels.

—— (2000d). *Social Policy Agenda*. Communication from the Commission, Brussels.

—— (2000e). *The Future Evolution of Social Protection from a Long-Term Point of View: Safe and Sustainable Pensions*. Communication from the Commission, Brussels.

—— (2000f). *Guidance on Work-related Stress. Spice of Life or Kiss of Death?* Luxembourg: Office for Official Publications of the European Communities.

—— (2001a). *Employment and Social Policies: A Framework for Investing in Quality*. Communication from the Commission, Brussels.

—— (2001b). *New European Labour Markets, Open to All, with Access for All*. Communication from the Commission, Brussels.

—— (2001c). *Employment in Europe 2001*. Luxembourg: Office for Official Publications of the European Communities.

—— (2001d). *Supporting National Strategies for Safe and Sustainable Pensions through an Integrated Approach*. Communication from the Commission to the Council, the European Parliament, and the Economic and Social Committee. Brussels, 3 July.

European Council (2000). *Nice European Council: Presidency Conclusions*.

—— (2001). *Stockholm European Council: Presidency Conclusions*.

Fajertag, G., and Pochet, P. (eds.) (2000). *Social Pacts in Europe (New Dynamics)*. Brussels: ETUI.

Falkner, G. (1998). *EU Social Policy in the 1990s: Towards a Corporatist Policy Community*. London: Routledge.

Fay, G. R. (1997). 'Making the Public Employment Service more Effective through the Introduction of Market Signals.' *Labour Market and Social Policy Occasional Papers*, no. 25. Organization for Economic Co-operation and Development.

Ferrera, M. (1993). *Modelli di Solidarita*. Bologna: Il Mulino.

—— (2000). 'Reconstructing the Welfare State in Southern Europe.' In S. Kuhnle (ed.), *Survival of the European Welfare State*. London: Routledge, 166–81.

—— and Gualmini, E. (2000). 'Italy: Rescue from Without?' In F. W. Scharpf and V. A. Schmidt (eds.), *Welfare and Work in the Open Economy*, ii: *Diverse Responses to Common Challenges*. Oxford: Oxford University Press, 351–98.

—— and Rhodes, M. (eds.) (2000). *Recasting European Welfare States*. London: Frank Cass.

—— Hemerijck, A., and Rhodes, M. (2000). *The Future of Social Europe: Recasting Work and Welfare in the New Economy*. Oeiras: Celta Editora.

Finegold, D., and Soskice, D. (1988). 'The Failure of Training in Britain: Analysis and Prescription.' *Oxford Review of Economic Policy*, 4(3): 21–53.

Flaquer, L. (2000). *Las politicas familiares en una perspectiva comparada*. Barcelona: La Caixa.

Flora, P., and Heidenheimer, A. (1981). *The Development of Welfare States in Europe and America*. Rutgers, NJ: Transaction Books.

Franzese Jr., R. J., and Hall, P. (2000). 'Institutional Dimensions of Coordinating Wage Bargaining and Monetary Policy.' In T. Iversen, J. Pontusson, and D. Soskice (eds.), *Unions, Employers and Central Banks. Macroeconomic Coordination and Institutional Change in Social Market Economies*. Cambridge: Cambridge University Press, 173-204.

Gallie, D. (1999). 'Unemployment and Social Exclusion in the European Union.' *European Societies*, 1: 1.

—— (2000). 'The Labour Force.' In A. H. Halsey and J. Webb (eds.), *Twentieth Century British Social Trends*. London: Macmillan, 281-323.

—— and Vogler, C. (1993). 'Unemployment and Attitudes to Work.' In D. Gallie, C. Marsh and C. Vogler (eds.), *Social Change and the Experience of Unemployment*. Oxford: Oxford University Press, 115-53.

—— Marsh, C., and Vogler, C. (eds.) (1993). *Social Change and the Experience of Unemployment*. Oxford: Oxford University Press.

—— Cheng, Y., Tomlinson, M., and White, M. (1994). 'The Employment Commitment of Unemployed People.' In M. White (ed.), *Unemployment and Public Policy in a Changing Labour Market*. London: Policy Studies Institute, 178-90.

—— and Russell, H. (1998). 'Unemployment and Life Satisfaction.' *Archives Européennes de Sociologie*, 39(2): 3-35.

—— White, M., Cheng, Y., and Tomlinson, M. (1998). *Restructuring the Employment Relationship*. Oxford: Clarendon Press.

—— and Paugam, S. (eds.) (2000). *Welfare Regimes and the Experience of Unemployment in Europe*. Oxford: Oxford University Press.

—— Paugam, S., and Jacobs, S. (2001). 'Unemployment, Poverty and Social Isolation: Is there a Vicious Circle of Social Exclusion?' Paper presented to the Euresco Conference on Labour Market Change, Unemployment, and Citizenship in Europe, Helsinki, 20-5 April.

Ganghof, S. (2000). 'Adjusting National Tax Policy to Economic Internationalization: Strategies and Outcomes.' In F. W. Scharpf and V. A. Schmidt (eds.), *Welfare and Work in the Open Economy*, ii: *Diverse Responses to Common Challenges*. Oxford: Oxford University Press, 597-646.

—— and Machin, S. (2001). 'The Relationship between Childhood Experiences, Subsequent Educational Attainment and Adult Labour Market Performance.' In K. Vleminckx and T. Smeeding (eds.), *Child Well-being in Modern Nations*. Bristol: The Policy Press, 129-50.

Garrett, G. (1998). *Partisan Politics in the Global Economy*. Cambridge: Cambridge University Press.

Gauthier, A. (1996). *The State and the Family*. Oxford: Clarendon Press.

Genschel, P. (2001). 'Globalization, Tax Competition and the Fiscal Viability of the Welfare State.' MPIfG working paper.

Gershuny, J. (2000). *Changing Times*. Oxford: Oxford University Press.

Gillion, C. (1999). 'Current Situation and Trends in Social Protection Financing Europe in 2035: The Financing of Pensions and Other Social Protection Programmes.' Paper presented at the 'Conference Financing Social Protection in Europe. A European

Way to Combine Sustainable Economic Growth, High Employment and Social Protection', Helsinki, 22–3 November.

Ginn, J., Street, D., and Arber, S. (eds.) (2001). *Women, Work and Pensions: International Issues and Prospects.* Buckingham: Open University Press.

Glyn, A., and Wood, S. (2001). 'New Labour's Economic Policy.' In A. Glyn (ed.), *Social Democracy in Neoliberal Times. The Left and Economic Policy since 1980.* Oxford: Oxford University Press, 200–22.

Goetschy, J. (1999). 'The European Employment Strategy: Genesis and Development,' *European Journal of Industrial Relations*, 6(2): 117–37.

Goldin, C. (1997). 'Career and Family: College Women Look to the Past.' In F. Blau and R. Ehrenberg (eds.), *Gender and Family Issues in the Workplace.* New York: Russell Sage, 20–58.

—— and Polacheck, S. (1987). 'Residual Differences by Sex: Perspectives on the Gender Gap in Earnings.' *American Economic Review*, 77: 143–51.

Gottschalk, P., McLanahan, S., and Sandefur, G. (1994). 'The Dynamics of Intergenerational Transmission of Poverty and Welfare Participation.' In S. Danziger, G. Sandefur, and D. Weinberg (eds.), *Confronting Poverty.* Cambridge, Mass.: Harvard University Press, 85–108.

Green, F. (1999). 'It's Been a Hard Day's Night: The Concentration and Intensification of Work in late 20th Century Britain.' Department of Economics, University of Kent, *Studies in Economics*, 99/13.

—— Felstead, A., and Gallie, D. (1999). 'Computers Are Even More Important than You Thought: An Analysis of the Changing Skill Intensity of Jobs.' Working Paper 99/13, Department of Economics, University of Kent.

Gregg, P., Hansen, K., and Wadsworth, J. (2000). 'Measuring the Polarisation of Work across Households.' Working Paper, Department of Economics, University of Essex.

—— and Machin, S. (2001). 'The Relationship between Childhood Experiences, Subsequent Educational Attainment and Adult Labour Market Performance.' In K. Vleminckx and T. Smeeding (eds.), *Child Well-being in Modern Nations.* Bristol: The Policy Press, 129–50.

Guillemard, A.-M. (1999). 'Work or Retirement at Career's End? A New Challenge for Company Strategies and Public Policies in Ageing Societies.' In S. Shaver and P. Saunders (eds.), *Social Policy for the 21st Century: Justice and Responsibility.* SPRC Reports and Proceedings, no. 141, vol. i, 22–40.

—— (2001). 'Continental Welfare States in Europe Confronted with the End of Career Inactivitiy Trap: A Major Challenge to Social Protection in an Ageing Society.' Paper presented to the Conference on Rethinking Social Protection, Centre For European Studies, Harvard University.

—— and de Vroom, B. (2001). 'From Externalisation to Integration of Ageing Workers on the Labour Market. A Comparison between France and the Netherlands.' Paper presented at the Euresco Conference 'Labour Market Change, Unemployment and Citizenship in Europe'. Helsinki, 20–5 April.

Gustafsson, B., Muller, R., Negri, N., and Voss, W. (2000). 'Paths Through and Out of Social Assistance.' Unpublished manuscript, University of Turin.

Gustafsson, S. (1994). 'Childcare and Types of Welfare States.' In D. Sainsbury (ed.), *Gendering Welfare States*. London: Sage, 45–61.

Gustavsen, B., Hofmaier, B., Philips, M. K., and Wikman, A. (1996) *Concept-Driven Development and the Organisation of the Process of Change. An Evaluation of the Swedish Working Life Fund*. Amsterdam/Philadelphia: John Benjamins Publishing Company.

Haber, Carole, and Gratton, Brian (1994). *Old Age and the Search For Security: An American Social History*. Bloomington, Ind.: Indiana University Press.

Hakim, C. (1987). 'Trends in the Flexible Workforce.' *Employment Gazette*, Nov: 549–60.

—— (1996). *Key Issues in Women's Work*. London: Athlone Press.

Hall, P. A. (1993). 'Policy Paradigms, Social Learning, and the State. The Case of Economic Policy Making in Britain.' *Comparative Politics*, 25(3): 275–96.

Hank, K., and Kohler, H. P. (2000). 'Gender Preferences for Children in Europe.' *Demographic Research*, 2.

Hannan, C. (1999). 'Beyond Networks: "Social Cohesion" and Unemployment Exit Rates.' Working papers of the ESRC Research Centre on Micro-social Change. Paper 99–7 Colchester: University of Essex.

Hardiman, N. (2000). 'The Political Economy of Growth: Economic Governance and Political Innovation in Ireland.' London: Society for the Advancement of Socio-Economics (SASE), July 7–9, 2000.

Hastings, D. (1997). 'Economic Activity of Working-Age Households.' *Labour Market Trends*. London: Office of National Statistics.

Hauser, R. (1997). 'Adequacy and Poverty among the Retired.' Organization for Economic Cooperation and Development, Paris.

—— Nolan, B., with Morsdorf, C., and Strengmann-Kuhn (2000). 'Unemployment and Poverty: Change over Time.' In D. Gallie and S. Paugam (eds.), *Welfare Regimes and the Experience of Unemployment in Europe*. Oxford: Oxford University Press, 25–46.

Haveman, R., and Wolfe, B. (1994). *Succeeding Generations. On the Effects of Investments in Children*. New York: Russell Sage.

—— —— (1995). 'The Determinants of Children's Attainments.' *Journal of Economic Literature*, 33: 1829–78.

Heckman, J., and Lochner, L. (2000). 'Rethinking Education and Training Policy.' In S. Danziger and J. Waldvogel (eds.), *Securing the Future. Investing in Children from Birth to College*. New York: Russell Sage, 47–86.

Heclo, H. (1974). *Modern Social Politics in Britain and Sweden: From Relief to Income Maintenance*. New Haven: Yale University Press;

Hemerijck, A., and Schludi, M. (2000). 'Sequences of Policy Failures and Effective Policy Responses.' In F. W. Scharpf and V. Schmidt (eds.), *Welfare and Work in the Open Economy—From Vulnerability to Competitiveness*. Oxford: Oxford University Press, 125–228.

—— and Visser, J. (2001). 'Learning and Mimicking: How European Welfare States Reform.' Manuscript.

Henz, U., and Sundstrom, M. (2001). 'Earnings as a Force of Attraction and Specialization in Sweden.' In H. P. Blossfeld and S. Drobnic (eds.), *Careers of Couples in Contemporary Society*. Oxford: Oxford University Press, 233–60.

Hernes, Gudmund (1976). 'Structural Change in Social Processes.' *American Journal of Sociology*, 32: 513–47.

Hinrichs, K. (2000). 'Combating Unemployment. What Can Be Learned from Whom?' Paper prepared for Conference 'Social Protection in the New Era: What Future for Welfare?' International Sociological Association, 24–7 August.

—— (2001). 'Elephants on the Move. Patterns of Public Pension Reform in OECD Countries.' In S. Leibfried (ed.), *Welfare State Futures*. Cambridge: Cambridge University Press, 77–102.

Hoem, B. (1997). 'The Way to the Gender-Segregated Swedish Labour Market.' In K. Mason and A. M. Jensen (eds.), *Gender and Family Change in Industrialsed Countries*. Oxford: Oxford University Press.

—— (2000). ' Utan Jobb—inga barn? Fruktsamhetsutvecklingen under 1990-talet.' In SOU (2000): ch. 4.

—— and Hoem, J. (1997). 'Fertility Trends in Sweden up to 1996.' Department of Demography, Stockholm University.

Huston, A. (1991). *Child Poverty, Child Development and Public Policy*. Cambridge: Cambridge University Press.

Iversen, T., and Wren, A. (1998). 'Equality, Employment and Budgetary Restraint: The Trilemma of the Service Economy.' *World Politics*, 50(4): 507–46.

Jahoda, M. (1982). *Employment and Unemployment: A Social-Psychological Analysis*. Cambridge: Cambridge University Press.

—— Lazarsfeld, P., and Zeizel, H. (1933). *Marienthal: The Sociology of an Unemployed Community*. London: Tavistock.

Johnson, J. V., and Johansson, G. (eds.) (1991). *The Psychosocial Work Environment: Work Organization, Democratization and Health. Essays in Memory of Bertil Gardell*. Amityville, NY: Baywood Publishing.

Joshi, H., and Davies, H. (2000). 'The Price of Parenthood and the Value of Children.' In N. Fraser and J. Hill (eds.), *Public Policy for the Twenty-First Century*. Bristol: The Policy Press, 63–76.

Karesek, R., and Theorell, T. (1990). *Healthy Work. Stress, Productivity and the Reconstruction of Work Life*. New York: Basic Books.

Kamerman, S., and Kahn, H. (1997). 'Investing in Children.' In A. Cornia and S. Danziger (eds.), *Child Poverty and Deprivation in Industrialized Countries*. Oxford: Clarendon Press.

Kangas, O. (2000). 'Distributive Justice and Social Policy. Some Reflections on Rawls and Income Distribution.' *Social Policy and Administration*, 34: 510–28.

Karoly, L., and Burtless, G. (1995). 'Demographic Change, Rising Earnings Inequality, and the Distribution of Personal Well-Being', 1959–1989. *Demography*, 32–3: 379–405.

—— et al. (1998). *Investing in our Children*. Santa Monica, Calif.: Rand Corporation.

Kaufmann, F.-X. (2001). 'Towards a Theory of the Welfare State.' In S. Leibfried (ed.), *Welfare State Futures*. Cambridge: Cambridge University Press, 15–36.

Kersbergen, K. van (1995). *Social Capitalism: A Study of Christian Democracy and the Welfare State*. London: Routledge.

Kohli, M. (1995). *Möglichkeiten und Probleme einer Flexibilisierung des Übergangs in den Ruhestand*. Berlin: Freie Universität.

—— (1999). 'Private and Public Transfers between Generations.' *European Societies*, 1: 81-104.

Kohn, M., and Schooler, C. (1983). *Work and Personality. An Inquiry Into the Impact of Social Stratification*. New Jersey: Ablex Publishing Corporation.

Korpi, W., and Palme, J. (1998). 'The Paradox of Redistribution and Strategies of Equality: Welfare State Institutions, Inequality and Poverty in Western Countries.' *American Sociological Review*, 63: 661-87.

Kuhnle, S. (ed.) (2000). *Survival of the European Welfare State*. London, Routledge.

Kunz, J., Villeneuve, P., and Garfinkel, I. (2001). 'Child Support among Selected OECD Countries.' In K. Vleminckx and T. Smeeding (eds.), *Child Well-Being in Modern Nations*. Bristol: The Policy Press.

Kvist, J. (2000). 'Welfare State and the Labour Market: Scandinavian Experiences in the 1990s.' Paper presented at the Conference 'The Welfare State and the Labour Market', Hanse Wissenschaftkolleg, Delmenhorst, 27-30 April 2000.

Lange, P. (1993). 'Maastricht and the Social Protocol: Why Did They Do It?' *Politics and Society*, 21(1): 5-36.

Larsson, A. (1998). 'The European Employment Strategy and EMU: You must Invest to Save.' The 1998 Meidner lecture, *Economic and Industrial Democracy*, 19: 391-415.

Laslett, Peter, and Fishkin, James (eds.) (1992). *Justice Between Age Groups and Generations*. New Haven: Yale University Press.

Leibfried, S., and Pierson, P. (eds.) (1996). *European Social Policy: Between Fragmentation and Integration*. Washington, DC: Brookings.

—— (2000). 'Social Policy.' In H. Wallace and W. Wallace (eds.), *Policy Making in the European Union*, 4th edn. Oxford: Oxford University Press, 267-92.

Levy, J. D. (2000). 'France: Directing Adjustment?' In F. W. Scharpf and V. A. Schmidt (eds.), *Welfare and Work in the Open Economy*, ii: *Diverse Responses to Common Challenges*, Oxford, Oxford University Press, 308-50.

Lipset, S. M., and Bendix, R. (1959). *Social Mobility in Industrial Societies*. Berkeley, Calif.: University of California Press.

Livi-Bacci, M. (1997). 'Scarsita e abbondaza. Le populazioni d'Italia e d'Europa al passaggio di millennio.' *Il Mulino*, 6: 993-1009.

Lødemel, I., and Trickey, H. (eds.) (2000). *'An Offer You Can't Refuse': Workfare in International Perspective*. Bristol: The Policy Press.

Lynch, L. (2000). 'Trends in and Consequences of Investments in Children.' In S. Danziger and J. Waldvogel (eds.), *Securing the Future. Investing in Children from Birth to College*. New York: Russell Sage, 19-46.

McDonald, P. (2000). 'The Toolbox of Public Policies to Impact on Fertility.' Paper presented at European Observatory on Family Matters, Seville, 15-16 September.

McIntosh, S. (2000). 'Skills and Unemployment.' Paper presented at the Workshop on Unemployment, Work and Welfare, Brussels, 9-11 November.

McLanahan, S., Casper, L., and Sorensen, A. M. (1995). 'Women's Roles and Women's Poverty.' In V. Oppenheimer and A. Jensen (eds.), *Gender and Family Change in Industrialized Countries*. Oxford: Clarendon Press, 258-78.

McNamara, K. (1998). *The Currency of Ideas. Monetary Politics in the European Union*. Ithaca, NY: Cornell University Press.

Manow, P., and Seils, E. (2000a). 'Adjusting Badly: The German Welfare State, Structural Change and the Open Economy.' In F. W. Scharpf and V. A. Schmidt (eds.), *Welfare and Work in the Open Economy*, ii: *Diverse Responses to Common Challenges*. Oxford: Oxford University Press.

Manton, K., and Stollard, E. (1994). 'Medical Demography: Interaction of Disability Dynamics and Mortality.' In L. Martin and S. Preston (eds.), *Demography of Aging*, Washington, DC: National Academy Press, 217-78.

Marmot, M., and Wilkinson, R. G. (eds.) (1999). *Social Determinants of Health*. Oxford: Oxford University Press.

Martin, A., and Ross, G. (eds.) (forthcoming). *EMU and the European Model of Society*.

Marx, I., and Verbist, G. (1998). 'Low-Paid Work and Poverty.' In S. Bazen, M. Gregory, and W. Salverda (eds.), *Low-Wage Employment in Europe*. Cheltenham: Edward Elgar, 63-86.

Mayer, S. (1997). *What Money Can't Buy*. Cambridge, Mass: Harvard University Press.

Meyer, Maddona Harrington (1996). 'Making Claims as Workers or Wives: The Distribution of Social Security Benefits.' *American Sociological Review*, 61: 449-65.

Meyers, M., and Gornick, J. (2001). 'Public or Private Responsibilities?' Unpublished paper, Columbia University School of Social Work, January.

Micklewright, J., and Stewart, K. (2000). *The Welfare of Europe's Children*. Florence: UNICEF.

Mills, C. W. (1956). *The Sociological Imagination*. New York: Basic Books.

Mincer, J., and Polachek, S. (1974). 'Family Investments in Human Capital: Earnings of Women.' *Journal of Political Economy*, 82: 76-108.

Mirowsky, J., and Ross, C. (1999). 'Economic Hardship Across the Life Course.' *American Sociological Review*, 64: 548-69.

Montanari, I. (2000). 'From Family Wage to Marriage Subsidy and Child Benefits.' *Journal of European Social Policy*, 10: 307-33.

Moore, K. (2001). 'The Best of Times and the Worst of Times: Lessons from Recent Reforms of the French Retirement System.' *Georgia Journal of International and Comparative Law*, 29: 443-71.

Moreno, L. (2000). 'The Spanish Developments of the Southern Welfare State.' In S. Kuhnle (ed.), *Survival of the European Welfare State*. London: Routledge, 145-65.

Morley, J. (1998). 'Unemployment in the EU: An American or a European Solution?' In J. Morley, A. Storm, with O. Cullmann and M. White (eds.), *Unemployment in Europe: The Policy Challenge*. The Royal Institute of International Affairs Discussion paper, no. 73. London: Royal Institute of International Affairs.

Morris, L. (1987). 'Local Polarisation: A Case Study of Hartlepool.' *International Journal of Urban and Regional Research*, 11(3): 331-49.

Morrison, D., and Ritualo, A. (2000). 'Routes to Children's Economic Recovery after Divorce.' *American Sociological Review*, 65: 560-80.

Murray, C. (1984). *Losing Ground*. New York: Basic Books.

Musgrave, Richard (1986). *Public Finance in a Democratic Society*, ii: *Fiscal Doctrine, Growth and Institutions*. New York: New York University Press.

Myles, J., and Pierson, P. (1997). 'Friedman's Revenge: The Reform of Liberal Welfare States in Canada and the United States.' *Politics and Society*, 25: 443-72.

—— —— (2001). 'The Comparative Political Economy of Pension Reform.' In P. Pierson (ed.), *The New Politics of the Welfare State*. Oxford: Oxford University Press.

Nahn, N., and Mira, P. (2001). 'Job Bust, Baby Bust? Evidence from Spain.' *Journal of Population Economics*, 14: 505–22.

Narendranathan, W., and Stewart, M. B. (1993). 'How Does Benefit Effect Vary as Unemployment Spells Lengthen?' *Journal of Applied Econometrics*, 8: 361–81.

Nickell, S. (1996). 'The Low-Skill Low-Pay Problem: Lessons from Germany for Britain and the U.S.' *Policy Studies*, 17(1): 7–21.

—— and Bell, B. (1997). 'Would Cutting Payroll Taxes on the Unskilled Have a Significant Impact on Unemployment?' In D. J. Snower and G. de la Dehesa (eds.), *Unemployment Policy*. Cambridge: Cambridge University Press, 296–328.

Nolan, B., Hauser, R., and Zoyem, J. P. (2000). 'The Changing Effects of Social Protection on Poverty.' In D. Gallie and S. Paugam (eds.), *Welfare Regimes and the Experience of Unemployment in Europe*. Oxford: Oxford University Press, 87–106.

—— and Marx, I. (2000). 'Low Pay and Household Poverty.' In M. Gregory, W. Salverda, and S. Bazen (eds.), *Labour Market Inequalities. Problems and Policies of Low-Wage Employment in International Perspective*. Oxford: Oxford University Press, 100–19.

—— and Whelan, C. T. (2000). *Loading the Dice? A Study of Cumulative Disadvantage*. Dublin: Oak Tree Press.

NOSOCO (2001). *Social Protection in the Nordic Countries, 1999*. Copenhagen: NOSOCO.

OECD (1988). *Reforming Public Pensions*. Paris: OECD.

—— (1994). *The OECD Jobs Study*. Part II, Paris: OECD.

—— (1995). *Employment Outlook*. Paris: OECD.

—— (1996). *Caring for Frail Elderly People*. Paris: OECD.

—— (1997). *Employment Outlook*. Paris: OECD.

—— (1998a). *Maintaining Prosperity in an Ageing Society*. Paris: OECD.

—— (1998b). *Education at a Glance*. Paris: OECD.

—— (1999a). *Preparing Youth for the 21st Century*. Paris: OECD.

—— (1999b). *Employment Outlook*. Paris: OECD.

—— (1999c). *A Caring World: The New Social Policy Agenda*. Paris: OECD.

—— (2000a). *Reforms for an Ageing Society*. Paris: OECD.

—— (2000b). *Literacy in the Information Age*. Paris: OECD.

—— (2000c). *Employment Outlook*. Paris: OECD.

—— (2000d). *Education at a Glance*. Paris: OECD.

—— (2001a). 'Firms' Contribution to the Reconciliation Between Work and Family Life.' *Labour Market and Social Policy Occasional Papers*, no. 48. Paris: OECD.

—— (2001b). *Aging and Income. Financial Resources and Retirement in 9 OECD Countries*. Paris: OECD.

—— (2001c). *Employment Outlook*. Paris: OECD.

—— (2001d). *Society at a Glance*. Paris: OECD.

Orloff, A. (2000). 'Gender Equality, Women's Employment and Welfare States.' Paper presented at the annual meetings of the American Sociological Association, Washington, DC, August.

Orzag, P., and Stiglitz, J. (1999). 'Rethinking Pension Reform: Ten Myths about Social Security Systems.' Washington, DC: The World Bank (September).

Osberg, L. (1998). 'Meaning and Measurement in Intergenerational Equity.' In M. Corak (ed.), *Government Finances and Generational Equity*, Ottawa: Statistics Canada.

Oxley, H., Dang, T., Forster, M., and Pellizzari, M. (1999). 'Income Inequalities and Poverty among Children and Households with Children in Selected OECD Countries.' Luxembourg: LIS Working Paper Series.

Palier, B. (2000). ' "Defrosting" the French Welfare State'. In M. Ferrera and M. Rhodes (eds.), *Recasting European Welfare States*. London: Frank Cass, 113–36.

Palmer, E. (1998). 'The Swedish Pension Reform Model: Framework and Issues.' Stockholm: National Social Insurance Board.

Paugam, S. (1996). 'The Spiral of Precariousness: A Multidimensional Approach to the Process of Social Disqualification in France.' In G. Room, *Beyond the Threshold: The Measurement and Analysis of Social Exclusion*. Bristol: The Policy Press.

Payne, J., Lissenburgh, S., Payne, S., and Range, M. (1999). 'The Impact of Work-Based Training on Job Prospects for the Unemployed.' *Labour Market Trends*, 107(7), July.

Petersen, T., and Morgan, L. (1995). 'Separate and Unequal: Occupational-Establishment Sex Segregation and the Gender Wage Gap.' *American Journal of Sociology*, 101(2): 329–61.

Peterson, P. (1993). *Facing Up: How to Rescue the Economy From Crushing Debt and Restore the American Dream*. New York: Simon and Shuster.

Pierson, P. (1994). *Dismantling the Welfare State? Reagan, Thatcher, and the Politics of Retrenchment*. Cambridge: Cambridge University Press.

—— (1998). 'Irresistible Forces, Immovable Objects: Post-Industrial Welfare States Confront Permanent Austerity.' *Journal of European Public Policy*, 5(4): 539–60.

—— (ed.) (2001). *The New Politics of the Welfare State*. Oxford, Oxford University Press.

Ploug, N., and Sondergaard, J. (1999). *Velfaerdssamfundets Fremtid*. Copenhagen: Socialforskningsinstituttet.

Porte, C. de la, Pochet, P., and Room, G. (2001). 'Social Benchmarking, Policy-Making and New Governance in the EU.' *Journal of European Social Policy*, 11(4): 291–307.

Pransky, G. (2001). 'Living Longer but Able to Work?' In P. Budetti, R. Burkhauser, J. Gregory, and H. A. Hunt (eds.), *Ensuring Health and Income Support for an Aging Workforce*, Kalamazoo, Mich.: Upjohn Institute.

Preston, S. (1984). 'Children and the Aged in the US.' *Scientific American*, 251: 44–9.

Rawls, J. (1971). *A Theory of Justice*. Oxford: Oxford University Press.

Regalia, I. (2001). 'Decentralizing Employment Protection in Europe: Territorial Pacts and Beyond.' Unpublished paper.

Reynaud, E. (1995). 'Financing Retirement Pensions: Pay-as-you-go and Funded Systems in the European Union.' *International Social Security Review*, 48: 41–58.

—— (1997). 'L'avenir des retraites en debat.' *Chronique International de l'IRES*, 48: 5–16.

Rhodes, M. (2000). 'Restructuring the British Welfare State: Between Domestic Constraints and Global Imperatives.' In F. W. Scharpf and V. A. Schmidt (eds.), *Welfare and Work in the Open Economy*, ii: *Diverse Responses to Common Challenges*, Oxford: Oxford University Press.

Rimlinger, G. (1971). *Welfare Policy and Industrialization in Europe, America and Russia.* New York: John Wiley and Sons.

Romanelli, E. (1999). 'Blind (but not unconditioned) Variation.' In J. A. C. Baum and B. McKervey (eds.), *Variations in Organization Science: In Honour of Donald T. Campbell.* Newbury Park, Calif.: Sage, 79–91.

Room, G. (ed.) (1995). *Beyond the Threshold: The Measurement and Analysis of Social Exclusion.* Bristol: The Policy Press.

Rosenfeld, R., and Kalleberg, A. (1990). 'A Cross-national Comparison of the Gender Gap in Income.' *American Journal of Sociology,* 96: 69–106.

Rubery, J., Smith, M., and Fagan, C. (1999). *Women's Employment in Europe.* London: Routledge.

Sainsbury, D. (ed.) (1999). *Gender and Welfare State Regimes.* Oxford: Oxford University Press.

Saraceno, C. (1994). 'The Ambivalent Familism of the Italian Welfare State.' *Social Politics,* 1.

Scharpf, F. W. (1997a). *Combating Unemployment in Continental Europe.* Florence, EUI, PP no 97/3.

—— (1997b). *Games Real Actors Play.* Boulder, Colo.: Westview Press.

—— (1999). *Governing in Europe: Effective and Democratic?* Oxford: Oxford University Press 1999.

—— (2000a). 'Economic Changes, Vulnerabilities and Institutional Capabilities.' In F. W. Scharpf and V. Schmidt (eds.), *Welfare and Work in Open Economies,* i. Oxford: Oxford University Press, 24–124.

—— (2000b). 'Notes Towards a Theory of Multilevel Governing in Europe.' MPIfG Discussion Paper, 00/5, Cologne, Max Planck Institute for the Study of Societies.

—— and Schmidt, V. (2000). *Welfare and Work in the Open Economy.* 2 vols. Oxford: Oxford University Press.

Schellenberg, G. (1994). *The Road to Retirement: Demographic and Economic Changes in the 90s.* Ottawa: Canadian Council on Social Development.

Schludi, M. (2001). 'Pension Reform in European Social Insurance Countries.' Paper prepared for delivery at the 2001 Biennial Meeting of the European Community Studies Association, Madison, 31 May–2 June.

Schmael, W. (1998). 'Social Security Pension Reforms in Germany.' Paper presented at the annual meetings of the National Academy of Social Insurance, Washington, DC.

Schmidt, G. J., O'Reilly, and Schömann, K. (1996), *International Handbook of Labour Market Policy and Evaluation.* Cheltenham: Edward Elgar.

Schmidt, V. (2000). 'Values and Discourse in the Politics of Adjustment.' In Scharpf and Schmidt (eds.) (2000), 229–309.

Shavit, Y., and Blossfeld, H. P. (1992). *Persistent Inequalities.* Boulder, Colo.: Westview Press.

Siebert, H. (1997). 'Labor Market Rigidities: At the Root of Unemployment in Europe.' *Journal of Economic Perspectives,* 11(3): 37–45.

Sloane, P., and Theodossiou, I. (2000). 'Earnings Mobility of the Low Paid.' In M. Gregory, W. Salverda, and S. Bazen (eds.), *Labour Market Inequalities. Problems and*

Policies of Low-Wage Employment in International Perspective. Oxford: Oxford University Press, 82–99.

Smeeding, T., and Sullivan, D. (1998). 'Generations and the Distribution of Economic Well-Being: A Cross-National View.' Luxembourg Income Study, Working Paper Series, no. 173.

Smolensky, E., Danziger, S., and Gottschalk, P. (1988). 'The Declining Significance of Age in the United States.' In J. Palmer, T. Smeeding, and B. Boyle Torrey (eds.), *The Vulnerable*. Washington, DC: Urban Institute, 29–54.

Socialministeriet (2001). *Socialpolitik som Investering. Socialpolitisk Redegoerelse 2000*. Copenhagen: Ministry of Social Affairs.

Sorensen, A. M., and McLanahan, S. (1987). 'Married Women's Economic Dependency.' *American Journal of Sociology*, 93: 659–86.

SOU (2000). Valfard vid Vagskal. Utvecklingan under 1990-talet. Stockholm: SOU (Sveriges Offentliga Utredningar).

Steinmo, S. (1996). 'The New Political Economy of Taxation: International Pressures and Domestic Policy Choices.' Center for Western European Studies, Working paper 19. Berkeley, Calif.: University of California.

Stewart, M. (1999). 'Low Pay in Britain.' In P. Gregg and J. Wadsworth (eds.), *The State of Working Britain*. Manchester: Manchester University Press, 225–48.

Stier, H., Lewin-Epstein, N., and Braun. M. (2001). 'Welfare Regimes, Family Support Policies, and Women's Employment Along the Life Course.' *American Journal of Sociology*, 106(6): 1731–60.

Streeck, W. (1992). *Social Institutions and Economic Performance: Studies of Industrial Relations in Advanced Industrial Economies*. Newbury Park, Calif.: Sage.

—— (1996). 'Neo-voluntarism: A New European Social Policy Regime?' In G. Marks, F. W. Scharpf, P. C. Schmitter, and W. Streeck (eds.), *Governance in the European Union*. London: Sage Publications, 64–124.

Street, D., and Ginn, J. (2001). 'The Demographic Debate: The Gendered Political Economy of Pensions.' In J. Ginn, D. Street, and S. Arber (eds.), *Women, Work and Pensions: International Issues and Prospects*, Buckingham: Open University Press, 31–43.

Sullivan, A. (2001). 'Cultural Capital and Educational Attainment.' *Sociology*: 893–912.

Svallfors, S., and Taylor-Gooby, P. (2001). *The End of the Welfare State? Responses to State Retrenchment*. London: Routledge.

Swank, D. (2001). 'Political Institutions and Welfare State Restructuring: The Impact of Institutions on Social Policy Change in Developed Democracies.' In P. Pierson (ed.), *The New Politics of the Welfare State*. Oxford: Oxford University Press, 197–237.

Tanzi, V. (1998). 'Globalization, Tax Competition and the Future of TaxSystems.' In G. Krause-Junck (ed.), *Steuersysteme der Zukunft*. Berlin: Duncker & Humblodt, 11–27.

Thompson, L. (1997). 'Predictability of Individual Pensions.' Paper presented to the Joint ILO-OECD Workshop: Development and Reform of Pension Schemes. Paris: OECD.

—— (1998). *Older and Wiser: The Economics of Public Pensions*. Washington, DC: The Urban Institute.

Thomson, D. (1996). *Selfish Generations? How Welfare States Grow Old.* Cambridge: White Horse Press.

Traxler, F., Blaschke, S., and Kittel, B. (2001). *National Labour Relations in Internationalized Markets. A Comparitive Study of Institutions, Change and Performance.* Oxford: Oxford University Press.

Trifiletti, R. (1999). 'Southern European Welfare Regimes and the Worsening Position of Women.' *Journal of European Social Policy*, 9: 1.

Tsaklogou, P., and Papadopoulos, F. (2001). 'Identifying Population Groups at High Risk of Social Exclusion.' Working paper, Athens University of Economics and Business (June).

Tuchszirer, C., and Vincent, C. (1997). 'Un consensus presque parfait autour de la reforme du systeme du retraite.' *Chronique Internationale de l'IRES*, 48: 26–30.

Turner, D., Giorno, C., de Serres, A., Vourch, A., and Richardson, P. (1998). 'The Macroeconomic Implications of Ageing in a Global Context.' Ageing Working Papers 1.2. Paris: OECD.

Vandenbroucke, F. (1999). 'The Active Welfare State: A European Ambition.' Den Uyl Lecture, Amsterdam, 13 December.

—— (2001). *Social Justice and Individual Ethics in an Open Society: Equality, Responsibility, and Incentives.* Berlin: Springer Verlag.

Visser, J., and Hemerijck, A., (1997). *'A Dutch Miracle.' Job Growth, Welfare Reform and Corporatism in the Netherlands.* Amsterdam: Amsterdam University Press.

Waldvogel, J. (1998). 'The Family Gap for Young Women in the United States and Britain. Can Maternity Leave Make a Difference?' *Journal of Labour Economics*, 16(3): 505–45.

Warr, P. (1987). *Work, Unemployment and Mental Health.* Oxford: Clarendon Press.

Wennemo, I. (1994). *Sharing the Costs of Children.* Stockholm: Swedish Institute for Social Research.

Whelan, C. T., Hannon, D. F., and Creighton, S. (1991). *Unemployment, Poverty and Psychological Distress.* Dublin: Economic and Social Research Institute.

—— and McGinnity, F. (2000). 'Unemployment and Satisfaction: A European Analysis.' In D. Gallie and S. Paugam (eds.), *Welfare Regimes and the Experience of Unemployment in Europe.* Oxford: Oxford University Press, 286–306.

—— Layte, R., Maitre, B., and Nolan, B. (2001). 'Persistent Income Poverty and Deprivation in the European Union.' The Economic and Social Research Institute working paper (EPAG, no. 17). Dublin.

White, M. (1998). 'Are Active Labour Market Policies Enough?' In J. Morley, A. Storm, and M. White (eds.), *Unemployment in Europe. The Policy Challenge.* The Royal Institute of International Affairs European Programme. Discussion Paper 73.

Wolf, D. (1999). 'The Family as Provider of Long-Term Care: Efficiency, Equity and Externalitites.' *Journal of Ageing and Health*, 11: 360–82.

Wolfson, M., Rowe, G., Lin, X., and Gribble, S. (1998). 'Historical Generational Accounting with Heterogeneous Populations.' In M. Corak (ed.), *Government Finances and Generational Equity.* Ottowa: Statistics Canada, 107-26.

Wood, A. (1994). *North–South Trade, Employment and Inequality: Changing Fortunes in a Skill-Driven World.* Oxford, Clarendon Press.

Wood, S. (2001). 'Labour Market Regimes under Threat? Sources of Continuity in Germany, Britain and Sweden.' In P. Pierson (ed.), *The New Politics of the Welfare State*. Oxford: Oxford University Press, 368–409.

World Bank (1994). *Averting The Old Age Crisis: Policies to Protect the Old and Promote Growth*. New York: Oxford University Press.

Zeitlin, J. (2001). 'Constructing Social Europe: Social Dialogue, Subsidiarity, and Open Coordination.' Comment presented to the European Conference 'Pour une politique européenne des capacités: Un cadre de travail entre chercheurs et acteurs du dialogue social européen', sponsored by Directorate General Employment and Social Affairs, European Commission, 12–13 Brussels, January.

Index